MENTORING ENGLISH TEACHERS IN THE SECONDARY SCHOOL

This practical guide will help school-based mentors of trainee or newly qualified English teachers in developing their own mentoring skills, whilst providing the essential guidance their trainees need as they navigate their new role in the secondary classroom. With analytical tools for self-evaluation, this is a key resource that will support and inspire mentors and help them identify both strengths and skill gaps to develop confidence and knowledge in their mentoring position.

By providing practical tools such as tasks, feedback guides, further readings and examples of dialogue with trainees, this volume covers the knowledge, skills and understanding every mentor needs. Key topics explored include:

- Roles and responsibilities of mentors;
- How to develop a mentor-mentee relationship;
- Developing beginning English teachers' subject knowledge and expertise, including planning for pupils' learning;
- Managing workload and student teacher well-being;
- Developing collaborative practice;
- Developing the wider, professional role of the teacher.

Filled with tried-and-tested strategies based on the latest research, *Mentoring English Teachers in the Secondary School* is a vital guide for mentors of English teachers, both trainee and newly qualified, with ready-to-use strategies that support and inspire mentors and beginning teachers alike.

Debbie Hickman is a senior lecturer and subject co-ordinator for Secondary English and Professional Studies for the PGCE at the Institute of Education, University of Chichester. Debbie taught in secondary schools for sixteen years prior to moving into Higher Education and she is currently a doctoral student at the University of Reading researching secondary pupils' perceptions of reading.

MENTORING TRAINEE AND NEWLY QUALIFIED TEACHERS

Series edited by: Susan Capel, Trevor Wright and Julia Lawrence

The **Mentoring Trainee and Newly Qualified Teachers** series offers subject-specific, practical books designed to reinforce and develop mentors' understanding of the different aspects of their role, as well as exploring issues that mentees encounter in the course of learning to teach. The books have two main foci: First, challenging mentors to reflect critically on theory, research and evidence, on their own knowledge, their approaches to mentoring and how they work with beginning teachers in order to move their practice forward. Second, supporting mentors to effectively facilitate the development of beginning teachers. Although the basic structure of all the subject books is similar, each book is different to reflect the needs of mentors in relation to the unique nature of each subject. Elements of appropriate theory introduce each topic or issue with emphasis placed on the practical application of material. The chapter authors in the subject books have been engaged with mentoring over a long period of time and share research, evidence and their experience. We, as series editors, are pleased to extend the work in initial teacher education to the work of mentors of beginning teachers.

We hope that this series of books supports you in developing into an effective, reflective mentor as you support the development of the next generation of subject teachers.

For more information about this series, please visit: www.routledge.com/series/MTNQT

Titles in the series

Mentoring Physical Education Teachers in the Secondary School
Edited by Susan Capel and Julia Lawrence

Mentoring Design and Technology Teachers in the Secondary School
Edited by Suzanne Lawson and Susan Wood-Griffith

Mentoring English Teachers in the Secondary School
Edited by Debbie Hickman

MENTORING ENGLISH TEACHERS IN THE SECONDARY SCHOOL

A Practical Guide

Edited by Debbie Hickman

LONDON AND NEW YORK

First published 2020
by Routledge
2 Park Square, Milton Park, Abingdon, Oxon OX14 4RN

and by Routledge
52 Vanderbilt Avenue, New York, NY 10017

Routledge is an imprint of the Taylor & Francis Group, an informa business

© 2020 selection and editorial matter, Debbie Hickman; individual chapters, the contributors

The right of Debbie Hickman to be identified as the authors of the editorial material, and of the authors for their individual chapters, has been asserted in accordance with sections 77 and 78 of the Copyright, Designs and Patents Act 1988.

All rights reserved. No part of this book may be reprinted or reproduced or utilised in any form or by any electronic, mechanical, or other means, now known or hereafter invented, including photocopying and recording, or in any information storage or retrieval system, without permission in writing from the publishers.

Trademark notice: Product or corporate names may be trademarks or registered trademarks, and are used only for identification and explanation without intent to infringe.

British Library Cataloguing-in-Publication Data
A catalogue record for this book is available from the British Library

Library of Congress Cataloging-in-Publication Data
A catalog record has been requested for this book

ISBN: 978-1-138-59135-6 (hbk)
ISBN: 978-1-138-59136-3 (pbk)
ISBN: 978-0-429-49047-7 (ebk)

Typeset in Interstate
by Newgen Publishing UK

CONTENTS

List of illustrations — viii
List of tasks — ix
List of contributors — xii
An introduction to the series: Mentoring Trainee and Newly Qualified Teachers — xiv

Introduction: A practical guide to mentoring in English — 1

SECTION 1 WHAT IS MENTORING? — 3

1 **Models of mentoring** — 5
Gill Golder, Alison Keyworth and Clare Shaw

Definitions of mentoring; The context in which you are working that underpins your mentoring practice; Effective mentoring models

SECTION 2 YOU AS A MENTOR — 15

2 **Understanding yourself and how your experiences influence your approaches to mentoring** — 17
Andrew Goodwyn

Purpose or purposes; Becoming an English teacher; Starting with literature; Not a conclusion but a beginning

3 **What subject and pedagogical knowledge, understanding and skills does a mentor of beginning English teachers need?** — 27
Sally Catchpole and Theresa Gooda

What is knowledge?; What is English?; Plugging the gaps in our own knowledge

4 Developing a mentor-mentee relationship 36
Rachel Roberts

The role of the mentor; Being an *English* mentor; Approaches to mentoring; Supporting your student teacher; Setting boundaries and expectations; Developing a professional identity; Navigating tricky relationships; Underpinning values

SECTION 3 WHAT A MENTOR DOES 51

5 Managing workload and student teacher well-being 53
Yvonne Williams

Managing assessment; Managing planning and preparation; Summary reflection on workload; Managing data; Listening, counselling and signposting; Supporting beginning teachers' well-being; Examples of interventions using cognitive thinking

6 Developing collaborative practice 67
Trevor Wright

Lesson observation and feedback; Collaborative work: The transfer of experience; Lesson planning; Wider collaboration

SECTION 4 SUPPORTING THE DEVELOPMENT OF BEGINNING ENGLISH TEACHERS' KNOWLEDGE, SKILLS AND UNDERSTANDING 77

7 What knowledge, skills and understanding do beginning English teachers need? 79
Debbie Hickman and Theresa Gooda

Outlining subject knowledge; Developing knowledge about speaking and listening; Developing understanding of reading; Developing a pedagogy for reading; Developing knowledge about writing; Developing a writing pedagogy; Supporting your mentee's developing subject knowledge

8 Supporting beginning English teachers to become reflective practitioners 92
Julia O'Kelly

Definitions of reflective practice; Reflexivity

9 Supporting beginning English teachers to support pupils' learning 101
Louise Beattie

Supporting the planning process; The planning process: The bigger picture; The planning process: Individual lessons; Teaching and evaluating lessons; Using data and assessment to inform planning and teaching; Moving from individual lessons to planning sequences of lessons

10 Observing beginning teachers' lessons 112
Rachel Roberts

Student teachers observing teaching; Being observed; Observing beginning English teachers; Effective feedback; Verbal feedback; Response to feedback; The purpose of written feedback

11 Holding weekly debriefs 126
Rachel Roberts

The reflective conversation; Knowing how to help; Barriers to progress; Topics for mentoring conversations; Evaluative language and praise; The role of emotions in mentoring conversations; Having difficult conversations; Values and the problem with progress

12 Developing the wider, professional role of the teacher 140
Debbie Hickman

What does it mean to be a professional and how does this relate to the role of the teacher?; Professional Studies and the wider role of the teacher; Pastoral care and the role of the form tutor; Working with others; Making a positive contribution to the wider life of the school

13 Continuing the mentoring of beginning English teachers beyond their initial teacher training 150
Yvonne Williams

The practicalities; What will be the demands on the mentor's time?; Documentation; Establishing expectations; Considering the expertise in your school; Conducting meetings; Planning; Marking and assessment; Lesson observation feedback; The wider professional role; Cross-curricular involvement; Supporting a weaker NQT; Mentoring an NQT to adapt beyond the induction year; Becoming a member of the professional community

References 163
Index 172

ILLUSTRATIONS

Figures

1.1	Developmental mentoring	13
8.1	Kolb's experiential learning cycle	94
8.2	Davis, Little and Thornton's Spectrum of teaching interventions and possible interpretations by students	99
10.1	Positioning feedback into a training process	119
10.2	Question boxes for written lesson observation feedback	125
11.1	The reflective cycle	127

Tables

1.1	Key external drivers influencing mentoring work	9
4.1	English trainee needs analysis	40
4.2	Using the Mentor Standards to set expectations of your relationship	45
5.1	Mentor-trainee conversation using CBT strategies	65
9.1	Thinking about the process behind the lesson plan	107
10.1	The REVIEW Process for structuring feedback conversations	122
11.1	Suggested questions to facilitate reflection	128
11.2	Examples of lesson objectives and outcomes	129
11.3	Topics for discussion in mentoring conversations	133

TASKS

1.1	Mentor reflection: Reflecting on your understanding of mentoring	6
1.2	Mentor reflection: Understanding the term 'mentoring'	7
1.3	The context in which you carry out your mentoring duties	8
1.4	Three different mentoring models	8
1.5	Responsibilities of the mentor and beginning teacher at each stage of Katz's development model	12
1.6	Helping a beginning teacher to learn using Clutterbuck's model	13
1.7	Attributes of an effective mentor	14
1.8	Mentor reflection: Reflecting on your mentoring practice	14
2.1	Reflecting on models of English	20
2.2	Considering literacy	21
2.3	Considering motivation	22
2.4	Personal reflection: Personal response	23
2.5	Reflecting on practice	25
2.6	Follow-up tasks	26
3.1	Beliefs about knowledge	28
3.2	Reflecting on your own knowledge in practice	29
3.3	Reflections on encoded knowledge	30
3.4	Reflection on the nature and purpose of English	32
4.1	Reflecting on your relationship with your own ITT mentor	37
4.2	Making a personal connection	38
4.3	Metaphors for teaching and mentoring	39
4.4	Identifying different types of support	41
4.5	Utilising reflective practice	43
4.6	Reflection on your mentor role	47
5.1	Overview	54
5.2	Reflection on the role of assessment, its role in practice and evaluation of the role of marking	55
5.3	Reflection on planning	56
5.4	Reflection on the role and purpose of data	57
5.5	Personal reflection	58
5.6	Mentor reflection: Understanding the place and purpose of theory-based tasks	60

5.7	Mentor reflection: Your understanding of well-being	61
5.8	Reflection on listening	62
5.9	Mentor reflection: Limitations and potential afforded by a cognitive approach	64
5.10	Mentor research	66
6.1	Agreeing feedback protocols	69
6.2	Considering and developing experience	70
6.3	Considering collaborative planning	74
7.1	Reflection on own knowledge and practice	80
7.2	Supporting student teachers' development	81
7.3	Reflecting on the role of talk in the classroom	83
7.4	What is reading?	84
7.5	Reflecting on reading	86
7.6	Reflection on own and mentee's reading knowledge and practice	87
7.7	Reflection on writing processes	89
7.8	Reflection on own and mentee's writing knowledge and practice	90
8.1	Reflecting on your understanding of reflective practice	92
8.2	Thinking about reflexivity	94
8.3	Thinking about the knowledge you use to help you to develop reflective practice	95
8.4	Starting to make tacit knowledge overt	96
8.5	Thinking about the knowledge your mentee can use to make sense of practice	97
8.6	Considering the value of written evaluations	99
8.7	Reviewing our understanding of reflective practice	100
9.1	Mentor reflection: Why plan?	101
9.2	Mentor reflection: What does planning mean?	102
9.3	Reconstructing planning	103
9.4	Supporting the planning through focused questions	105
9.5	Reflection on promoting learning over time	110
10.1	The purpose of observation	113
10.2	Joint observation	114
10.3	Being observed	115
10.4	Using deliberate practice as part of training	117
10.5	The feedback conversation	120
10.6	Framing feedback	123
11.1	Barriers to progress	130
11.2	Using reappraisal	135
11.3	Having a difficult conversation	137
12.1	Reflection on roles and responsibilities	141
12.2	Considering Hoyle and John's model	142
12.3	Reflection on cognitive dissonance	143
12.4	Professional Studies programme	145
12.5	Reflection on the pastoral structure and the role of the tutor	147
12.6	Reflecting on relationships	147
12.7	Introduction to others	148
13.1	Setting up the NQT induction	152

13.2	Reflection on time management	153
13.3	Reflecting on the language and expectations of the DfE's Statutory Guidance	154
13.4	Supporting planning	157
13.5	Considering assessment of progress over time	158
13.6	Some prompts for focused observations	159

CONTRIBUTORS

Louise Beattie is a senior lecturer and subject lead for the PGCE Secondary English course at the University of Worcester. She is a Fellow of the Higher Education Academy. For details, please visit www.worcester.ac.uk/about/profiles/louise-beattie.aspx

Sally Catchpole is an experienced secondary school teacher of English and Subject Lead in Health and Social Care. She has several years of experience mentoring PGCE, Schools Direct and GTP students, as well as NQTs, in both subjects since 2007.

Gill Golder is director of teacher education, department head for education and programme leader for secondary education at the University of St Mark and St John, Plymouth. For details, please visit www.marjon.ac.uk/about-marjon/staff-list-and-profiles/golder-gillian.html

Theresa Gooda is a secondary English teacher with over 20 years' classroom experience, who has been mentoring beginning English teachers since 2003. She is also currently a doctoral researcher in education at the University of Sussex. Theresa is regional co-ordinator for the National Association for the Teaching of English (NATE) and leader of the Sussex branch of the National Writing Project.

Andrew Goodwyn is a Professor and Head of The School of Education and English Language and also Director of The Institute for Research in Education, at The University of Bedfordshire. He is also Emeritus Professor at The University of Reading where he was Head of Education [2007–15]. After 12 years teaching English in comprehensive schools in Coventry and London, he moved to work in teacher education and research and ran a PGCE English course for 20 years. He has been a member of NATE for 35 years and is a former Chair. His research focuses on first language education and on the concept of teacher expertise. He has published extensively including single authored and edited books, contributed to many scholarly journals and given lectures and presentations around the world. He is on the editorial board of numerous journals.

Debbie Hickman is a senior lecturer and subject co-ordinator for Secondary English and Professional Studies for the PGCE at the Institute of Education, University of Chichester. Debbie taught in secondary schools for 16 years prior to moving into Higher Education and she is currently a doctoral student at the University of Reading researching secondary pupils' perceptions of reading.

Alison Keyworth is a senior lecturer in postgraduate and professional development at the University of St Mark and St John, Plymouth. For details, please visit www.marjon.ac.uk/about-marjon/staff-list-and-profiles/keyworth-alison.html

Julia O'Kelly was head of secondary PGCE at the university of Chichester for 13 years. She is now retired and is continuing her EdD research into Initial Teacher Education.

Rachel Roberts is lecturer in Secondary English and lead for the Secondary English PGCE at the Institute of Education, University of Reading. Rachel taught in secondary schools for ten years prior to moving into Higher Education and she has recently completed her doctorate exploring the role of evaluative language in mentoring conversations. She is also Chair of the NATE Initial Teacher Education Committee.

Clare Shaw is a senior lecturer in primary initial teacher education at the University of St Mark and St John, Plymouth. For details, please visit www.marjon.ac.uk/about-marjon/staff-list-and-profiles/shaw-clare.html

Yvonne Williams is Head of English and Drama at Portsmouth High School, a member of the Post-16 committee for NATE and an experienced mentor. She was a member of the Department for Education independent workload review group for marking in 2016 and has written articles on teacher development, well-being and marking for the English Association, NATE and TES online.

Trevor Wright was a senior education lecturer at the University of Worcester, in charge of secondary English training. His research interests include literacy, teaching poetry and advanced mentoring skills. He was a secondary English teacher before moving into higher education. He is the author of *How to be a Brilliant English Teacher*, *How to be a Brilliant Teacher* and *How to be a Brilliant Trainee Teacher*, as well as editor of *How to be a Brilliant Mentor* and series editor of *Mentoring Teachers in the Secondary School*, all published by Routledge.

AN INTRODUCTION TO THE SERIES: MENTORING TRAINEE AND NEWLY QUALIFIED TEACHERS

Mentoring is a very important and exciting role. What could be better than supporting the development of the next generation of subject teachers? A mentor is almost certainly an effective teacher, but this doesn't automatically guarantee that he or she will be a good mentor, despite similarities in the two roles. This series of practical workbooks covers most subjects in the secondary curriculum. They are designed specifically to reinforce mentors' understanding of different aspects of their role, for mentors to learn about and reflect on their role, to provide support for mentors in aspects of their development and enable them to analyse their success in supporting the development of beginning subject teachers (defined as trainee, newly qualified and early career teachers). This book has two main foci: first, the focus is on challenging mentors to reflect critically on theory, research and evidence, on their own knowledge, how they work with beginning teachers, how they work with more experienced teachers and on their approaches to mentoring in order to move their practice forward. Second, the focus is on supporting mentors to effectively facilitate the development of beginning teachers. Thus, some of the practical activities in the books are designed to encourage reflection, whilst others ask mentors to undertake activities with beginning teachers.

This book can be used alongside generic and subject books designed for student and newly qualified teachers. These books include Capel, Leask and Younie's *Learning to Teach in the Secondary School: A Companion to School Experience*, 8th edition (2019) which deals with aspects of teaching and learning applicable to all subjects. This generic book also has a companion Reader: *Readings for Learning to Teach in the Secondary School* by Capel, Leask and Turner (2010) containing articles and research papers in education suitable for master's-level study. Further, the generic book is complemented by two subject series: *Learning to Teach [subject] in the Secondary School: A Companion to School Experience*; and *A Practical Guide to Teaching [subject] in the Secondary School*. These books are designed for student teachers on different types of initial teacher education programmes (and indeed a beginning teacher you are working with may have used/currently be using them). However, these books are proving equally useful to tutors and mentors in their work with student teachers, both in relation to the knowledge, skills and understanding the student teacher is developing and some tasks which mentors might find it useful to support a beginning teacher to do.

It is also supported by a book designed for newly qualified teachers, Capel, Lawrence, Leask and Younie's *Surviving and Thriving in the Secondary School: The NQT's Essential*

Companion (2019), as well as Capel, Heilbronn, Leask and Turner's *Starting to Teach in the Secondary School: A Companion for the Newly Qualified Teacher* (2004). These titles cover material not generally needed by student teachers on an initial teacher education course, but which is needed by newly qualified teachers in their school work and early career.

The information in this book should link with the information in the generic text and relevant subject book in the two series in a number of ways. For example, mentors might want to refer a beginning teacher to read about specific knowledge, understanding and skills they are focusing on developing, or to undertake tasks in the book, either alone or with their support, then discus the tasks. It is recommended that you have copies of these books available so that you can cross-reference when needed.

In turn, the books complement a range of resources on which mentors can draw (including other mentors of beginning teachers in the same or other subjects, other teachers and a range of other resources including books, research articles and websites).

The positive feedback on *Learning to Teach* and the related books above, particularly the way they have supported the learning of student teachers in their development into effective, reflective teachers, encouraged us to retain the main features of that book in this series. Like teaching, mentoring should be research- and evidence-informed. Thus, this series of books introduces theory, research and professional evidence-based advice and guidance to support mentors as they develop their mentoring to support beginning teachers' development. The main focus is the practical application of material. Elements of appropriate theory introduce each topic or issue, and recent research into mentoring and/or teaching and learning is integral to the presentation. Tasks are provided to help mentors identify key features of the topic or issue and reflect on and/or apply them to their own practice of mentoring beginning teachers. Although the basic structure of all the subject books is similar, each book is different to reflect the needs of mentors in relation to the unique nature of each subject.

The chapter authors in the subject books have been engaged with mentoring over a long period of time and are aiming to share research/evidence and their experience. We, as series editors, are pleased to extend the work in initial teacher education to the work of mentors of beginning teachers. We hope that this series of books supports you in developing into an effective, reflective mentor as you support the development of the next generation of subject teachers.

Susan Capel, Julia Lawrence, Trevor Wright and Sarah Younie
February 2019

Introduction
A practical guide to mentoring in English

The importance of mentoring

The growing significance of the role of mentors in supporting beginning teachers in England is reflected in the publication in 2016 of mentoring standards (Teaching Schools Council, 2016), which provide guidance and support for those engaging in mentoring. The profile of mentors in supporting the development of beginning teachers is rising. Concerns regarding, for example, recruitment, retention, workload and work-life balance are all contributing towards a need to support those joining the profession not only during their beginning years, but also longer term.

The purpose of this workbook

Being a mentor is both rewarding and challenging. The role of the mentor is one of influence and privilege. As a mentor, you will work with beginning English teachers with differing needs and differing rates of development and have a significant impact on their perceptions of their role as an English teacher.

Your own experience and practice as a mentor may well be shaped and influenced by your own experience, as a mentee and as a teacher. There are many similarities between the role of a teacher and that of a mentor and therefore you may draw, in your mentoring, on your knowledge, skills and experience from teaching. However, your role as a mentor is not just to pass on your experience and shape a teacher in your own image: what works or worked for you might not work for the beginning teacher you are mentoring. You might, therefore, identify different ways to do things through, for example, engaging with research and literature about mentoring and the pedagogy and practice of teaching English. You might develop your practice alongside other mentors in your department or school, or through regional networking. You will certainly develop your understanding of mentoring and teaching your subject working alongside your beginning English teacher.

This workbook is designed to offer practical support in your own professional learning and development. As such, it aims to enable you to be able to support beginning English teachers in their development towards becoming effective, reflective practitioners. It emphasises and supports you in reflecting on your own practice so that you can develop your knowledge and understanding, offering advice on different approaches you may use to meet the needs of a beginning teacher at particular points in their development or training year.

Introduction

This book draws on a variety of contributors with a broad range of expertise. The chapter authors have been invited to contribute because of their experiences as mentors and/or tutors of beginning English teachers and/or their work in supporting the development of effective mentors, as well as their work in developing practice in the teaching of English. Each chapter, in turn, draws on the expertise of the wider English and educational community, through reference to research, evidence and case studies.

This workbook explores a range of themes and ideas which are particularly relevant to mentoring beginning English teachers. This book recognises the recursive and iterative nature of development and practice and as such you will find that themes and ideas are revisited across chapters. The ideas and advice in the workbook are not intended to be prescriptive, acknowledging the contextual need for professional judgement. You will, therefore, likely refine the suggestions offered to suit the particular circumstances of each beginning teacher with whom you work and adapt these to their own specific situation. It is hoped that the workbook will support your thinking and practice and afford opportunities for your own development, as well as that of your beginning English teacher, as you consider your practice as an English teacher from a different perspective. The reference and further reading lists therefore offer recommendations to allow you to pursue lines of enquiry as required.

SECTION 1
What is mentoring?

1 Models of mentoring

Gill Golder, Alison Keyworth and Clare Shaw

Introduction

Your job as a mentor is to develop a positive working relationship with a beginning teacher to enable them to grow and develop both professionally and personally. How you go about this will be influenced by a number of factors, such as your own experience of being mentored in the past and your common-sense opinions of the role. These are important starting points, but you are likely to grow as an effective mentor when you also base your approaches on evidence. This chapter (and this book) are designed to support you in considering the evidence to underpin your practice.

The chapter starts by looking at different definitions of mentoring. It then looks at the importance of the context in which you are working as a mentor, highlighting a number of documents from England and other countries that impact on your mentoring practice. The chapter then considers three mentoring models a mentor could adopt to inform their practice. These models underpin various roles you undertake and hence the other chapters in this book.

Objectives

At the end of this chapter, you will be able to:

- Have a greater understanding of what is meant by the term 'mentoring' for a beginning teacher;
- Have an appreciation of the key context in which you work that may influence the manner in which you act as a mentor in school;
- Have an awareness of the plethora of mentoring models that exist;
- Compare and contrast three developmental mentoring models and how these could be used to support your role as a mentor.

> **Task 1.1 Mentor reflection: Reflecting on your understanding of mentoring**
>
> Reflect on what you understand by mentoring by considering the following questions:
>
> - How would you define mentoring?
> - How does your definition inform your practice as a mentor?
> - How do the various policy and guidance documents relevant to your context influence your mentoring practice?
> - Do you base your mentoring practice on personal experience or on a model or models of mentoring? If a model, which? Why?

Definitions of mentoring

Mentoring is widely used in many contexts for the purpose of helping people to learn and develop, both professionally and personally. There are numerous and frequently contradictory definitions of mentoring, with accompanying models of how mentoring is best approached (Haggard, Dougherty, Turban and Wilbanks, 2011). Whilst different models might utilise different terminology and vary in emphasis regarding the role of a mentor, what remains consistent is the view that mentoring is a supportive, learning relationship. The mentor, with his or her more extensive experience, is there to support the learner's development. The quality of the relationship between mentor and mentee is extremely important.

The terms mentoring and coaching are at times used interchangeably. Both aim to develop the professional competencies of the client or colleague. Although mentoring and coaching have much in common, an important difference between the two is the focus of developmental activities. In mentoring the focus is on development at significant career transitions whereas in coaching the focus is on the development of a specific aspect of a professional learner's practice (CUREE, 2005).

Montgomery (2017) suggested that definitions of mentoring often involve the concept that advice and guidance to a novice, or person with limited experience, is given by an experienced person. In this way, mentoring can be seen to be hierarchical; a top-down approach largely based on a one-way flow of information.

> Mentoring involves the use of the same models and skills of questioning, listening, clarifying and reframing associated with coaching. Traditionally, however, mentoring in the workplace has tended to describe a relationship in which a more experienced colleague uses his or her greater knowledge and understanding of the work or workplace to support the development of a more junior or inexperienced member of staff.
>
> (CIPD, 2012, p.1)

In contrast, other definitions of mentoring follow a less hierarchal structure. These include peer mentoring (Driscoll et al, 2009) and group mentoring (Kroll, 2016). In these approaches to mentoring the flow of information is more bidirectional. Montgomery (2017) suggested they are more personalised as mentoring is adapted more effectively to an individual mentee's goals and needs. Higgins and Thomas (2001) suggested that top-down mentoring had greater impact on short-term career outcomes and individually driven mentoring more effectively supported long-term career development. Whether the focus is on short- or long-term tailored development of a mentee, there are common aspects to all forms of mentoring. CIPD (2012, p.1) identified four characteristics of mentoring:

- It is essentially a supportive form of development.
- It focuses on helping a person manage their career and improve skills.
- Personal issues can be discussed productively.
- Mentoring activities have both organisational and individual goals.

In education, school-based mentors play a vital role in the development of student teachers and induction of newly qualified teachers. They also support other staff at points of career development. As with mentoring in other contexts, there is a focus on learning, development and the provision of appropriate support and encouragement. The definition of a mentor outlined in the *National Standards for School-based Initial Teacher Training (ITT) Mentors* in England (Department for Education (DfE), 2016b, p.11) is someone who 'is a suitably experienced teacher who has formal responsibility to work collaboratively within the ITT partnership to help ensure the trainee receives the highest quality training'. However, in initial teacher education in many countries, including England, assessment of the beginning teacher is integral to the mentor's role. This is supported by Pollard (2014), who suggested that the role of the mentor in ITT has developed because of three aspects: the complexity of the capabilities teachers need to meet; the focus on high professional standards in school; and the transfer of knowledge from one generation to another.

Task 1.2 Mentor reflection: Understanding the term 'mentoring'

1. Research the terms 'mentoring' and 'coaching'.
2. List a variety of terms that you associate with coaching and mentoring.
3. Make a list of common and unique characteristics for both.

The context in which you are working that underpins your mentoring practice

Mentoring is increasingly important in a range of fields, both in the UK and internationally, as a tool to support recruitment into a profession, retention in that profession, professional learning, networking and career development. In teaching, it is widely recognised that there is a strong relationship between professional learning, teaching knowledge and practices, educational leadership and pupil results (Cordingly et al. 2015). As such, there has been an increase in development of policy and guidance documents as well as frameworks, toolkits and factsheets produced over the past few years to support educators and others in fulfilling their roles as mentors.

As a mentor, it is important to recognise and embed current policy and statutory guidance into your mentoring practice. There are a number of key documents that underpin the mentoring process in initial teacher education and beyond in England and elsewhere. These constitute the key external drivers in shaping mentoring practice in school. Being aware of these is important, but knowing how to use them to support your work with a beginning teacher can add purpose and validity to what you do (there are examples of how to do this in other chapters in this book). They also enable you to recognise the value of being a mentor in school, as 'effective professional development for teachers is a core part of securing effective teaching' (DfE 2016a, p.3).

Table 1.1 highlights policy and guidance documents that influence the work you do in school with a beginning teacher in England but also signposts you to examples of international equivalence documents to enable you to make comparisons internationally.

Task 1.3 The context in which you carry out your mentoring duties

Reflect on the context in which you carry out your mentoring duties. Ensure you are familiar with the relevant documents listed in Table 1.1 (or their equivalents if you are working elsewhere). What aspects of these documents do you identify as being of most use to your work and why?

Effective mentoring models

As alluded to above, there are a number of mentoring models which a mentor could adopt in order to support the growth and development of a beginning teacher. Attempts have been made to categorise different approaches to mentoring. For example, Maynard and Furlong (1995a) suggested that there are three categories of mentoring, the apprentice model, the competence model and the reflective model. The apprentice model argues that the skills of being a teacher are best learned by supervised practice, with guidance from imitation of experienced practitioners. The competence model suggests that learning to teach requires learning a predefined list of competences (the current Teachers Standards in England (DfE, 2013b) could be described as a competence model). In this model, the mentor becomes a systematic trainer supporting a beginning teacher to meet the competences. In the reflective model, the promotion of reflective practice through mentoring is key. This requires a beginning teacher to have some mastery of the skills of teaching to be able to reflect upon their own practice and for the mentor to be a co-enquirer and facilitator rather than instructor.

Task 1.4 Three different mentoring models

- What are the features of practice for each of these models: apprentice, competence and reflective?
- Which features of these models do you use/want to use in your mentoring?
- When do/would you use each model of mentoring?

Table 1.1 Key external drivers influencing mentoring work

	Policy/guidance document	Author and date introduced	Key purpose
Teacher standards documents	Teachers' Standards (England)	DfE (2011)	Used to assess all student teachers working towards qualified teacher status (QTS) as well as newly qualified teachers completing their statutory induction period. 'Providers of ITT should assess trainees against the standards in a way that is consistent with what could reasonably be expected of a trainee teacher prior to the award of QTS' (DfE, 2013b, p.6).
	The Australian Professional Standards for Teachers	Australian Institute for Teaching and School Leadership (AITSL) (2011)	The Standards are designed so that teachers know what they should be aiming to achieve at every stage of their career; to enable them to improve their practice inside and outside the classroom. 'The Standards do this by providing a framework which makes clear the knowledge, practice and professional engagement required across teachers' careers' (AITSL 2011, p.2)
Core content requirements for Initial Teacher Education	Framework of Core Content for Initial Teacher Training (England)	DfE (2016)	The aim of this framework is to improve the consistency and quality of ITT courses by supporting those involved in training teachers and student teachers themselves to have a better understanding of the key elements of good ITT content (DfE, 2016a)
	Differentiated Primary and Lower Secondary Teacher Education Programmes for Years 1-7 and Years 5-10 (Norway)	Ministry of Education and Research (2010)	These regulations apply to universities and university colleges that provide primary and lower secondary teacher education. They aim to ensure that teacher education institutions provide integrated, professionally oriented and research-based primary and lower secondary teacher education programmes of high academic quality.
National or regional standards for educators acting as mentors	National Standards for School-based Initial Teacher Training (ITT) Mentors (England)	DfE (2016)	The standards were developed to bring greater coherence and consistency to school-based mentoring arrangements for student teachers. They set out the minimum level of practice expected of mentors. They are used to foster consistency in the practice of mentors, raise the profile of mentoring and build a culture of mentoring in schools (DfE, 2016b).
	The New York State Mentoring Standards Albany (USA)	The State Education Department/ The University of the State of New York (2011)	A set of standards that guide the design and implementation of teacher mentoring programmes in New York State through teacher induction.

(continued)

Table 1.1 (Cont.)

	Policy/guidance document	Author and date introduced	Key purpose
National or regional guidelines for general coaching and mentoring practice	National Framework for Mentoring and Coaching (England)	Centre for the Use of Resource and Evidence in Education (CUREE) (2005)	The framework was developed in order to help schools implement mentoring and coaching to assist with continuing professional development and other activities. It sets out ten recommended principles based on evidence from research and consultation to inform mentoring and coaching programmes in schools. The framework provides a tool for reflection on existing practice and further development and assists a mentor in self-regulation and monitoring of their own practice.
	NTC Continuum of Mentoring Practice (USA)	New Teacher Centre (NTC) (2011)	Designed to assist programme leaders as they seek to implement mentoring to support induction programmes that are capable of accelerating the development of beginning teacher effectiveness, improving teacher retention, strengthening teacher leadership and increasing pupil learning. 'It presents a holistic view of mentoring, based on six professional standards... The continuum of mentoring practice describes three levels of development, labelled Exploring/Emerging, Applying, Integrating/Innovating' (New Teacher Center, 2011, p.2)
Professional development expectations for teachers	Standards for Teachers' Professional Development (England)	DfE (2016)	This is intended for 'all those working in and with, schools in order to raise expectations for professional development, to focus on achieving the best improvement in pupil outcomes and also to develop teachers as respected members of the profession' (DFE 2016c, p.4). There is an emphasis on using the standards to support regular reflection on existing practice and discussion between all members of the teaching community. There are five parts to the standards, which, when acted upon together, ensure effective professional development.
	Ohio Standards for Professional Development (USA)	Ohio Department for Education (2015)	These define the essential elements of a strong professional learning system which is one way that school systems can support all educators and encourage improved teaching and learning.

Maynard and Furlong (1995a, p.18) acknowledged that these three models exist but suggested that they should be taken together, in order to contribute to 'a view of mentoring that responds to the changing needs of trainees'. It is this recognition that mentoring practices and approaches evolve as a beginning teacher develops and it is the need for an examination of different stages of development that leads us to exploring three models of mentoring in more detail. We explore three well-known models (Daloz, 2012; Katz, 1995; and Clutterbuck, 2004), all of which focus on the need for the mentor to be flexible in their style and approach to best fit the needs of a beginning teacher at any given stage of their development, in initial teacher education and/or their teaching career.

Daloz's (2012) developmental model identifies two key aspects that need to be present in order for optimal learning to take place: **challenge** and **support**. The challenge aspect refers to your ability as a mentor to question a beginning teacher to enable them to reflect critically on their own beliefs, behaviours and attitudes. The support aspect relies on you being able to offer an empathetic ear, actively listen and encourage a beginning teacher to find solutions in order to continue to develop and progress.

Daloz (2012) argues that a combination of high challenge and high support need to be offered by you as the mentor for a beginning teacher to learn effectively and to '**grow**' (high challenge + high support = **growth**). At the opposite end of this spectrum is what Daloz refers to as '**stasis**'. A beginning teacher's learning in this zone is very limited indeed as a result of their mentor offering low levels of challenge and support (low challenge + low support = **stasis**). Where challenge is high but support is low, a beginning teacher is likely to '**retreat**' from development (high challenge + low support = **retreat**). However, where challenge is low but support is high, a beginning teacher is unlikely to move beyond their present situation despite their potential for growth. Daloz refers to this as '**confirmation**' (low challenge + high support = **confirmation**). You therefore need to be aware of both the level of challenge you offer and the level of support needed by the beginning teacher.

The second model is Katz's stages of development model (1995) which describes a model for professional growth in four stages:

1. Survival stage
2. Consolidation stage
3. Renewal stage
4. Maturity stage

During the first stage, '**Survival**', a beginning teacher is likely to show signs of being very self-focused and just 'getting by' or coping from day to day. They are likely to experience their practice from a position of doubt and to ask questions like 'can I get to the end of the week?' or 'can I really do this day after day?'. During this initial stage, a beginning teacher may show a reluctance to take responsibility for things and, instead, look to blame others, for example, the pupils, colleagues, the school. As a mentor, observing a beginning teacher during the survival stage, you are likely to see elements of confusion and a lack of any clear rules and routines in their lessons. The beginning teacher may also demonstrate little, if any, consistency in their approach to managing behaviour. Their teaching style is often very teacher-centric and they show a reluctance to deviate from their 'script' in any way.

By the second stage, '**Consolidation**', it is likely that a beginning teacher will have begun to implement clearer rules and routines into their classrooms. There is evidence of them starting to question their own practice and being more open to alternative ways of doing things. Whilst observing a beginning teacher at this stage, you are likely to notice that their classes are generally well managed and that the needs of the average pupil are predominantly well catered for. In addition, the beginning teacher is likely to demonstrate a greater awareness of individual pupils and their learning needs. However, they are unlikely to have gained a true grasp of how to support and cater for the needs of pupils within specific subgroups, for example, those with special educational needs and disability (SEND), English as an Additional Language (EAL) and Gifted and Talented (GandT).

The '**renewal**' stage is the point at which a beginning teacher is becoming much more self-aware and self-critical. They have generally mastered the basics and are now striving for ways in which they can improve their practice. They are looking for strategies and ideas of how to introduce more creative and innovative activities into their lessons. As a general rule of thumb, at the 'renewal' stage beginning teachers are often at their most self-motivated and are eager to contribute to departmental discussions, offer suggestions, design additional resources and/or become involved in the running of lunchtime and after-school clubs.

The final stage of Katz's model, '**maturity**', is where a beginning teacher is demonstrating signs of developing their own beliefs, teaching style and strategies. They are regularly asking themselves a number of questions which support deeper levels of reflection, both in and on practice (Schön, 1983). They are still looking to improve their practice and are still interested in new ideas and resources. However, their focus has shifted from an inwards perspective to a much broader one. They are now very much interested in the impact of their teaching on their pupils' learning and progress.

Task 1.5 Responsibilities of the mentor and beginning teacher at each stage of Katz's development model

In each of Katz's stages, there are responsibilities for both the mentor and beginning teacher. Identify what you would do to support a beginning teacher at each stage.

And finally, Clutterbuck's (2004) model of developmental mentoring suggests that an effective mentor wants to draw on all four of the 'helping to learn' styles: guiding, coaching, counselling and networking (see Figure 1.1). Figure 1.1 shows that in any given mentoring relationship, a mentor may need to adopt a different style and/or approach to challenge and support a beginning teacher at various stages of their development. In developmental mentoring the beginning teacher sets the agenda based on their own development needs and the mentor provides insight and guidance to support the beginning teacher to achieve the desired goals. A more expert mentor will be able to select the right 'helping to learn' style for a beginning teacher's needs.

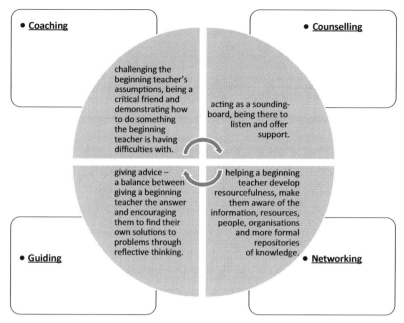

Figure 1.1 Developmental mentoring
(Source: Adapted from Clutterbuck's model (2004, p.9))

Task 1.6 Helping a beginning teacher to learn using Clutterbuck's model

- Consider which of the four 'helping to learn' styles you feel most comfortable with and why.
- Which do you use the least often and/or feel the least comfortable with and why?
- What could you do to overcome this?

Your ability to assess and identify the developmental stage in which a beginning teacher is operating at any given point is a significant aspect of your role in becoming an effective mentor and ensuring growth takes places. Of equal importance, however, is your skill in adapting your own approach to fit the developmental needs of a beginning teacher. It is worth remembering that none of the three models (Daloz (2012), Katz (1995) or Clutterbuck (2004)) is linear in structure and, therefore, it is likely that a beginning teacher will move 'to and fro' between stages or zones when, for example, teaching different aspects of the curriculum in which they have greater or less knowledge and/or confidence, or starting at a new school. With each of the models considered above it is possible to see elements of all three approaches to mentoring described by Maynard and Furlong (1995a). Regardless of the mentoring model on which you prefer to base your practice, the attributes of the mentor play a crucial role in making decisions about the approach to mentoring.

There have been a number of attempts to characterise attributes of mentors. For example, Child and Merrill (2005) sought to generate an understanding of the attributes of a mentor in initial teacher education. Cho et al. (2011) described personal qualities that lie at the core of the mentor's identity and professional traits that relate to success in work-related activities. The DfE (2016b) described four separate but related areas in the *National Standards for School-based Initial Teacher Training (ITT) Mentors*, i.e. personal qualities; teaching; professionalism and self-development; and working in partnership. Ragins (2016) described the attributes of a mentor as an antecedent to high quality mentoring; as something that needs to be in place before a mentor–mentee relationship begins.

Task 1.7   Attributes of an effective mentor

1. Considering the context and models of mentoring outlined in this chapter, reflect upon what you think the attributes of an effective mentor are. Attach a level of significance to each attribute, using three categories of significance: *essential*, *highly desirable* or *desirable*.
2. Having identified the attributes and the levels of significance, place five of the attributes in a prioritised list that best captures the ideal profile of a mentor of a beginning teacher.
3. Reflect on your own practice as a mentor. How might you develop the attributes you have prioritised?

Task 1.8   Mentor reflection: Reflecting on your mentoring practice

After having read this chapter, reflect how your understanding of definitions of mentoring, relevant policy and guidance documents and models of mentoring have or will have an impact on your practice.

Summary and key points

Effective mentoring is a complex and demanding task, but, as with any role that enables you to have a positive impact on the development of others, it is hugely rewarding. In this chapter, we have considered the importance of:

- being aware of different definitions of mentoring
- understanding the context in which you are carrying out your role and what moral, political or theoretical drivers might influence the education system that you work in and/or your work as a mentor
- having a broad understanding of different models of, or approaches to, mentoring in order to make decisions about how to carry out your role as a mentor

SECTION 2
You as a mentor

2 Understanding yourself and how your experiences influence your approaches to mentoring

Andrew Goodwyn

Introduction – English: 'The quicksilver' subject

English as a school subject was once characterised as being the 'quicksilver' subject (Dixon, 1967) because of its liquidity and capacity to stay 'liquid', to stay mobile, moving and elusive to definition. This characterisation is now more than 50 years old but it remains a valuable insight into the way English refuses any neat and prescribing definition. Perhaps in official terms it is much less mobile and now more fixed, certainly being formed by examination demands such as GCSE. Back in the late 1980s we had the first National Curriculum for English (NCE), something that produced huge debate amongst teachers at the time; the said NCE has been revised numerous times, revealing, in different ways, that there are ongoing attempts to define English by various interested parties. But exactly what English is – and is for – remains valuably elusive, allowing for teacher agency to work in the open space that is the subject. What emerges from this is absolutely not a problem. What emerges is that English is so fascinating to teach, and to study, because it is broad and inclusive and provides exciting flexibilities in the hands of a good English teacher; whatever the authorities are demanding, you still make it your own in your classroom every day and in partnership with your students.

This chapter asks you to think carefully about your own genuine views about English, how you formed (and continue to form) those views and how they will influence your role as a mentor. The chapter deliberately looks at the 'big picture', the really formative influences on the subject and how its rich and complex history still plays out in the daily practice of teachers. There are a series of stopping points where you are invited to pause and actively reflect on your relationship to English as a subject; not just the school subject as it exists now, but many versions of English you have experienced from being a school student yourself to later forms of study, including your own teacher training. More often questions are posed to prompt continual reflection and material is introduced about the history and formation of the subject to stimulate a recognition that the subject is, itself, continually changing and that mentees' potential obsession with the present needs to be mediated towards beginning to develop a longer and more informed view. Rather than try to define the indefinable, we should start with purpose; it will help lead towards a definition at least of content, as in what should we study in English?

Objectives

At the end of this chapter, you will have:

- A greater understanding of the influences that have shaped the nature of English as a school subject;
- A greater understanding of the influences that have shaped your own experiences of and views about English;
- An appreciation of how this understanding might support you in your work as a mentor of a beginning teacher of English.

Purpose or purposes

When Dixon (1967) coined the quicksilver characterisation he also discussed the purposes of English. At that time, he identified two existing and well-established purposes. One was the idea of the Literary Heritage, something that has continued to dominate teaching English since the 1920s, and adult literacy, often called Adult Needs – that is the need for adults to function in the world, to read and write and communicate as responsible and active citizens. Whilst this need has not changed, the nature of the literacies of the twenty-first century are certainly more complex and multimodal than they were 50 years ago. What are the exact literacy skills in reading and writing on Twitter or profiling your life on Instagram and Facebook (probably soon to be replaced)? Equally, how can we ensure our citizens can cope with the demands of 'reading' in the digital universe that envelops most of them? No doubt you will have views about such matters.

English is always engaging with the real lives of students. English is not abstract, it is not a strict 'discipline': it is not understanding algebra or quantum mechanics; it does not make such concrete knowledge claims about itself nor does it distance itself from the critical reality of young people, asking real-life questions such as, 'how should I live?', 'why does this book upset/ anger/soothe/enchant me?' English involves good ideas to help young people think about these important matters and that is why they cannot be reduced to a formula; no wonder it is such fun to teach.

All teachers are purposeful; English teachers are both professionally purposeful and personally engaged with that purpose. When they can, they take great care, for example, over the choice of a text to work with in a class. Such a choice is both professional – *this text is appropriate for these students at this stage of their development* – but also personal – *I believe this is the right text (chosen from many) for this purpose for these students and I own that choice*. This leads us to consider Dixon's new model, that of Personal Growth. For him and his generation of influential thinkers about English such as James Britton, Harold Rosen, Douglas Barnes, Nancy Martin and a host of others, Personal Growth was a new student-centred view of English as a dynamic element in the emotional and intellectual development of each individual student.

So, what is the purpose of your English teaching? What is it you want to encourage your mentee to do in the classroom when learning to teach English?

Here is a first reflective opportunity – one we will return to throughout the chapter.

These 'models of English' were produced to inform the production of the first NCE. Research over the last 30 years (Goodwyn, 2010, 2016a, 2016b) suggests that – in one form or another – they remain influential and significant, regardless of changes to curriculum prescriptions and examination criteria. They remain useful 'versions' of the purpose of English that English teachers themselves recognise and think about when planning English work:

- A 'personal growth' view focuses on the child: it emphasises the relationship between language and learning in the individual child, and the role of literature in developing children's imaginative and aesthetic lives.
- A 'cross-curricular' view focuses on the school: it emphasises that all teachers (of English and of other subjects) have a responsibility to help children with the language demands of different subjects on the school curriculum: otherwise areas of the curriculum may be closed to them. In England, English is different from other school subjects, in that it is both a subject and a medium of instruction for other subjects.
- An 'adult needs' view focuses on communication outside the school: it emphasises the responsibility of English teachers to prepare children for the language demands of adult life, including the workplace, in a fast-changing world. Children need to learn to deal with the day-to-day demands of spoken language and of print; they also need to be able to write clearly, appropriately and effectively.
- A 'cultural heritage' view emphasises the responsibility of schools to lead children to an appreciation of those works of literature that have been widely regarded as amongst the finest in the language.
- A 'cultural analysis' view emphasises the role of English in helping children towards a critical understanding of the world and cultural environment in which they live. Children should know about the processes by which meanings are conveyed, and about the ways in which print and other media carry values (Department of Education and Science and the Welsh Office, 1989).

Whilst these models were developed in the UK, another model that has emerged – especially in Australia and the USA – is Critical Literacy. (As an aside, I suggest here that mentors should always engage with broader horizons than their own – never be merely parochial – it is part of your job to help mentees see beyond the local 'this is what works here'. Who knows where they will be going next?) A possible definition (there are many variants):

> 'Critical literacy' is the ability to read texts in an active, reflective manner in order to better understand power, inequality and injustice in human relationships. For the purposes of critical literacy, text is defined as a 'vehicle through which individuals communicate with one another using the codes and conventions of society'. Accordingly, songs, novels, conversations, pictures, movies, etc. are all considered texts. The development of critical literacy skills enables people to interpret messages in the modern world through a critical lens and challenge the power relations within those messages. Teachers who facilitate the development of critical literacy encourage students to interrogate societal issues and institutions like family, poverty, education, equity, and equality in order to critique the structures that serve as norms as well as to demonstrate how these norms are not experienced by all members of society.
>
> (Goodwyn, 2016b, p.18)

> **Task 2.1 Reflecting on models of English**
>
> What, in your view, is the purpose of English?
> How do you view these models in relation to your own beliefs about teaching English?
>
> Consider the following:
>
> Does one stand out as the key model?
> Are they complementary or contradictory?
> Are some more to do with what you **have to do** than with **what you want to do**?
> Are some models more important at Key Stage 3 (KS3) than Key Stage 4 (KS4) or Key Stage 5 (KS5)?
> Are some models related more to public expectations, rather than your personal aspiration?
> Is one model your core model, or are they all 'you'?
> Finally, do you see these models in any of the documentation you work with, such as school schemes of work, NCE, GCSE specifications?

You may feel that the pressure in mentor meetings is almost entirely on practical matters, planning lessons, considering assessment tasks for classes and so on. However, it would be valuable in your mentor meetings, perhaps in the initial stages of training, to offer these models as prompts to reflection and the basis for a discussion about your views, and the mentee's views, of English. Perhaps just select one at a time to begin with – and at a session later in the year of their ITT course or NQT year – offer them all together and consider the bigger picture.

Becoming an English teacher

As has become apparent in the opening section, English is a personal subject for its teachers – and its students – and its teachers regularly use the word 'love' about it. This is not in any way to say that Maths teachers do not love Maths. On the contrary, they are equally passionate about its beauty and aesthetics (Goodwyn, 2018) and its fundamental significance in human history, but its content (expressed simplistically) is numbers and variations on that theme. Equally we can all love music – without reading or ever playing a note of it. When our students leave school or university they will no longer 'DO' English. They will do some Maths every time they check their credit bill, they will be doing Music if they are making it or listening to it but, even though they are dealing with language and messages almost every second, they will not be doing some simple thing called English. Yet they will be 'doing' so many things that are a part of it: the four language modes of reading, writing, speaking, listening (we might include 'viewing' if you see media-related work as a part of the school subject English (see the section Starting with literature below for further thinking on that topic)).

It is not accidental that English is the subject that principally prioritises autobiography. It has its place in other subjects, perhaps, but it would be emphatic that in most subjects, even History, it will be biography that is key. So English in every sense is the autobiographical subject and its teachers bring their personal histories into their teaching.

This next section is deliberately framed through a generalisation to enable you to position yourself in relation to that. Research demonstrates (Goodwyn, 2010, Gibbons, 2016) that most English teachers express their motivation for becoming an English teacher as a 'love of reading' and a wish to pass that love on to their students. Generally, they are less motivated by a love of writing, a love of language or grammar or spelling – or even a love of 'literacy'. Within that 'love' is a love of reading literature and how the literature is defined varies a good deal. It was striking that in the period of the National Literacy Strategy and Framework for English, 1997–2007, English teachers were adamant that they were not teachers of 'Literacy' (Goodwyn, 2010; Goodwyn & Fuller, 2011). Of course, they are teachers of literacy in the traditional sense of teaching reading and writing, but what they were objecting to was a narrow version of Literacy being prescribed by the government and a pedagogy that they found patronising.

Task 2.2 Considering literacy

'Literacy', like school subject 'English' is harder to define than parents and politicians like to think. We touched above on the 'Adult Needs' model of English, deriving as it does from a notion of a level of functional capability with language enabling an adult to be a successful citizen. Your mentees, whatever their age, have experienced many years of the digital environment. Some teachers welcome the proliferation of e-readers (iPads, Kindles etc.), whereas others see them as threatening real reading.

So, what is your stance on twenty-first-century literacy?
What might you learn from conversations with your mentees about literacy that will keep you in touch with how it is evolving?

As a colleague once pointed out when being interviewed for an English teacher training programme, no interviewee has ever said their motivation for joining the profession was writing perfect objectives on the board. The 'love of literature' has a long history in English teaching and, if it does not express your own inspiration for becoming a teacher of English, it does express the majority motivation. Therefore it is a serious and important consideration in reflecting on the purpose of the profession and what it sees students as engaging with when they 'do English'. One thing you might explore with your mentee is that they do have a powerful motivation but they may not be fully aware of it; they may have several motives, some conflicting, even confusing. They need to work these through and discussion of purpose and motivation, including your own, are vital. If you are honest, why are you still teaching English after x number of years? What started you off down that path?

> **Task 2.3 Considering motivation**
>
> Consider the following:
>
> What motivated you to become an English teacher?
> Have any of these motivations changed with time and experience? Are any the same?
> Why does your mentee want to be an English teacher?

Starting with literature

In the history of English teaching two broadly expressed paradigms have been present in relation to teachers' passion and purpose about teaching English. The first was literature, the second, more of a hybrid purpose but with more attention to, language. The first can be traced principally to the work of F.R. Leavis and I.A. Richards in the 1920s and 30s. Terry Eagleton, a very celebrated literary critic and theorist, observed that 'all English teachers are Leavisites whether they know it not' (Eagleton, 1975). What he was getting at was the 'mission' of many English teachers, over a number of generations, to introduce their students to literature and especially 'Great Literature' as a transformative experience, highly moral and elevating. One of the first expressions of this mission was as long ago as 1921 in The Newbolt Report, the first ever official, national review of the place of English in the national education system.

What his colleague, Richards, added was the idea of critical analysis of why literature is great and how we know. His famous experiments with Cambridge undergraduates (Richards, 1929), asking them to evaluate the quality of short texts or extracts, sight unseen, led to his formulation of the concept of 'Practical Criticism', which has been a dominating practice in English since that time. His idea was that properly trained readers could discriminate between texts, even texts which had their authorship and date of writing and all context stripped away. Readers, it was implied, should have developed the perfect critical judgement to know what was great and what was not.

Richards' pioneering work on the real responses of readers and analysing them for their own sake produced a body of research unequivocally demonstrating that readers really do respond very personally to texts. However, in doing so they draw on both literary knowledge and also personal, life knowledge. These findings were first picked up in 1967 by Louise Rosenblatt (1995), who developed Reader Response Theory, the chief principle of which is that readers necessarily generate a response that starts from the personal and that at different stages in life their responses will change. Equally, she showed that initial responses to a text are constantly modified by rereading and by engaging with the responses of other readers. Considering these ideas gives us something that sounds like pedagogy: first, getting readers to engage with a text; second, getting them to articulate their response through speech and writing; third, the teacher's input at all stages and, perhaps, finally, asking students to produce a summative response as work on the text comes to an end (this might take many forms but tends to be something like a literary essay). In the UK, English teachers tend not to use Reader Response as a guiding paradigm but they actively use the approach, tending more often to emphasise the term personal response.

> **Task 2.4 Personal reflection: Personal response**
>
> Consider the following:
>
> How important is personal response to you in your teaching, especially in relation to literature?
>
> To what extent do you feel that students' often desperate desire for a right answer should be encouraged or discouraged?

In the background to this development of Practical Criticism, Leavis was working on teaching his students (many of whom went on to be English teachers) to resist the allurements and the seductions of popular culture. 'Popular culture', epitomised most of all by advertising and the commercialisation of culture through mass media via newspapers, magazines and so on, were, to Leavis, a corrosive development. Building on Richards' work, he developed the battle cry 'discriminate and resist' (Leavis and Thompson, 1933). English teachers, research demonstrates, still struggle with their relationship to popular culture. An influential research study of English teachers in the 1970s (Mathieson, 1975), when popular culture was pressing in on the classroom through the increasing influence of movies, television and 'pop' music, characterised English teachers revealingly as 'The Preachers of Culture'. Leavis, paradoxically, was a kind of father to media studies. His 'discriminate and resist' battle cry was powerful, not least because he did sense the emergent power of the media, even back in the 1930s. His approach was later renamed as 'inoculation theory' – the metaphor suggesting that injecting young minds with evidence that popular media was bad for you would then lead to healthy adults who could, indeed, resist popular culture.

Is this approach still a valuable element of English teaching? Do our students need to be protected from fake news and daytime television? Where do you stand on including media-related work in English? These questions become especially relevant as there are no longer any direct references in the National Curriculum or GCSE. This is certainly paradoxical because, since the first NCE in 1989, the presence of media-related work has increasingly been a part of English, perhaps culminating with the 2000 version where it became statutory for English teachers to teach their students about the moving image (Goodwyn, 2004). Again, we are reminded how much external influences impose change on what English teachers are supposed to teach.

So, will you encourage your mentee to plan and teach some lessons which are media related or will you discourage them from that kind of work – and why?

At the time of writing, the official curriculum of English is dominated once more by not just a focus on cultural heritage but actually the 'English Literary Heritage'. Mentees may well be very concerned about how to teach dense and difficult nineteenth-century texts. Although this is knowledge that they will need to thrive in current circumstances, this will always be valuable subject pedagogical knowledge. However, the current heavyweight dominance of the English Literary Heritage is a problem and not a solution to becoming a well-balanced and authentically committed English teacher.

It was recognition of this dominance that led to the development of what might be seen as the other or complementary paradigm that continues to be fundamental to good English teaching. Although the society that Leavis was addressing was heavily structured by class and the establishment, in many respects it was relatively homogeneous. So much so that George Sampson, a member of the Newbolt Committee, wrote his book *English for the English* in 1922, a passionate argument for the centrality of English language and literature to replace the old model of Classics as key to social glue, after the social traumas of World War One.

But after World War Two and further trauma, the 1960s was a decade that tried to come to terms with an emergent multicultural society, a nationalising imperative meant to deliver social justice, to remove class barriers and to deal with an extraordinary impetus from young people to create a new popular culture. One outcome was the move to comprehensive schooling, part of the nationalising, social justice impetus.

English led the way as a school subject determined to stay relevant to young people and society. Equally new theories and new research challenged many of the received wisdoms of the elitist academic model of research. The psychological work of Piaget and Vygotsky, of William James and John Dewey, offered totally new perspectives on how we learn and what we mean by knowledge. The work of Richards and Rosenblatt was part of this move away from narrowly received wisdoms to the ideas of experience and personal expression.

Dixon's third model of English was Personal Growth. Its central principle is that English is student centred, that the point of 'doing English' is to learn as an individual in a social context, how to use language powerfully and how to understand the power of language. Literature, as one of the key cultural linguistic artefacts, is thus naturally central to both textual analysis and textual production. However, this model treats students as readers with personal responses, not just 'appreciative' responses. It also considers students as writers of many genres of text, some of which (poems, for example) are in the literary mode of expression. It encourages personal expression and personal response, but not, as some critics argue, in some romanticised, vague way suggesting we can all be poets. What it argues is that the local linguistic resources of the students' communities are vital. Thus, the idea of Heritage is transformed to heritages and multilingualism. One of the more formal expressions of this paradigm is partly evidenced in the hugely influential Bullock Report of 1975, 'A Language for Life'. It was then strongly emphasised in the Cox Report, as one of the '5 models of English'. Research over many years (Goodwyn, 2016b) shows that Personal Growth remains the perspective that best fits with English teachers' views of their subject and of how they believe children learn. Indeed it has been called a holistic view of education rather than just a view of English. What the research has also demonstrated is that the first version of the NCE in 1989, was actually the closest official version of English to teachers' own views, beliefs and values (Goodwyn, 1997).

So, where do you stand on this question of whether English fundamentally is about Personal Growth? As mentioned above, most new English teachers cite a 'love of reading' as their motivation for becoming an English teacher and usually they have never heard of Personal Growth, or its informing spirit, John Dewey, before they started their teacher training (they may not have heard of it there, either, given how much time may be spent on very instrumental techniques). Most experienced English teachers pride themselves on their relationships with students as individuals and they have knowledge of the student as a person, usually enhanced by some knowledge of their social situation such as friends and family.

That English is a personal subject has been one powerful reason why students have valued it. In its lessons they have a voice in both talking situations and writing. However, this is far from some verbal 'free for all'; students have to learn how to talk in small groups, how to engage purposefully in whole class discussion, how to listen intently to others, especially those they disagree with. The reduction of the status of speaking and listening in the current NCE and GCSE is another relatively recent narrowing of the scope of English. Mentees often find the kinds of lesson that involve a good deal of student talk especially hard to construct and manage. You can be a powerful role model in relation to that challenge. How might you model, for them, a lesson which is principally about speaking and listening in both senses: that is, students actively participating in speaking and listening activities as well as learning something about the nature of speaking and listening and the kinds of skill needed to be a successful participant? This is an essential in the English classroom, being clearly a vital skill set for further study, for working life and for being a future parent.

Task 2.5 Reflecting on practice

Reflect on your own teaching and your lessons.

- What kind of English are you modelling for your mentees?
- How do lessons demonstrate a love of reading and literature in particular?
- Do they prioritise the individuality of students?
- Do you model 'immediacy', that being where the teacher brings her life in to the lessons as a connective to the lives of students?
- When asked by your mentee about aspects of your practice, are you able to ground these in a clear rationale for English as a subject?

Not a conclusion but a beginning

One way of approaching an understanding of English is by exploring the subject with a novice teacher as they seek answers and words of wisdom. Many experienced mentors explain (Goodwyn, 1997) that they value mentees because they ask questions in a naive way but which demands an articulation of often profoundly complex ideas. A model of expertise was created by the Dreyfus brothers as they were contesting, back in the 1980s, the claims that Artificial Intelligence would replace humans in many professions, including teaching. Their argument was ahead of its time, pointing out that human intelligence and our emotions make our authentic expertise irreplaceable. However, what they also showed was that expert practitioners (in a number of professions) become so highly expert that much of their thinking is 'automatic' – but not 'robotic'. What it means is that the highly skilled teacher is doing many excellent things in a kind of routine way, especially aspects of classroom management, which liberates their mental space to focus on what really matters in a lesson, and especially to 'see' all the students as individuals and to anticipate and solve problems (Goodwyn, 2010). To the mentee, highly accomplished teaching looks effortless and marvellous and I would argue that this is especially true of English teachers.

As a result, mentees can observe an excellent English lesson and learn almost nothing from it because they cannot see the deftness and nuances of the teacher's work. To get the meaning, they need to ask simplistic questions but also to have you draw their attention to where they can see the meaning of the lesson. In this respect English may be harder to 'read' than some other subjects. That is partly why some discussions need to be about the subject itself and its history and your history as an English teacher. Mentees want stability and predictability and must develop confidence in order to develop competence. But they also need to start to realise that English is a flexible subject that provides much spontaneous opportunity for student learning and teacher enjoyment. They must also be helped to accept that the subject will not sit still. External influences will come and go, but much that is its core has a long history of evolution and development and needs to be valued and understood.

Task 2.6   Follow-up tasks

There are many ways in which you might follow up some of the ideas in this chapter. Here are some suggestions:

- Ask your mentee, in early mentor sessions, to reflect on and articulate their reasons for becoming an English teacher.
- Return to these on a regular basis, asking your mentee to reflect on how and where this motivation is reflected and demonstrated in their emerging practice.
- Make explicit and draw attention to, for your mentee, the opportunities in your own practice.
- Review different curriculum frameworks (NCE, GCSE, A Level, DfE's long-term planning) in the light of the different models of English considered. Discuss the differing priorities and how different models might be foregrounded.

Further reading

Davison, J., Daly C. & Moss, J. (2010). *Debates in English Teaching*. London: Routledge.
This book discusses a number of topics and debates related to English teaching, to encourage teachers to reflect on and consider their views on teaching English in the light of theoretical knowledge and understanding.

The English and Media Centre (www.englishandmedia.co.uk/blog) publishes regular blog posts discussing pertinent topics and concerns centred on the nature and purpose of the study of English.

3 What subject and pedagogical knowledge, understanding and skills does a mentor of beginning English teachers need?

Sally Catchpole and Theresa Gooda

Introduction

As introduced and discussed in Chapter 2, English as a subject sits upon shifting sands. Its domain is not fixed. The English language itself is in constant metamorphosis and the subject encompasses much more than language. The skills, knowledge, even texts that might form foundations are themselves malleable. English studies are extensive, complex, often contentious and continually changing (Stevens & Lowing 2008). Depending on your perspective, English may straddle creative, humanistic, growth, cultural, literacy, linguistic, heritage, critical thinking and functional models. The national curriculum, and the canon, are themselves both inherently problematic in relation to English content; and subject knowledge clearly cannot be limited to these spheres alone. Moreover, subject knowledge of English is inevitably bound up with classroom and pedagogic knowledge; at times they appear to be so integrated as to be indivisible. Teachers' knowledge is both nuanced and unsystematic (Yandell, 2017).

Chapter 1 identified the importance of recognising and embedding current policy and statutory guidance in your mentoring practice and considered a number of associated key documents. Chapter 2 has dealt with the ways in which influences have shaped the subject of English and therefore your understanding of the subject. This chapter considers what knowledge you, as mentor, require in order to undertake the role, offers some approaches for identifying knowledge, skills and understanding, and considers ways that you might keep you own subject knowledge updated in order to support beginning English teachers who themselves are more likely to have concerns about their levels of subject knowledge in particular (Stevens & Lowing 2008). There are significant links between the ideas of this chapter and Chapter 7, which specifically addresses supporting and developing the subject pedagogical knowledge of beginning English teachers.

If you are, in part, responsible for a new teacher's entry into the profession then it stands to reason that a certain degree of subject knowledge must be in place and yet, as we have already identified, there is no recognised single body of knowledge that constitutes 'English'. You are, however, more likely to operate as an effective mentor when you are able to be honest about your subject knowledge; when you are open to understanding what you *don't* know, as well as being realistic about the contested nature of 'knowledge', including within English itself.

Objectives

At the end of this chapter, you will be able to:

- Have a greater understanding of the nature of knowledge and of different types of knowledge;
- Have reflected on the nature of knowledge in English and on which your practice is built and developed;
- Have considered your own knowledge, including ongoing development in order to address 'gaps';
- Have considered your specific development of knowledge of mentoring.

What is knowledge?

Before we can begin to consider how we might support beginning English teachers, it is useful to consider in more detail what it is that we mean by knowledge and its significance in our position as English teachers.

Task 3.1   Beliefs about knowledge

Consider the following questions:

> What is knowledge in and of English?
> What is knowledge of teaching and learning?
> Where does it come from?
> Why do you need it?

Discuss these questions with your mentee at an early stage in their placement.

Your responses to these questions will reveal a great deal about your understanding of knowledge broadly *and* within English. Your ideas about and attitudes towards the nature of knowledge will very likely inform the decisions and choices that you make daily as a teacher of English. There may be many similarities between your ideas and those of the student teacher that you are supporting, but there may also be differences. More significantly, as the mentor with responsibility for supporting the development of the beginning teacher, you may well be in a position to make recommendations about their subject knowledge and how it might be developed. In order to be able to effectively manage this, it might be helpful to spend a little time considering the idea of how we acquire and develop knowledge, and how this relates to our professional development and practice.

Wilson (2017) and Philpott (2013) discuss variously the different types of knowledge that might be associated with working in education. These types of knowledge are not separate and distinct. Neither are they fixed or permanent. They are perhaps better understood as being flexible, interrelated and dynamic:

Encoded knowledge – this is codified, sometimes academic, knowledge which allows us to communicate increasingly complex ideas and understandings, often in the form of theories. Encoded knowledge might also include rule-based information such as might be found in policy documents. Encoded knowledge is likely, therefore, to form the foundation of much of your professional practice.

Craft knowledge – this is often practical knowledge, presented in the form of strategies or actions and sometimes tacit in teacher practice. It is usually context based. This knowledge can sometimes be difficult to articulate, because teachers may not always be aware of what it is that they are doing. Sometimes such knowledge may be presented as simple or straightforward, but it is often only acquired through significant and localised experience.

Cultural knowledge – this includes knowledge of the conventions and etiquette that govern the way that we interact with each other. This exists in many different forms and at different levels, including knowing and understanding the way a particular society or group works. A school is a particular community with its own culture, ethos and behaviours, some of which may be very specific to the institution. Some of the cultural expectations and practices might be made explicit in formal policy and practice documents whereas others might be more tacit.

Personal knowledge – Another type of knowledge upon which teachers and student teachers will depend is knowledge of self. Student teachers will already have some clear personal beliefs and views about teaching, which may become clearer when they talk about why they want to be a teacher. Some may have already worked in a school. All will have had significant experience of education in terms of their own schooling. These experiences will have developed particular views and ideas about teaching which they will bring to the course and to their practice. Considering these and where they come from is part of the reflexive, and therefore critical, thinking discussed in Chapter 8.

Subject knowledge – this is often specific, domain-based knowledge, commonly identified as academic in form, which might include that which was gained in the study of a specialist degree. You will know from your own experience and from your experience of working with student teachers that academic subject knowledge alone does not prepare the student teacher explicitly or wholly for teaching. They will need additional knowledge, including knowledge within the subject domain of Education, and knowledge of pedagogy, so that they can make sense of their own and others' practice. These particular aspects of knowledge and how they might be developed in a beginning teacher of English are addressed in more detail in Chapter 7.

Task 3.2 Reflecting on your own knowledge in practice

Reflect on a recent day in school, including lessons that you taught.

Which of the above forms of knowledge are identifiable in your reflection?
Which forms of knowledge are more dominant?

You might find it useful to ask your student teacher to reflect on their own understanding of knowledge in a similar way, as an introduction to or alternative way of discussing their subject knowledge development.

The different types of knowledge discussed at the start of the chapter might also prove a useful starting point for reflecting on the different types of knowledge with which you will want your student teacher to become more confident. For example, in relation to encoded knowledge, there will undoubtedly be a number of policy and practice documents with which your student teacher will need to be familiar. Not only will they need to understand and follow the policies which underpin practice in your particular setting, they will also need to understand some of the statutory frameworks and guidance which underpin practice in English more broadly, such as the National Curriculum (DfE, 2013a) and GCSE specifications. In terms of cultural knowledge, student teachers are likely to have some ideas of the ways in which education in the UK works. They will have knowledge of the general ways that schools work, because of their own schooling experience. However, they may need specific guidance and advice about the culture of your own school. This might include, for example, advice about tea and coffee routines in the department, as well as seating arrangements at break time. There might also be more formal cultural knowledge into which they will need induction, such as dress and behaviour codes, or planning and marking protocols which might then overlap with aspects of encoded knowledge.

Task 3.3   Reflections on encoded knowledge

Compile a list of the different documentation which underpins your practice and with which your student teacher will need to be familiar.

> How will they be introduced to these?
> Is there a logical sequence or priority for their introduction? How do you decide?
> Are these documents to be read independently or to be discussed and dissected as part of your mentoring sessions?

Student teachers will also need, as part of their development, support with developing their professional knowledge. Understanding the wider role of the professional is discussed in more detail in Chapter 12. However, within this chapter, the role of the professional also relates to the role and development of knowledge as an English teacher.

For many academics theorising about teaching as a profession, engaging with debate about the nature of knowledge is essential. Lunt, for example, argues that membership of a profession requires the acceptance of 'the contested and provisional nature of knowledge' (Lunt, 2008, pp. 88-89). Doecke argues that knowledge should be seen to 'signify a field of inquiry with certain protocols for arriving (provisionally) at a better understanding of the world' (Doecke, 2016, p. 296). In attempting to better understand the world of school and the classroom, accepting the uncertain, complex and contested views of knowledge, however, can be challenging for teachers, particularly in the early stages of their career. Green argues that 'the realities of working within the corporate context of the school and department' mean that 'personal constructs of subject must be submitted to a further (and sometimes draconian) process of moderation by consensus' (Green, 2006), p. 118). Brindley develops this idea further, suggesting that the 'relocation of knowledge to state control ... results in a dislocation of the professional values and beliefs held by the individual' so that 'the identity of the English teacher is shaped by knowledge through policy demands, and our identity is that of the "good teacher" as effective deliverer of this type of knowledge' (Brindley, 2015, p. 50).

In Chapter 2 you began to reflect on some of the influences that have shaped the nature of English as a subject in school and understood how these influences might have shaped your experience and ideas as a teacher yourself. How have your ideas about effective teaching been further shaped, as distinct from and/or as part of your understanding of your subject?

What is English?

Academics continue to critique successive government policies for the teaching of English as manifested in various inceptions of the National Curriculum (Brindley & Marshall, 2015; Davison, Daly & Moss, 2010; Goodwyn & Fuller, 2011; Lindsay & Yandell, 2014). Furthermore, many argue that various attempts to create a supposedly objective view of the curriculum are problematic (Fleming & Stevens, 2015; Ward & Connolly, 2008). This is because the subject of English in the secondary school is difficult to define, containing different epistemologies and philosophical viewpoints (Clarke et al., 2010; Fleming & Stevens, 2015). The debates about what might, could and should constitute a curriculum for English recognise 'the subject's awkward status as a medium as well as object of study, a debate which is still rife in the battle between subject skills and subject content' (Green & Mcintyre, 2011, p. 8).

Thus, if academics agree that the subject is difficult to define, and problematise successive attempts to do so, this makes more complex the question of how to support a beginning teacher of the subject.

Cliff Hodges (2016) asserts that:

> when researchers and teachers of reading engage in discussions about English as a discipline, they inevitably acquire deeper understanding about the complexity of the domain in which they are working and of the other domains in which their students are learning (Cliff Hodges, 2016, p. 15).

This assertion suggests that supporting a beginning teacher's understanding of the complexity of teaching and their development would be enhanced by discussion about the nature of the subject. So, what is English and why should students study it in school? You were probably asked a question similar to this at the interview for your own teacher training. You may have been asked about your views and ideas about teaching English as part of the interview for your current job. You began to reflect on this question during Chapter 2. It is likely that your student teacher will have been asked a similar question at interview for the training programme in which they are now participating. They may have discussed, during initial subject study sessions in their training, their view of English and its position and have been asked to consider and discuss some readings that gave them the opportunity to reflect on the nature of English in the secondary classroom.

> **Task 3.4 Reflection on the nature and purpose of English**
>
> In Chapter 2 you reflected on the purpose of English and your views about the subject. How might you discuss and compare these ideas with your mentee?
>
> Consider how your conclusions compare with the presentation of English in the National Curriculum and within the curriculum of your school. What are the key similarities and differences? Why do you think these have emerged? How might you reconcile any key differences or tensions?

You might find that your student teacher has to consider some of these questions as part of a formal assignment for their ITT provider. The rationale for this is perhaps best summarised in the following Doecke quotation:

> As members of 'a scholarly community' teachers have a solid understanding of 'the structures of subject matter, the principles of conceptual organisation, and the principles of inquiry' of their fields. Their knowledge of their fields provides a necessary framework for the learning they facilitate (Doecke, 2016, p. 295).

The assignment or task, regardless of its form and formality (informal discussion to formally assessed academic writing) is likely included as part of the student teacher's induction to this scholarly community. As a result, you might find that discussing subject knowledge development in these broader terms are a foundation of the student teacher's beginning professional development. Brindley (2015) argues that subject knowledge development as such 'requires an approach to the subject in ways that demonstrate critical engagement with a network of concepts, rather than discrete "units" of knowledge' (Brindley, 2015, p. 50). Thus, professional development as an English teacher requires a critical engagement with the nature of the subject and its underpinning concepts as much as understanding its more immediate component parts.

There is a need to be honest, therefore, about potential differences in ideas and positions and also to have engaged with different models of English teaching. It is also important to understand one's own theoretical perspective. That might seem a strange thing to say to the mentor as it is often (mis)understood that the partner training institution is where 'theory' happens. However, all teaching is rooted in theory. Scholes contends that nothing we do in a classroom exists in isolation or without theory, arguing that 'practice is never natural or neutral; there is always a theory in place, so that the first job of any teacher of criticism is to bring the assumptions that are in place out in the open for scrutiny' (Scholes, 1985, pp. x–xi).

As well as understanding and acceptance of different perspectives, empathetic skills are vital. Memories of what it was like to feel like you didn't know anything, and to feel that even what you did know was redundant, or not easily translatable to the classroom, are important, as are skills in reconciling difference. Understanding where your own ideas come from is crucial. This requires a holistic approach, considering the role, contribution and place of various forms of knowledge.

Plugging the gaps in our own knowledge

Having accepted the responsibility of mentoring as a reality, there is a duty, often unthought of, to consider your own knowledge gaps, to become aware (once more) of your own strengths and weaknesses as a teacher. There is an assumption, often untrue, that subject knowledge is balanced in terms of both literature and language and that knowledge is somehow 'competent'. An honest audit, such as considering some of the questions posed in the previous tasks, will find most mentors in a position where they have a preference, albeit unintentional, for some aspects of English.

Tomlinson (1995, in Brooks et al., 2012, p. 10) presents a model of learner development that moves from unconscious incompetence to conscious competence, arguing that there are four distinct stages:

Unconscious incompetence: learners start by not knowing what they don't know;
Conscious incompetence: learners come to recognise what they don't know;
Conscious competence: learners know in theory but apply only with difficulty;
Unconscious competence: involves knowing how to but not being fully aware of what you're doing.

In Chapter 2, Goodwyn describes the deftness and nuances of an effective teacher which might go unnoticed by the novice teacher. Both teachers in this situation might be described as at different stages in their development: the experienced teacher, unconsciously competent, teaches effectively without always clearly making explicit what they are doing and why and, when asked, they may themselves not be clear. The novice teacher, by contrast, is not able to discern the deftness, because they do not yet know how and why a lesson might be effective. One of the many jobs of the mentor is to help and support the mentee to move from one position to another, so that the beginning teacher can develop into at least a competent practitioner. This may involve making more explicit the whys and wherefores of practice, some of which may not be explicitly known.

It may be, too, that our own knowledge has actually, and paradoxically, *declined* or been diminished over time in teaching, due to the need to achieve, for example, good assessment outcomes or inspection reports. Some schools have 'neither the time nor the capacity to devote to focused study of the subject but are very focused on structures and strategies which they think meet Ofsted requirements' (Hodgson 2014, p.13). Our own practice may have become reductive through curriculum and specification requirements. It is worth, therefore, returning to the breadth of English as a subject. It is a living, conceptualised thing, beyond English pedagogy, re-engaging with the bigger picture, the stuff of which dreams are made.

What we do, implicitly and therefore tacitly, is to use our own subject knowledge in order to support gaps in student knowledge. As discussed already, teachers use a variety of different types of knowledge in order to formulate what they teach and the way in which they teach it. As practitioners we quickly become used to being self-critical, reflecting and adjusting our attitudes and skills to the needs of our students. We self-examine: 'that was a good lesson/ lesson planning/evaluation/observation'.

Many of us as practitioners will be in a position where the 'reflection *in* action' is a relatively well-established control mechanism, discussed in more detail in Chapter 8. Schön

(1983) describes this as reflecting on a process whilst it can still benefit the situation: we adapt within the actual practice, in real time, drawing upon our wide range of subject knowledge and pedagogical skills and adjust accordingly. This is how we become aware of gaps and we may have to reflect after the matter (reflection *on* action) and make professional attempts to fill those gaps. It is the acknowledgment of the deficiencies (large or small) and the need for reconciliation of them that is important.

How do we plug those gaps in our own knowledge? The questions of and about knowledge may not be something that we have considered holistically since our own experiences of initial teacher training. It is worth taking time at this point to achieve clarity about exactly what you do know. When teachers are faced with teaching entirely new texts or unfamiliar skills, our response is often to 'fire-fight', to find a quick fix to plug the gap. You may have 'gone on a course' or done some independent research. It is at these points that we return to our academic skills as part of our continuing professional development. Working 'smartly' means knowing where to source the most efficient way in. Establishing what you need to know to get the job done entails clarity of understanding. For example, curriculum change may necessitate development which includes identification of the curriculum expectations for the identified gap and researching the wealth of current information. Sources to plug the gap might include: academic studies; subject organisations such as NATE; subject networks on social media; CPD courses; Teach Meets; and tried and tested single sources (both contributors will thank Stephen Fry (2007) for *The Ode Less Travelled* as a starting point in relation to understanding and teaching poetry, for example).

Mentoring, and developing the knowledge of a student teacher, requires a different approach. It requires a deeper understanding of your own knowledge in order to be able to effectively support and guide someone else. But the act of mentoring is a form of professional development in itself and this is indeed part of the mentor's reward – mentoring challenges your currency both in terms of pedagogy but also in framing, honing and increasing your subject knowledge. In order to get to a position where you understand what you need to do to fill gaps or support, you have to reflect on your own practice.

Every teacher – and every mentor – will have their own specialist knowledge or preferred specialisms. Mentoring is a two-way process and you are not mentoring to create a mentee in your own image. It is important to be aware of your biases so that you are able to support your mentee, with confidence, to bridge their gaps. How you draw on your resources to support the training teacher is vital and not merely concerned with pedagogy and behaviour management.

We have to be honest with ourselves. It is quite simple to establish a list or audit of what you have read and which areas of the broad subject of English you are most comfortable with. Your mentee cannot be expected, and neither can you, to know everything. An experienced mentor we interviewed found themselves in a position of teaching a full drama unit at KS5 with little or no experience from their previous degree and academic study to fall back on – in such a case there is little need for auditing and every need for recognising and reconciling in full. The need for self-auditing is perhaps more complex where the gaps are more subtle and require more reflection after our teaching. We require integrity and a personal honesty to acknowledge what we do not know, and also specifically how *current* our views are. Old Spanish customs in terms of the texts, exemplars and literary critics upon which we have come to rely are as important in the audit as the texts in the canon. They need to be as current and challenging as those being taught in the Universities and School Alliance training. Occasionally and happily, we may have to accept that a trainee's recent study may be more relevant than our own experience. Hooray!

Most mentees will experience a period of training in the stages that precede and succeed their chosen teaching key stages. With the increasing of standards inherent in the new curricula it is vital that you know what is being taught in the stages sandwiching your mentee's training. Making an assumption about what has and has not been taught at KS1 and 2, for example, can result in either a duplication of student experience or, worse still, provide an under-nourishing experience for the student. Your understanding of the arc of the experiences studied will enable you to secure the mentee's perception of the overall journey and their part in that. Close co-operation with feeder primary schools will in any case really support the mentee and make them feel part of the holistic literary experience. This is also true of the language elements of the teaching - an awareness of the skill levels and localised methods of teaching will enable you to help the mentee direct the pedagogy in a way that is already familiar to the learners, and make the teaching more effective. Non-fiction and topic-based texts are often well displayed in primary schools and regular visiting is very beneficial and not that time-consuming. It can also often bring joy.

As a mentor it is incumbent upon you to have an innate understanding of the training institution requirements, and, indeed, their pedagogical and cultural styles in order to support the student teacher. Naturally, the training institution will expect of the mentor attendance at subject-specific training schemes to ensure that not only are the national training standards maintainable and auditable, but that the mentee receives the consistent quality of input they not only deserve but also now pay for. In addition, it is important that the internal initial teacher training structure of the school maintains strong and positive relationships with the personnel from the training institution. The cross-fertilisation of experience and knowledge between mentors coming from a wide range of institutions will ensure the mentor's personal development can support the mentee: 'The more impressive course models focused on preparing teachers for a lifelong career, rather than simply "meeting the (teaching) standards" and passing the course' (DfE, 2017, p. 63).

Further reading

Wright, T. (2016). *How To Be a Brilliant Mentor*. Routledge: London.
Part of the 'How to be a brilliant ...' series, this book offers a range of guidance and advice on mentoring and effective mentor practice.

4 Developing a mentor-mentee relationship

Rachel Roberts

Introduction

This chapter will explore the role of the mentor and the specific aspect of being an English mentor. Aspects of mentor support are considered, including professional, pedagogic and emotional, and strategies are discussed. The relationship between mentor and trainee, which is not a straightforward one, will be explored and ways of setting expectations and boundaries covered. Finally, we will consider how to navigate difficult mentor-trainee relationships. Each section contains practical strategies that mentors can use to establish and maintain positive working relationships with their trainees.

Objectives

At the end of this chapter, you will:

- Have a greater understanding of the nature of the relationship between mentor and mentee;
- Have understood a range of strategies and approaches that you might utilise in developing and maintaining an effective relationship.

The role of the mentor

Definitions of mentorship exist in abundance, yet one to which I regularly return is: 'off-line help from one person to another in making significant transitions in knowledge, work or thinking' (Megginson & Clutterbuck, 1995, p.12). Its starting point is that the mentor-trainee relationship is 'off-line' - that is to say, non-hierarchical; 'help' emphasises the supportive nature of the role; 'significant transitions' is suggestive of the fantastic progress that it is possible to see in a novice teacher over the course of a year. It isn't just about 'doing the do', either: teaching is more than *just* what happens in the classroom, this definition's incorporation of 'thinking' is important. Mentoring a beginning teacher is as much about enabling them to make informed choices as it is about technical skill. How best to capture the attention of 9z3 when teaching Shakespeare? Should you start with 'knowing the story' (through doing a 'whoosh', for example); or play some games around the language used in the opening of *Romeo and Juliet*; or watch a range of productions and consider how their difference in staging highlights key themes? (Wright's (2012) chapter on 'Shakespeare: first contact' provides some sound advice on this.) Supporting the mentee in thinking about why will help to transform their practice from doing and knowing to understanding. Guiding someone through the process of learning to teach requires quite a lot of *thinking* and this starts with the complexity of the relationship between mentor and trainee, as 'Those who *can*, do. Those who *understand*, teach' (Shulman, 1986, p.14).

Task 4.1   Reflecting on your relationship with your own ITT mentor

Think back to your own training.

> What was the relationship like with your mentor?
> How did they support you?
> Are there elements of their practice that you would like to emulate or avoid?
> Can you identify what made the relationship work (or not)?

There is plenty of research that indicates the importance of the mentor–trainee relationship (CUREE, 2005; Lord, Atkinson & Mitchell, 2008), and this importance is now recognised by the government in the form of the non-statutory Mentor Standards (DfE, 2016b) referenced in Chapter 1. The problem with Megginson and Clutterbuck's 1995 definition is that, in the context of teacher training in England, the mentor's role isn't truly 'off-line': in recent years, the move towards more school-based Initial Teacher Training has increased the responsibility of a greater number of mentors, as they will usually be the person with sole or primary responsibility for assessing the progress of their trainee, rather than this being a role shared with a provider such as a university. Given the significance of the mentor's role in the development of the trainee, it is unsurprising that the evaluative nature of the relationship can be problematic (Rehman & Al-Bargi, 2014), and even a source of conflict between a mentor and trainee (Roberts, 2019). As mentor, you have quite a lot of power and influence over your beginning teacher and this shouldn't be underestimated. As a qualified, experienced teacher, comfortable in your professional environment, much of what you do will seem effortless to a novice. It may seem obvious, but for a mentor–trainee relationship to work, it needs to be positive, bearing in mind the power differential.

Being an *English* mentor

How is an English mentor different from any other mentor? Could a specialist in another subject support a beginning English teacher just as well? Shulman (1986) identified a category of teacher knowledge that he described as pedagogical content knowledge, or PCK. This is distinct from content (or subject) knowledge, as it is the knowledge of *how to teach* subject content. It is likely that a mentor with a different subject specialism could support an English trainee in lots of ways: behaviour management strategies; employing different types of differentiation; developing positive relationships with pupils... What they would be missing is the

English bit, and of course this doesn't just mean knowledge of a text (perhaps they've read plenty of Shakespeare, regularly visit the theatre and even studied *Romeo and Juliet* themselves at school). They certainly have general pedagogic knowledge, but even if they had enough content knowledge, they won't have deep knowledge of what Shulman (1986, p. 9) describes as 'an understanding of what makes the learning of specific topics easy or difficult'. It is this knowledge and understanding that belongs uniquely to the subject-specialist mentor. If learning might be said to be participation in discourse using subject-specific concepts (Winch, 2013) then learning to be an English teacher can be conceived as being inducted into a discourse community (Swales, 1988); a community that shares both values and vocabulary. Schools have their own language and jargon in which student teachers must become fluent. Your job as mentor will be, in part, to act as translator and guide through the PCK of English, firstly as it is taught in your school and then as it might be taught differently in other contexts. Chapter 8 offers some ideas for developing this aspect of your role in more detail.

As discussed in Chapter 2, English teachers tend to cite their love of English and desire to pass on this passion to the next generation as their key motivation into teaching. As a mentor, subject knowledge can be a point of connection in the early days of your relationship. However, many beginning English teachers do not have a straightforward 'English' degree: I have trained those with drama, creative writing, film or even law as their first-degree subject. Many more students with language or linguistics qualifications apply to PGCE courses. You will have your own English subject journey, too. Recently the government has funded Subject Knowledge Enhancement courses for English, to support those who may have gaps in subject knowledge to complete before they start teacher training. Your student's route to English teaching is likely to vary considerably from individual to individual and may not mirror your own (see Chapter 2).

Task 4.2   Making a personal connection

Ferrier-Kerr's (2009, p. 792) research suggests that a positive mentoring relationship is founded in 'personal connectedness'. In an early conversation with your trainee, discuss their subject specialism and passions and share your own. This might be part, or an extension of, one of the conversations suggested in Chapter 2.

Approaches to mentoring

The metaphors we use both influence and indicate how we understand the world around us (Lakoff & Johnson, 1980); metaphor is a function of how we communicate and, as English teachers, we are likely to be sensitive to the use of metaphor. Izadinia (2017) researched the metaphors that mentors and mentees used to describe their relationships. Many were categorised as parent-child or teacher-student, which indicates a clear hierarchy. Some used more equal analogies to describe their relationship, such as colleagues. How you and your trainee think of your relationship is important because a mismatch in the understanding of the relationship is likely to affect how it works.

> **Task 4.3 Metaphors for teaching and mentoring**
>
> Think about how *you* would characterise teaching English and being a mentor. Finish the following sentences, creating your own metaphors or similes:
>
> - Teaching is (like) ...
> - Teaching English is (like) ...
> - The mentor-trainee relationship is (like) ...
>
> This might be a good exercise to do with your mentee; it would allow you to talk about your expectations of them, their expectations of you and how your relationship might function.

Peters and Austin (1986) suggest adopting the following behaviours makes for effective mentors:

- Provide **latitude** (freedom to try, courage to fail).
- Push limits (**challenge**, demand excellence).
- Recognise success and effort (give **praise**, highlight achievement).
- **Counsel** (advise and give feedback, encourage self-analysis).
- Set personal **example** (offer role models, set standards).

These suggestions could also apply to what makes an effective teacher; being a mentor is not like teaching children, however, because your mentee is an adult. Understanding some of the key drivers for adult learning (andragogy) can be helpful:

1. In terms of their self-concept, adults tend to see themselves as more responsible, self-directed, and independent;
2. They have a larger, more diverse stock of knowledge and experience from which to draw;
3. Their readiness to learn is based on developmental and real-life responsibilities;
4. Their orientation to learning is most often problem centred and relevant to their current life situation;
5. They have a stronger need to know the reasons for learning something;
6. They tend to be more internally motivated (Kiely, Sandmann & Truluck, 2004, p. 20).

Therefore, spending time getting to know your mentee (what motivates them in wanting to be an English teacher and the qualities and experiences they may bring) is important in enabling you to know how to best support them.

In addition, the process of becoming a teacher is not as simple as imitation and trying to create a 'mini-you' should be avoided: 'The question is not "how can this student teacher become like me?" but "How can this student teacher learn to start becoming a good teacher?"' (Goodwyn, 1997, p. 49). As the school-based mentor, you create the training plan for your mentee's school experience. Depending on how much school experience your beginning teacher has had prior to starting training and their subject specialism at degree level, their needs will be unique to them. Try creating an initial needs analysis (which can be updated periodically) with your trainee; Table 4.1 is an example of one completed at the beginning of a placement. This is a highly personalised exercise, and you will need to contextualise the training for your school and department. It is possible that the provider with which your school and student teacher are working in partnership will already have a proforma for such needs analysis and action planning.

The more specific you can both be regarding the mentee's needs, the more targeted support can be. They can also be related to the Teachers' Standards, so that the beginning teacher can begin to understand their development towards, and then gather evidence of meeting, the Teachers' Standards from the start.

You will not wish to do all of the training yourself and therefore you will need to co-ordinate with other members in your department and beyond. How might you ensure that other members of staff working with your mentee do so in a productive way? Each of these members of staff will develop a relationship with the student teacher. Could you provide a training session for your department on ways to support student teachers on placement? Does the provider with which you are working in partnership provide training on supporting student teachers that you might attend and/or share with your team?

Table 4.1 English trainee needs analysis

Mentee's needs	Support strategies	Date for completion
Subject knowledge – Standard 3 (*such as: knowledge of contemporary children's literature*)	Mentee to read three books typically taught to Year 8. Discuss with mentor/Key Stage 3 co-ordinator why they are taught to this year group. Mentee to read some of the Carnegie Award book winners to develop a wider knowledge of current fiction for young adults.	
Curriculum knowledge – Standard 3 (*such as: knowledge and understanding of the current GCSE syllabus you use in your school*)	Mentee to read GCSE syllabus and the department's programme of study for Key Stage 4. Discuss with mentor/Key Stage 4 co-ordinator/Head of Department the rationale for the order of teaching and choice of texts for sets (if relevant). Participate in webinar training provided by the exam board.	
Behaviour management – Standard 7 (*such as: your school's sanctions and rewards policy*)	Mentee to read school policy and attend training session provided by the assistant head. Mentee to observe specific members of staff to see how the policy works in practice (mentor to suggest staff to observe).	
Understanding how school systems function for assessment – Standards 6 and 8 (*such as: the collation of data and reporting systems*).	Mentee to attend training session provided by data manager. Mentor to demonstrate how this works in English by showing a recent report cycle and explaining how it works.	

Supporting your student teacher

The mentor's role has a number of different facets: role model (Anderson & Shannon in Kerry & Mayes, 1995); guide (Izadinia, 2017); provider of assistance (Tomlinson, 1995); developer of reflective practice (Ballantyne, Packer & Hansford, 1995); emotional supporter (Marable & Raimondi, 2007). This section will focus on the different types of support that you might provide for your beginning teacher.

Schutz (1994) suggests that positive relationships are dependent on both parties showing that the other is important, competent and likeable. As a mentor, you need to demonstrate to your student teacher that they are *important* by making time for them; that they are *competent* by showing that you believe in them and *likeable* by showing an interest in them. (The latter is not the same as becoming their best friend!) These features are reflected in the first Mentor Standard: 'be approachable, make time for the trainee, and prioritise meetings and discussions with them' (DfE, 2016b, p. 11).

When you have conversations with your beginning teacher, whether formal discussions in weekly meetings (discussed in Chapter 11) or more casual chats in the staffroom, it is likely that the main characteristic of these conversations will involve some kind of support (Israel, Kamman, McCray & Sindelar, 2014). Support could be divided into the following categories:

- Professional support (such as showing the trainee how to put 'praise points' onto the database and discussing when this would be appropriate);
- Pedagogic support (such as demonstrating how to model some writing during a lesson and discussing how it worked afterwards);
- Academic support (such as suggesting a book on basic grammar knowledge that you've read);
- Emotional support (such as comforting them if they have a difficult lesson).

Whilst these types of support seem to divide neatly, in reality they are likely to blend into or overlap with one another.

Task 4.4 Identifying different types of support

Read the following scenario and try to identify the different types of support provided by the mentor. In what ways do they overlap and why might this make supporting a student teacher more complex?

Jenny, a young and keen recent graduate, in the middle of her first school placement, asks to speak to you in private. Her face is red and it looks as though she has been crying. You find an empty classroom and you ask her what the matter is. She tells you that she has just been 'told off' by a teaching assistant at the end of a lesson for not speaking to her about the content of the lesson. You ask her how she feels about this and Jenny replies that she feels small and embarrassed about the confrontation with the teaching assistant and is now afraid of speaking to her and dreading the next lesson with this class. You offer her a tissue and reassure her that you're sure the teaching assistant wasn't 'telling her off'. You explain to her that this member of staff is a very experienced TA who has been working with an individual pupil for a long time and therefore knows the needs of this child well.

Having worked with this TA yourself in the past, you recognise that she can come over as abrupt occasionally, but that she is highly professional, genuinely interested in learning and enjoys assisting in English lessons. You ask Jenny for the exact words that the TA used, and Jenny reports that she said: 'It would be helpful if you could send me the worksheet in advance, as I can have it altered for John so that he can read it himself.' You ask what plans Jenny had for using the TA in her lesson and she looks surprised, saying 'I didn't realise that I had to. I thought they knew what they were doing.' You look at Teachers' Standard 8 together, which requires teachers to work with colleagues, and discuss ways in which she might include the TA in her planning and how she might speak to her about it.

'But I feel embarrassed talking to her now,' Jenny says. You describe that teaching is teamwork; that all staff have the interests of children at heart and that she needs to build a professional relationship with the TA. You offer to speak to the TA yourself but encourage Jenny to email her to ask how she might best deploy her in lessons and whether she would have time to discuss the needs of individual pupils in the class before their next lesson.

My own research into conversations between mentors and mentees suggests that around 30 per cent of the conversation could be categorised as 'support'. This was broken down into the following subcategories, using the gerund verb form to describe what the support was doing; they are listed here from the most to least frequent type of support:

- **Checking** – showing concern, generic or specific, regarding mentee's well-being or progress. Usually in the form of a question.
- **Reassuring** – comments that 'things will be fine'; that what the mentee is experiencing is normal. Empathetic in tone.
- **Encouraging** – comments that suggest the mentor has confidence or faith in the mentee's ability; to bolster the mentee's confidence.
- **Caring** – showing concern, often through using a question and related to mentee's well-being.
- **Positive reframing** – the mentor repositions a negative self-evaluation that the mentee has into a positive.
- **Protecting** – the mentor's suggestions protect the mentee from possible threats (Roberts, 2019, p. 108).

The unifying approach here is this tacit acknowledgement of the role of emotions; teaching involves emotions (Day & Leitch, 2001; Hargreaves, 1998) and the main motivation for going into teaching tends to be intrinsic (Lortie, 1975; Nias, 1996). Teachers care about their pupils; they care about their academic progress and their general welfare. They want them to do well and therefore when things go wrong (poor behaviour in a lesson, for example), it is easy for teachers – particularly beginning teachers – to take it very personally. Although the relationship between mentor and mentee is not the same as that of a teacher and pupil, it certainly has similar elements which does mean the relationship is 'emotionally charged'

(Hawkey, 2006, p.145). Your relationship with your mentee should be characterised by your care for them, although this can be made more complex by other pressures, including your own teaching workload and the need for you to assess your mentee's progress.

You may already be familiar with the concept of emotional labour; Hochschild's (2012) research with workers in the service industry identified aspects of work that expected particular kinds of emotional interaction or management or emotions. For example, a waitress or shop assistant would be expected to smile and wish the customer a 'nice day', even if they didn't feel like it. This emotional labour is not confined to service industry jobs; Hochschild argues that it features in any job that requires interaction with people. Nurses, librarians, social workers, police and teachers and other, similar occupations will require a certain amount of emotion regulation. Mentoring similarly requires some emotional labour: training to be a teacher is an emotional process (Yuan & Lee, 2016), as beginning teachers are making a significant transition in their professional identity. How your mentee feels about themselves and aspects of their training, and how they react to different situations in school is an important and necessary part of that transition. As a mentor, you will have to manage your own emotions in front of your mentee and to help them manage *their* emotions if they find things overwhelming. A significant part of mentoring might be described as a kind of *affective practice* – that is, a way of understanding and using emotions as part of professional interpersonal relationships. This is discussed in more detail in Chapter 12.

Ideally, the process of initial teacher education should lead to the student teacher becoming more independent and able to reflect on their own practice with increasingly less structured support from mentors and other colleagues. Like support, there are different kinds of reflection and it can be helpful to consider this when talking to your trainee. Green suggests the following four types of reflection:

- **Personal** – think about the relationships you are developing with students and a variety of colleagues;
- **Professional** – consider the meaning of professionalism and what this constitutes within the school environment;
- **Academic** – seek to develop your understanding of your subject;
- **Pedagogic** – explore the wide range of ways in which learning can be mediated and enhanced (Green, 2011, p.1).

Task 4.5 Utilising reflective practice

Read the following scenario and, using Green's different types of reflection, think of the different kinds of responses or questions that you might use to help Angela reflect on her lesson.

Angela has just taught a lesson with a middle-set Year 9 class on the opening of Macbeth. Her immediate feeling is that the lesson was a disaster: she didn't cover everything that was in her lesson plan; there was a lot of chatter, particularly when the class were supposed to be writing quietly, and she is not sure that the learning objectives were achieved.

The value of reflective practice and supporting student teachers to develop it is discussed in more detail in Chapter 8.

Setting boundaries and expectations

A little like your first lesson with a new class, the first meeting with your mentee is a good opportunity to set the tone for your working relationship, as well as a starting point for forging a connection. Once you have established your mentee's background in terms of subject strengths and school experience, and perhaps shared your own, it is worth setting out what you *both* hope to get out of the relationship. The Mentor Standards (DfE, 2016b) might be useful in helping you to structure this conversation with your mentee. You might also have additional guidelines from your ITT provider.

Table 4.2 is an example of how you might use the Mentor Standards to set out your working relationship with your trainee. This is set out as a kind of contract, but you could rephrase this in any way that suits you.

Developing a professional identity

If this is your first time as a mentor, then you are likely to experience a shift in how you see your teacher identity; as previously argued, being a mentor is similar to being a teacher of children, but it is certainly not identical. As a mentor, your professional identity will have to move away from being pupil-centred towards being mentee-centred (at least for the times that you are working directly with your student teacher). The starting point for this identity shift is, as Ferrier-Kerr (2009, p. 796) suggests, for mentors to 're-examine their own beliefs and assumptions by examining their own learning and performance as teachers and [mentors]', so that they can enable reflection in their trainees. This is exemplified in Chapter 2 and reflected in a number of activities across a number of chapters in this book.

This may feel quite uncomfortable at first; scrutinising the minutiae of your everyday practice can be difficult and exhausting (Schön, 1983). As much of what you do is likely to be automatic (unconsciously competent), it can take time to deconstruct what you do, and you may even feel threatened by this process (this topic is further explored in Chapter 8). The cycle of working with a student teacher will include reflection on your own practice, modelling approaches in the classroom and making the thinking behind your decisions transparent to your trainee. As a mentor, you are learning too (Grimmett, Forgasz, Williams & White, 2018). Grimmett et al.'s work with mentors in Australia found that more productive mentor–trainee relationships were forged where mentors conceived themselves as 'teachers of teaching' (2018, p. 341). This involved moving away from a view of teaching purely as a skill and focusing more on care for, rather than assessment of, the student teacher. This could be conceived as a continuum:

Table 4.2 Using the Mentor Standards to set expectations of your relationship

Mentor Standard	Expectations in your mentor-mentee relationship
Standard 1 - Personal qualities *Establish trusting relationships, modelling high standards of practice, and understand how to support a trainee through initial teacher training* The mentor should: • Be approachable, make time for the trainee, and prioritise meetings and discussions with them; • use a range of effective interpersonal skills to respond to the needs of the trainee; • offer support with integrity, honesty and respect; • use appropriate challenge to encourage the trainee to reflect on their practice; and • support the improvement of a trainee's teaching by modelling exemplary practice in planning, teaching and assessment.	I (the mentor) will meet with you (the mentee) at least once a week for our designated meeting. I will meet with you at other times if needed and try to 'check-in' with you every day, although I won't necessarily have time to spend very long every day. You can email me at any time and you can call me up until 7pm, although I'd rather you didn't phone unless it is an emergency. Because I have additional responsibilities, sometimes I will be very busy and may seem distant or stressed; please don't take this personally and remember that I am still here for you if you need me. Do also use other members of the department for advice or asking how things work. When you start teaching, I will observe you at least three times a week and provide verbal and written feedback. Please don't be discouraged by suggestions for improvement; this is meant to help you improve. I am very happy for you to observe me teaching any of my classes and will arrange for you to observe other staff (both in and out of English) throughout the year. If you aren't able to observe a lesson for any reason, please let me or the member of staff know, as we may have planned something especially for you to see! Each week we will spend some time talking and thinking about what is being taught in each year group, where resources can be found, etc. It would be great to hear your ideas or approaches that you've learnt at university or through your own study. We are always happy to experiment.
Standard 2 - Teaching *Support trainees to develop their teaching practice in order to set high expectations of all pupils and to meet their needs* The mentor should: • support the trainee in forming good relationships with pupils, and in developing effective behaviour and classroom management strategies;	I will help you with getting to know your classes; initially by observing them and then gradually teaching small groups and team teaching before embarking on whole-class teaching. I will show you the school behaviour policy and explain how this works in lessons. When you observe me teaching, and other members of staff, we'll discuss some of the strategies used to manage a class well.

(continued)

Table 4.2 (Cont.)

Mentor Standard	Expectations in your mentor-mentee relationship
• support the trainee in developing effective approaches to planning, teaching and assessment; • support the trainee with marking and assessment of pupil work through moderation or double marking; • give constructive, clear and timely feedback on lesson observations; • broker opportunities to observe best practice; • support the trainee in accessing expert subject and pedagogical knowledge; • resolve in-school issues on the trainee's behalf where they lack the confidence or experience to do so themselves; • enable and encourage the trainee to evaluate and improve their teaching; and • enable the trainee to access, utilise and interpret robust educational research to inform their teaching.	I will show you all of our programmes of study and relevant Schemes of Work and demonstrate how I plan individual lessons. We can try some co-planning first, then I will give you advice on the plans that you create for classes. In the first three weeks of you teaching, I would like to see these in advance - at least 24hrs so that I will have time to look at them. I can then give you some suggestions before you teach. Towards the end of the term, once we are both more confident in your planning, then I won't need to see them in advance (although I'll still be happy to give you advice if you want it!). We have lots of resources, and you are welcome to use these. However, you will need to adapt them to suit your classes and this should be shown in your planning. It is really good practice to do some planning from scratch and I will help you do this initially. Hopefully, by the end of the term you will be able to do this independently. We have a strict marking policy that we need to adhere to, so I will sit down with you and co-mark a few times. As you begin to take over classes, you should start to do some marking (with the help of the main class teacher). This will help inform your planning too. When we do moderation (and sometimes training from the exam board), you will be fully involved. We have an extensive subject library, including books on English pedagogy, and I would like you to read from here regularly. We can discuss what you've read in our meetings. If you have any problems or issues with other members of staff, I will help you; please don't be afraid of talking to me about any issues that you have. I promise to be positive and supportive in our conversations.
Standard 3 - Professionalism *Set high expectations and induct the trainee to understand their role and responsibilities as a teacher* The mentor should: • encourage the trainee to participate in the life of the school and understand its role within the wider community;	I will make sure that you are able to contribute to some of our afterschool clubs (such as creative writing) and do some work with our feeder primary school. I will tell you if I feel that your conduct is at odds with our expected codes of conduct - please don't be offended - but we do expect you to be on time, to be polite and dress appropriately.

Table 4.2 (Cont.)

Mentor Standard	Expectations in your mentor–mentee relationship
• support the trainee in developing the highest standards of professional and personal conduct; • support the trainee in promoting equality and diversity; • ensure the trainee understands and complies with relevant legislation, including that related to the safeguarding of children; and • support the trainee to develop skills to manage time effectively. Standard 4 – Self-development and working in partnership *Continue to develop their own professional knowledge, skills and understanding and invest time in developing a good working relationship within relevant ITT partnerships.* The mentor should: • ensure consistency by working with other mentors and partners to moderate judgements; and • continue to develop their own mentoring practice and subject and pedagogical expertise by accessing appropriate professional development and engaging with robust research.	*Our ITT tutor will ensure that you're attached to a tutor group and will be able to attend meetings with the head of year and any training we have on safeguarding etc. We'll discuss things like diversity and the curriculum in English department meetings and how we try to encourage reading for pleasure through making a focus of our new library.* *We will provide you with a diary and teacher's planner. You can then keep track of all aspects of your school week; keep a 'to do' list and start a markbook.* *I will work closely with other members of the department to make sure that they understand how your training course works and that they regularly observe and give you feedback.* *I will read all of the training materials from the ITT provider and keep your university tutor informed of your progress. I will attend the mentor training provided by the university and keep my subject and pedagogical knowledge up to date by reading relevant research, such as the College of Teaching's* Impact *magazine.*

As mentors moved more towards understanding their role as 'teacher of teaching', rather than as supervisor or assessor, their professional identity shifted.

Task 4.6 Reflection on your mentor role

Reflect on how you see yourself as mentor. What are your most pressing concerns or anxieties? These will vary depending on your own experiences of being mentored and being a mentor.

Did you volunteer for the role or were you asked to take it on (or even *told* to)? How has this affected your understanding of the role? How might this impact on your relationship with your student teacher?

Navigating tricky relationships

Much of the discussion in this chapter regarding relationships assumes that, with the right approach, they will be positive. Sometimes the relationship between a mentor and mentee can be challenging. There are a range of factors that can affect the quality of this relationship and if you find yourself in a situation where you feel that the relationship isn't working it is worth trying to identify what specifically is affecting it. Some of the factors that might affect your relationship include:

- lack of time to spend with your mentee
- lack of support from colleagues
- mismatch of expectations (yours of your mentee or your mentee's of you)
- evaluation being perceived as judgement
- personality clash.

The first two areas can be addressed through support from the structures of the training programme – either through a school-based colleague, such as the professional tutor, or from the provider, who may be a university tutor. If you feel that you don't have enough time to spend with your mentee or that other members of staff could help with aspects of training, then redress should be sought through the systems within school. It is rare for a mentor to be allocated timetabled lessons to work with their mentee outside a single designated meeting time. Your role will necessarily entail more time than you are officially allocated; this can cause strain in your relationship if you are managing a number of different responsibilities in addition to being a mentor. Feedback may seem rushed; you might feel that you keep having to 'put off' your trainee because you have so many other things to do. Talk to your senior leadership team or line manager to see if some of your workload could be re-distributed.

Whilst it may seem easier and more practical to give your mentee your classes, it is a better idea to allow them the chance to work with a range of different teachers and classes within your department. This might pose problems if your colleagues have not worked with student teachers before; you may need to run some in-house training for them, so that they are able to provide high-quality, focused feedback and support your mentee in similar ways to yourself. If you find that there are issues arising from your mentee working with other staff, you can either approach this directly with the member of staff concerned or via your school structures. A solution may be as simple as sitting down with your colleague to explain how the systems of the ITT programme work.

A mismatch of expectations could occur in a variety of areas: you think that your mentee frequently misses deadlines while the mentee thinks that they prioritise the important things; your mentee feels they need more encouragement whereas you feel you provide sufficient positive feedback. Having a conversation at the beginning of the training programme could address this kind of issue before it takes root. If you find that things are slipping, such as your mentee not meeting deadlines, return to the agreement that you set up (see Table 4.2). This will allow you to discuss *why* they are finding this difficult; perhaps there is an underlying issue with time management and they need support with organisation and making the best use of their time in school. There may be issues at home that are preventing them from working effectively in the evenings. If this is the case, you'll need to ask sensitively what you can do to help. Could the trainee have a designated work area in school and arrive earlier in the morning to work? If they are feeling generally overwhelmed by workload, you may need to sit down with them and discuss how they can prioritise elements of their work, for example: using medium-term plans for teaching, so that they are not rushing around at the last minute for resources, or using a planner or diary to ensure they are aware of deadlines for reports or assignments. Turner and Braine's (2016) research with beginning teachers found that making use of the teacher planner enabled beginning teachers to manage their time better, and develop a better work-life balance. Further guidance for having difficult conversations is provided in Chapter 11.

Underpinning values

Most people who enter the teaching profession are motivated by an altruistic desire to help others, to pass on their passion for their subject and to make a difference to children's lives. Aristotle (2014) identified different kinds of virtue or intelligence: *techne* (skills), *episteme* (knowledge) *and phronesis* (practical wisdom). To consider teaching simply as a set of skills (*techne)* reduces it complexity and ignores its fundamentally *ethical* component. Mentors can embody a kind of *phronesis*, as they make choices based on their experience.

Summary

The key to developing a productive mentor-trainee relationship is finding common ground and setting and adhering to expectations. This could start with shared reasons for going into teaching and a passion for English and from there the setting of expectations (on both sides) can be established. The role of the mentor is complex, because mentors are required to support and assess their student teachers. The role is vital to the progress of the beginning teacher and support should begin with their needs, in terms of school experience and subject knowledge.

The range of support mentors provide is diverse: from professional to emotional and these often overlap in practice. Emotional support should not be underestimated: it is connected to reflective practice as you help mentees realise what they can and cannot control in their professional practice.

The Mentor Standards can be useful to set up expectations of professional support and behaviour as well as set boundaries for your relationship. Taking on the role of mentor will require you to develop a different facet of your professional identity – from that of teacher to teacher of teaching.

If you encounter difficulties in your relationship with your mentee, draw on existing support structures. Fundamentally, relationships are about communication and, if we assume that those who enter into the profession of teaching have others' best interests at heart, we need to remember that what drives us should bring us together.

Further resources

Teachers' TV video: What to do if you don't get on with your mentor (Trevor Wright): http://archive.teachfind.com/ttv/www.teachers.tv/videos/you-do-not-get-on-with-your-mentor.html

SECTION 3

What a mentor does

5 Managing workload and student teacher well-being

Yvonne Williams

Introduction

In this chapter, although workload has been placed ahead of well-being, this does not diminish the over-arching importance of attending to mentees' mental and physical health and stamina. That workload is an issue is well documented in recent government surveys and studies. The Workload Challenge questionnaire of 2014 was completed by almost 44,000 teachers, leading to the setting-up of three working groups (Marking, Planning, Data Management) and the subsequent publication of their reports. The Workload Survey of 2016 led to research into ways of reducing workload, undertaken by 12 schools in 2017 and published on the Department for Education (DfE) website. Finally, the Workload Toolkit was published in July 2018 in response to research funded by the DfE. (See the web page, detailed at the end of the chapter, which indexes all relevant documents).

Objectives

At the end of this chapter, you will:

- Have understood a range of strategies and approaches that you might utilise in supporting your mentee to manage their workload;
- Have a deeper understanding of well-being in order to direct the support and guidance you provide for your beginning teacher;
- Have a deeper understanding of the drivers of excessive workload, including a greater understanding of recent surveys of and recommendations for teacher workload;
- Have a toolkit of possible coping and improved strategies taken from nationally available case studies and various websites;
- Help your beginning teacher to select strategies and approaches that are most appropriate to their environment;
- Understand ways in which you could offer support through enhanced listening and joint problem-solving, using some appropriate counselling skills;
- Have an understanding of some external support available to beginning teachers who are struggling to cope with professional and personal problems, and of how to refer a struggling mentee to the appropriate agency.

As a mentor you will have prepared your mentee for the sometimes seemingly relentless nature of their classroom role. There will be various safeguards in place, such as limitations on the proportion of a full timetable she will teach. In itself this should limit the time spent on planning, marking and data-tracking. However, alongside these activities will go professional projects and more monitoring than exist for fully qualified teachers. Thus the mentee's workload is wider and more consistently intense than for most teachers. They will be writing very detailed plans and reflections on their teaching, analysing the data from their lessons much more explicitly, marking in depth and maintaining written records of their progress beyond the remit of qualified teachers.

When the DfE published the reports and recommendations for the independent working bodies on marking, planning and data management (DfE, 2016d, 2016e, 2016f) the recommendations were to slim down these processes as far as possible. This was because some schools had inflated practice: via dialogic or "deep" marking; demands for detailed weekly plans submitted to the head on Sunday afternoons and excessive data entries, which tended to obscure rather than illuminate progress.

Obviously, at this developmental stage, beginning teachers need to externalise their thinking, but it would be worth comparing their workload with that of an experienced teacher.

Task 5.1   Overview

Mentor reflection on legislation affecting your mentee's working time and safeguards within your institution

How many hours a year constitute the directed hours a teacher should work?
What are the limits on tasks undertaken outside those hours?
What was the average working week for classroom teachers in the UK in 2017?

Evaluation

How confident were you of your own knowledge in answering these questions?
Did these results surprise you? See *Reducing Workload in Your School* (DfE, 2018a (updated 2019)). (At this stage you might reflect on the extent to which the findings in the survey reflect your own weekly hours).
What might be the implications for your mentee's workload?

In the light of these figures it is very important to put in place some practical strategies to enable the mentee to get into good productive habits from the start, but where to begin?

Managing assessment: Understanding and evaluating the role of marking in good practice

Teachers of English face a substantial marking load. Because the written word, increasingly moving towards the extended essay, is the most usual assessment focus, there is a larger "outcome space" – that is, a wider range of possible approaches and material, as well as a perceived need to write more detailed, differentiated comments to enable pupils to improve. Additionally, English teachers are expected to deal with technical accuracy and enable pupils to remedy and pre-empt errors. Other teachers may have a lesser role to play in this, even though all GCSE qualifications include assessment of accuracy.

Helping to define and describe the expectations for what teachers do are the Teachers' Standards (DfE, 2013b). The relevant standard for marking and assessment is Standard 6: "Make accurate and productive use of assessment". The last of the four points of this Standard is "Give pupils regular feedback, both orally and through accurate marking, and encourage pupils to respond to the feedback."

A good starting point for reflection on the implications of the standard for practice would be the word "productive". Reference to the reports of the review groups from the DfE Workload Challenge indicates that many schools have misinterpreted *productivity* to mean *quantity* of written feedback, which has become extended and often fruitless written dialogue. The use of different colours in marking adds to the burden. Ofsted (2015) has been keen to distance itself from these onerous practices; and it is worth bringing to the attention of your beginning teacher the videos and tweets of Sean Harford, the National Director.

It might be a good idea to devote a mentor session to these Workload Reports, using questions such as those in Task 5.2 to guide reflection.

Task 5.2 Reflection on the role of assessment, its role in practice and evaluation of the role of marking

1. What is the role of marking within assessment?
2. Who is the intended audience of marking and assessment? How does this shape the kind of comments given?
3. What are the alternatives to written feedback? How and where are these most effective?

These questions may be pertinent not only to your mentee's workload but your own, so you may want to try these out before the mentoring session.

The most useful advice within the Report of the Marking Policy Review Group (DfE, 2016d) is that all marking should be:

> Meaningful: marking varies by age group, subject, and what works best for the pupil and teacher in relation to any particular piece of work.
>
> (DfE, 2016d, p8)

> Manageable: marking practice is proportionate and considers the frequency and complexity of written feedback, as well as the cost and time-effectiveness of marking in relation to the overall workload of teachers
>
> (ibid.)

Motivating: Marking should help to motivate pupils to progress. If the teacher is doing more work than their pupils, this can become a disincentive for pupils to accept challenges and take responsibility for improving their work.

(DfE, 2016d, p10)

A further source of good advice is the Education Endowment Fund's report *A Marked Improvement* (Elliott et al., 2016, p5). Its recommendations divide marking into several categories, which include: dealing with careless errors; the value of awarding marks; and providing comments and setting targets.

Discussing these recommendations and advice will help your student teacher understand not just the role and workload, and will also contribute to their understanding of what might constitute best practice. Similarly, you might use your school's marking and assessment policy as the focus for constructive discussion – not just so that the procedure can be followed, but also to consider good and effective practice. Such activity would be an example of developing the mentee's cognitive problem-solving strategies to develop professional judgement about what works best and when. Further reflection and metacognitive development could focus on evaluating the sources of advice within the context of the mentee's institution(s). If on a second placement, the mentee could make useful comparisons of practice within contrasting environments.

Managing planning and preparation: Understanding and evaluating its role in good practice

Inevitably, beginning teachers will spend a lot more time than long-serving teachers on lesson-planning (see Chapter 9), and the basics need to be fully covered from the start. The time needed for these can be cut down by reference to online resources, textbooks and existing schemes and plans within the department. English teachers are notorious "magpies" who take materials from a variety of sources and enjoy the creativity of planning and preparation. At this stage of their careers, beginning teachers will benefit from guidance as to how to balance wider research with pragmatism. There are not enough hours in the day to research and create everything afresh. Cost-benefit analysis would be useful here. As a mentor you might want to consider the demands you make in terms of the level of detail in the planning and how many plans you ask to see.

Task 5.3 Reflection on planning

Consider what constitutes good practice in lesson planning and evaluate its impact on pupils in order to direct effective use of time in constructing and using lesson materials.

Consider, in an early mentor session, a cost-benefit analysis of the first plans produced by the mentee:

What are the benefits derived from the methods, materials and strategies in terms of pupil outcomes?

How long did it take to create and compile the materials for the lesson?

Compare the first three lessons for a class, and consider which lesson has been the most productive and why. What can be learned for the future?

Summary reflection on workload

The Workload Planning Report indicates that the "tick-box" approach to planning is one cause of its becoming an increasing burden, and suggests that instead of producing *individual lesson plans* teachers should concentrate on *planning sequences of lessons*. This means taking an overview of the sequence and evaluating pupil outcomes regularly. However, in the initial stages of the beginning teacher's development, the focus will be on planning individual lessons. Good practice within schools involves access to good-quality materials. Joint planning can be an excellent learning opportunity for the beginning teacher and increase resilience through the social and cognitive aspects of the activity (see Chapter 6 for further ideas and guidance on collaborative working). It would be useful to reflect with the beginning teacher what has been learned from the joint endeavour and the impact on their resilience. See Chapter 9 for further ideas about supporting student teachers with planning.

Finally, of course, lesson-planning often needs to be adjusted in the light of pupil learning in previous lessons, which is where effective, relevant use of data comes in:

Managing data: Understanding and evaluating its role in good practice

The Workload Report on Data Management defines data as "numerical measure of pupil progress that can be tracked and used to draw a wide range of conclusions about pupil and teacher performance, and school policy" (DfE, 2016f, p8).

Such numerical data is seen as playing an important role in the life of the modern teacher because it proports to show how pupils have progressed over time and highlight some learning gaps. You could use the table (Section 21 on pages 8-9 of the Data Management Review Group Report) to evaluate your use of data in relation to the mentee's context. Alternatively, you could complete Task 5.4.

Task 5.4 Reflection on the role and purpose of data

Which types of data exist in your institution?

How would you rank these data in terms of their effectiveness in enabling the teacher to keep track of pupil learning and progress?

What is the cost-benefit analysis of these different types of data and the frequency and nature of their collection?

Listening, counselling and signposting

The workload reports mentioned in this chapter are full of good advice, amalgamated by the DfE from reports from the studies undertaken by various schools across the country in 2016-2017. These can be accessed on the DfE website and contain numerous strategies and recommendations. There are times, however, when the workload can become too much, or your beginning teacher becomes overwhelmed by professional or personal problems which detracts from their effectiveness in the classroom and their feelings of efficacy. At such a point it is time to consider what additional help you or your school are able to offer or whether you need to signpost them to an outside agency.

Supporting beginning teachers' well-being

Just by taking on the demanding role of mentor within your organisation, you have demonstrated professional competence and personal success in your teaching career thus far. On your professional journey you have weathered crises and used opportunities to develop your expertise, experiences on which you have reflected and learnt and which you will use to guide those who are just setting out. The chances are that through experience and/or intervention you have an understanding of what constitutes your own well-being and are therefore well placed to consider the well-being of others.

This section of the chapter starts by considering recent studies on what constitutes well-being and the ways in which definitions might shape the overall direction and support you are able to offer your mentee. The chapter also covers common problems that can arise when new teachers experience excessive workload and offers some sources of help and advice which you and your mentee can access on your joint journey. It is important to realise early on that, although your responsibility as a mentor is considerable, you cannot cope with all issues that arise. At the end of the chapter there is a list of agencies to whom you can refer your mentee if problems arise that are outside your areas of expertise as a mentor.

Task 5.5   Personal reflection

Cast back your mind to your own training and list three key concerns that were uppermost in your mind at the time.

- Do you think they are the same and of the same priority at this stage of your working life as they were at the outset of your career?
- What do you think might have changed and why?
- How might these realisations impact on the ways in which you can support your mentee?

Well-being

Maintaining a positive outlook and resilience is key to the beginning teacher's success in their training: in the classroom, on placement and beyond. Mentors fostering mentees' well-being in these very early career stages can put in place positive developmental strategies, alongside coping strategies, to extend qualities of optimism and resilience.

One pragmatic reason for adopting wellbeing techniques is to fulfil the school's duty of care to protect the mental health of teachers as employees. Health and Safety is not just about avoiding physical harm, for example. The Teacher Toolkit 2014 (www.theteachertoolkit.com/) cites a research study by Briner and Dewberry (Birkbeck University 2007) which shows a positive correlation between staff well-being and school success. Some commentators may see cultivating well-being as a moral imperative that ethical organisations owe to their members at all levels, including beginning teachers whose membership of the community may be temporary.

Well-being definitions

In 1947, the World Health Organization (WHO) defined wellbeing as: "a state of complete physical, mental and social wellbeing and not merely the absence of disease or infirmity in which the individual realises his or her own abilities, can cope with the normal stresses of life, can work productively and fruitfully, and is able to make a contribution to his or her community" (WHO, 2014).

Physically, well-being could be about the individual looking after their health through ensuring regular and sufficient sleep, healthy eating and exercise. Mentally, it could be about keeping unhelpful and overwhelming stress at bay. Socially, it could be about ensuring that mentees are well integrated into a range of social networks: within a school; within a subject association; with other beginning teachers at a similar stage of development; and with the provider responsible for the oversight of the beginning teacher's development, such as the university, teaching school or School-Centred Initial Teacher Training (SCITT) provider. All of these well-being needs are seen as complementary and holistic, contributing, according to the WHO, to a "complete" state.

Research into well-being has been expanding and deepening recently. One review of the literature (McCallum & Price, 2017) advocates well-being as a positive strategy shared between sectors, schools and individuals, thus indicating an ongoing interaction beyond the mentor/mentee context. This does not absolve the mentor of responsibility for making efforts to support their charge's mental health, but it does make it less emotionally onerous to know that there are others who can help and offer advice, and in addition share responsibility.

McCallum and Price's work also suggests that well-being is developmental and cognitive and that activities which might enhance memory and problem-solving, and therefore well-being, could include "tasks that involved information processing, doing puzzles, conducting inquiries into teaching and learning, thinking laterally, and being committed to lifelong learning" (McCallum & Price, 2010, p13).

The emphasis on the cognitive has its attractions in that mentors can provide support by engaging beginning teachers in intellectual activity, expanding their mental capacity. In this context, the projects that beginning teachers might be completing could be integrated into professional dialogue. Assignments and tasks set and marked by PGCE and PGDE providers, for example, might be seen by the mentee as chores or even bolt-on obligations that impede rather than enhance the development of their practice. Time spent on discussing and reinforcing the value and contribution of such activities to understanding and therefore practice will not only make the enquiries more relevant to the whole placement, but will also ensure that they become more satisfying. The work on and completed assignments such as these therefore provide material for future reference as well as a methodology to support future questioning, reflection and problem-solving. The attraction of this emphasis is its potential impact on the beginning teacher's sense of agency and control. Thinking their way out of difficulties relieves emotional pressure and provides possible solution(s); most importantly, cognitive thinking of this nature maintains the mentee's feeling of being in control.

Task 5.6 Mentor reflection: Understanding the place and purpose of theory-based tasks

How familiar are you with the tasks that your beginning teacher needs to complete as part of their initial training?

Read through the assignment list and associated guidance in the beginning teacher's documentation. For each, consider the following:

- How clear are the instructions and criteria for successful completion of the task?
- How far would your own knowledge allow you to address the tasks?
- Where might you go to find out more about recent aspects that you may not have covered?
- How supportive is the provider (your link with your SCITT or university) in helping you as a mentor to understand these tasks (e.g. access to published materials, clarification by your contact, further explanation of the relevance of the tasks)?
- To what extent do the tasks support and develop the practice of the beginning teacher as the placement unfolds?

At this stage you might reconsider the structure of mentor sessions at key points in the development of the assignments to take in the following:

- What further experiences in school could be undertaken by the beginning teacher to support their understanding of the relationship between theory and practice?
- Where could you build in space for the beginning teacher to raise issues from written assignments that illuminate their practice or make them question their methodology? How might you support this?

McCallum and Price discuss further the significance of the cognitive role when reviewing previous studies and perceptions of well-being: "Long et al. (2012) describe a 'move away from a narrow, technical, and fixed goal-oriented framework of inducting beginning teachers towards conceptualizing the development of becoming a new teacher as a process'" (McCallum & Price, 2017, p49).

This has implications for the overall perspective that mentors have. Often mentoring is seen as a succession of tasks which are structured by a timetable of deadlines for completion of reports to the relevant bodies on the progress of the beginning teacher. To turn a chain of events into a narrative within a broader, more personalised philosophy requires a joint undertaking by the mentor and mentee. Connelly and Clandinin (1999, p19) conceptualised this identity process as "stories to live by". The process attends to both the personal context of teachers and the cultural contexts of school with attention to a time span. The need to shape relational places on school landscapes that allow beginning teachers' spaces to reconfigure their ongoing identities as teachers is critical.

Thus, for beginning teachers it is particularly important to build a sense of identity derived from their knowledge of their own background and character, strengths and weaknesses, their values and expectations of the institution in which they work. This sense of who they are and their purpose, as discussed in previous chapters, combined with an understanding of how these might play out in an educational context, vital in establishing their own narrative and integrating it into their environment, is thus essential in supporting and maintaining well-being.

It is undoubtedly challenging for a first-time mentor to undertake an over-arching discussion about identity and personal narrative at the point where the mentee is most eager to get on with the tasks related to the classroom. Careful thought might be given as to how this vital conversation can be conducted and what consequent benefit might be seen over the course of the mentoring. Further advice on this aspect has been offered in previous chapters.

One key difficulty in addressing the issue of wellbeing is that a plethora of definitions exists. So for you, as a mentor of a beginning teacher, it is important to consider which aspects relate to your relationship with your mentee.

> **Task 5.7 Mentor reflection: Your understanding of well-being**
>
> Reflect on what you understand by well-being by considering the following questions:
>
> - How do you define well-being, taking in to account the ideas above?
> - How do the various aspects of the ideas reflect the strategies and mindset you have built up so far for yourself?
> - Which elements will you take forward to support and develop your beginning teacher?

Identifying difficulties

In the first instance as mentor, you might have picked up that something is not quite right. Before considering how to proceed, it is useful to get some idea of the nature and size of the problem. It is also important to realise that few mentors have any training in counselling and should not attempt to take on this task single-handedly if the problems are complex and outside the mentor's capability to joint problem-solve. It is also worth remembering that counsellors themselves have co-counsellors to help offload problems and any distress that may accrue from the counselling process.

There are stages of the counselling process that all teachers use in helping pupils with problems, which involve careful listening, reflecting the problem back, gauging the emotional state and pressure and helping or guiding towards a solution that can be "owned" by the person with the problem. It is important to remember that, unlike coaching, counselling is non-directional. The most important skill is *listening* so that you can understand the issue and its emotional impact. Advice-giving is different.

There is a place for all of these strategies, which your experience with others will help you to judge, as will your growing experience in the role of mentor.

Task 5.8   Reflection on listening

Consider the following prompts, as and when required:

What is the problem? You may like to make notes as you listen to your beginning teacher.

Have you checked back by reflecting to your beginning teacher what s/he has said to you?

What does the beginning teacher feel about the problems?

Are there any immediate solutions that you might help or guide the beginning teacher towards?

Is the problem beyond your capability? Can you signpost? If so, have you a helpful list of agencies to whom you can refer your beginning teacher?

Although different problems require different follow-up conversations, would it be a good idea to list possible problems and timescales to follow-up here?

Examples of interventions using cognitive thinking

Inevitably, many beginning teachers experience strong feelings of self-doubt as the early experience of the classroom – once the "honeymoon" is over – can be challenging. The usual means of conducting feedback, in which the mentee articulates first their impression of the lesson, can result in a list of things they perceived as going wrong, and profuse apologies. This practice, if left to continue unchecked, can be detrimental in the long term.

So, using the theory set out in McCallum and Price's (2017) research, it is a good idea to refocus the mentee onto what actually happened in the classroom. One strategy I have used to good effect was to sharpen the objective observation powers of the mentee, who was asked to say what a number of individual students did and said when they were directed by the teacher.

This strategy had at least two very useful outcomes. Firstly, instituting targeted observation of specific students took the emotional heat out of the situation: once the intellect was engaged, it was possible to see beyond the feelings of failure. Secondly, the beginning teacher was able to see more objectively what was actually going on. From this, a more realistic picture of the lesson enabled the mentee to draw more helpful conclusions and to make a better evaluation, which fed into a more optimistic and sustaining narrative. Shifting the perspective provided clarification and enhanced progress substantially. As a footnote, the mentee was able to sustain this cognitive approach to bring about a very successful conclusion to the placement and go on to find further success.

But there is an important warning note to be struck here.

All of the thinking and research undertaken into well-being seem to imply that, with the right strategy at their finger-tips and a kind of growth mindset, all teachers (including beginning teachers) can cope with everything that modern teaching throws at them. At the very least, schools can implement "protective factors" to support management of stress and these do have their place. But, as McCallum and Price point out, these are "a reaction to a state of unwell-ness" (McCallum & Price, 2010, p31). They advocate promoting a more positive view by: "focusing on a stable emotional state and a sense of harmony between context and teacher, whereby teachers attune themselves to specific school context factors and demands" (2010, p23).

It is sometimes suggested that problems might just be a matter of perception. So it is more than useful that McCallum and Price (2010) refer to the work of Margolis, Hodge and Alexandrou (2014) to repeat a note of caution. They suggest that strategies for coping, framed as developing resilience, often serve to benefit the institution rather than the individual. At this stage you might reflect back on your self-evaluation and the tasks you listed at the start of this chapter. How did and do you cope with the combination of demands placed on you in your teaching, managerial and mentoring role? If you are simply making lists on a need-to-do-by-the deadline basis, this might indicate a coping strategy. If you are looking at the ways in which the tasks relate to each other (another narrative to work by!) then you are likely exerting some cognitive control and working according to your conception of the role and job function. If you are then synthesising these into a framework that is in alignment with your values and emerging priorities, you are likely to have a fuller understanding of the way the components of the job fulfil a central and personal mission.

The implications for lack of attention to beginning teacher well-being cannot be underestimated. Teacher 'burnout' can begin in the training year (Turner & Braine, 2016), related to mental health problems, a lack of a work-life balance, and stress. Cognitive Behaviour Therapy (CBT) offers some useful techniques that you might use with a mentee who is experiencing mild anxiety, for example. Essentially, CBT focuses on changing the relationship between an event and its result through a person's perceptions. A good way of thinking about this is as follows:

A = an event
B = one's perception of the event
C = one's emotional or behavioural reaction

Events trigger thoughts, which provoke feelings, that generate actions that influence aspects of one's life. CBT challenges the assumption that A leads directly to C (Lam & Gale, 2000); it is one's *perception* of events that will affect feelings. Imagine your trainee teaches a lesson in which she has to send a pupil out of the classroom for refusing to comply with a request (A). She thinks she has failed because she has had to remove the pupil and feels that she is not able to fully control the class (B). She becomes uncertain in her authority in the classroom and she is less decisive in her behaviour management in the following lesson (C). This could easily become a downward spiral in her self-efficacy (that is: her belief in her own ability to be successful in a particular capacity) and progress.

You can help your mentee to address this kind of negative cycle of thinking by talking through some of the following steps exemplified in Table 5.1, using strategies adapted from Riggenbach (2013). In the scenario, the mentor (Sunita) has noticed that her trainee (Grant) has been withdrawn in his interactions with staff and his lessons have been rather 'flat', so she initiates a conversation with him.

Task 5.9   Mentor reflection: Limitations and potential afforded by a cognitive approach

Reflect on your understanding of the possibilities and drawbacks offered by recent research.

How far do you think that holistic well-being strategies which promote resilience and problem-solving can work in your environment?

List the times when cognitive approaches have helped you, and instances in which the problem has been beyond what the individual can do.

For the mentor looking for material on which to draw for help and advice, there are advice sheets from the Education Support Partnership and Teacher Toolkit Blog. The Education Support Partnership is a charity which undertakes and publishes research into many aspects of teachers' lives. It is referred to extensively by many writers about education and offers a helpline as well as other services. The Teacher Toolkit (link included in the further reading list at the end of the chapter) offers a range of blogs with useful advice on well-being as well as other topics. It might be useful for you as a mentor to take time out to consider which aspects of well-being belong within the mentoring relationship. For example, you might consider the difference in approach between the extent to which you consider the mentee's health and home circumstances and those of your pupils. Is it appropriate to adopt the same approach for both? How far can you solve the problems of either?

On the other hand, you may well take steps to help the mentee build the most positive relationships with all those with whom they come into contact. McCallum and Price (2017) provide a very useful discussion of the impact on well-being of relationships between teachers and their pupils, parents and colleagues at all levels.

In these materials you will find that well-being does not just relate to the individual's capacity to cope with the stressors of teaching, which are common to all teachers. There

Table 5.1 Mentor-trainee conversation using CBT strategies

Mentor-trainee conversation	CBT strategy
In this scenario, the mentor (Sunita) has noticed that her trainee (Grant) has been withdrawn in his interactions with staff and his lessons have been rather "flat".	
Sunita: I've noticed that you've been a bit withdrawn over the last few days and wondered whether anything was wrong.	Identify triggers
Grant: Um, I don't know.	
Sunita: It seemed to start from the lesson feedback that you had from Nancy when you taught her Year 12 class. Can you talk to me about that?	
Grant: It - it didn't go well. I got a bit muddled when discussing The Songs of Innocence and Experience. I didn't study Blake at university, so I don't know his poetry that well.	
Sunita: What did you discuss with Nancy in the feedback from the lesson?	
Grant: That I need to prepare more thoroughly. She gave me some things to read but ...	
Sunita: How did you feel about what she said?	Identify feelings
Grant: I felt quite disappointed in myself; like I'd let her down and let the class down.	
Sunita: That's a bit hard on yourself! Do you think that has affected you in other ways?	
Grant: I'm just really worried that I'm not doing a good job. I'm almost scared to have any feedback now, as I know it's going to be bad.	
Sunita: So you feel anxious about receiving criticism because you think you're going to get everything wrong?	Identify distorted thoughts
Grant: Yeah.	
Sunita: I'm sorry to hear that; let's think about how we can address how you feel. **What has your reaction been to this feeling? How has it impacted on your interactions here at school?**	Identify unhealthy coping mechanisms
Grant: I've withdrawn a bit - hidden away.	
Sunita: What impact do you think that has had?	
Grant: **I think it has meant that my teaching has lacked energy - I keep thinking "what's the point?" - it'll go wrong anyway.**	Recognise consequences
Sunita: Have you mentioned that this is how you're feeling to anyone?	
Grant: No.	
Sunita: Ok; let's think about where this anxiety is coming from. You seem to be saying that you're worried that everything is going to go wrong and that has made you particularly wary of receiving feedback. Why do you think that it's all going to go wrong?	
Grant: Teaching is hard; harder than I thought it would be. I have failed before when I've found something hard. I'm going to fail again. **I am a failure.**	Identify core beliefs
Sunita: That's quite a powerful negative belief to have about yourself. It isn't a very healthy belief to have. **What would be a healthy belief to have?**	Identify healthy beliefs
Grant: That I can be successful?	
Sunita: Yes! You said that you have failed before; **how do you think you failed?**	
Grant: I failed my A Levels and had to re-take.	Think of evidence of unhealthy beliefs
Sunita: Ok, but you worked hard and you succeeded in the end?	
Grant: Yes.	
Sunita: And you went to university and did well in your degree?	
Grant: Yes: **I got a 2:1.**	Think of evidence of healthy beliefs
Sunita: That sounds like good evidence for having a healthy belief - you have been successful and resilient!	
Grant: I hadn't thought about it like that, but yes, you're right.	
Sunita: So as you're learning to teach, **you do need to have feedback - positive feedback but also constructive criticism**, as that's part of how you learn. How do you think you can hear that criticism without it destroying your confidence?	Face your fears
Grant: I think **I need to remind myself of the things that went well.**	Use your resources
Sunita: Yes, perhaps write down the positives as a reminder. Remember that we all want you to do well and targets for improvements are intended to help you progress.	
Grant: It might help to have a specific focus in each lesson when I'm observed; I think that will help me not to feel overwhelmed.	
Sunita: Good idea.	

are frequent references to workload, from which it can be inferred that the number and dimensions of tasks now undertaken by classroom teachers have grown out of proportion.

Task 5.10   Mentor research

You might find it useful to spend some time looking at and considering the advice offered in Teacher Toolkit, the TES and Teacher Support networks. Look at the further reading list at the end of the chapter for additional advice.

What are the features of each web page that are applicable to your context?
When might you use some of the advice offered?

Conclusion

In many ways, a mentor is a mediator between the school and the individual mentee, so the process of mentoring in the context of well-being reflects the ethos and practice of the organisation. If the mentee is to thrive in a number of schools, probably across sectors, then it is likely that the experience of mentoring will itself be a focus, providing metacognition of the processes involved and strategies learned. The construction of a sustainable narrative and strong teacher identity will help to provide a supporting mechanism during the many challenges that will exist throughout a teaching career.

Further reading

Hawkins, K. (2017). *Mindful Teacher, Mindful School*. London: SAGE.
Offers useful advice for teachers on developing self-care and maintaining well-being for pupils in school.

The Teacher Toolkit. Available at:
www.theteachertoolkit.com

Workload Reduction Toolkit. Available at:
www.gov.uk/government/collections/workload-reduction-toolkit

6 Developing collaborative practice

Trevor Wright

Introduction

It's arguable that all mentoring is based on collaborative practice. In that sense, the whole of this book is about how mentors and mentees work together. This chapter considers in detail the nature of this collaboration and offers specific examples and suggestions for building sharing protocols which will enhance the mentee's confidence and abilities. For our purposes here we are considering a collaborative relationship to be one which reduces as much as possible the sense of hierarchy between mentor and mentee. As well as a basic system of lesson observation and feedback, the successful mentor will develop a wide repertoire of joint activities which develop the mentee's reflection across many professional contexts.

This range of collaborative activity will provide rich development as well as enhancing the mentor/mentee relationship. Maynard and Furlong (1995b) suggested that we may encounter three approaches to mentoring – based on competence, apprenticeship or reflection. A collaborative relationship in which mentor and mentee explore together the issues that face a teacher in building skill and professionalism moves beyond the first two of these attitudes and sees *reflection* as fundamental to full development. Essential to the mentor's role is developing experiences which will generate reflective opportunities, as well as supporting and structuring that reflection when it happens.

Objectives

By the end of this chapter, you will be able to:

- Recognise a wide range of collaborative activities;
- Devise collaborative feedback systems;
- Devise complex inputs for mentees;
- Devise a range of lesson-planning collaborations;
- Devise collaborations with and beyond the classroom.

Lesson observation and feedback

We have said that lesson observation and feedback is a staple of this process, and other chapters in this book focus on many aspects of it. In this chapter I want to go beyond it. But nevertheless we could begin by considering some opportunities which it provides for specifically collaborative working. In some senses, observation and feedback are a microcosm of the mentor/mentee relationship; a genuinely collaborative approach here will support a broad range of successful joint activity elsewhere.

Of course observation and feedback are not always collaborative, and indeed it can sometimes seem restricted to the competence or apprenticeship versions of mentoring. It can generate what Hobson and Malderez (2013) call "judgmentoring", especially if the essential purpose of mentoring is believed to be limited to the judgment of competence and the improvement of the mentee through emulation. Your mentee may understandably feel intimidated by these attitudes, and stress is not a good basis for clear thought and improvement. I'm suggesting that your job is to generate a sense of mutuality and of shared endeavour. Here are some suggestions for rendering this tense process of lesson observation more collaborative.

Arranging a visit

A collaborative approach requires agreement. Instead of informing your mentee of your intention to visit her classroom, you should agree on a date and time. It may be that your mentee wants feedback on a particular class, a particular piece of subject knowledge or pedagogy.

Observation focus

Let your mentee suggest the main focus for the observation. She may want advice on starting Shakespeare, on teaching sentence grammar or on creating pupil response to poetry. You may of course have agreed on such a topic during a previous feedback discussion.

Feedback protocols

At an early stage, you should agree on the nature of your post-observation feedback conversations. These agreements should be reached before the first observation. You should work together to establish a regular feedback system, and you should stick to this until, by agreement, you evaluate it and modify it. The protocol will vary, according to individuals, but (as an example only) you and your mentee may agree at an early stage that each lesson feedback will be based on:

- Three positive points
- Two developmental targets
- Explicit comment on progress regarding previously agreed targets
- Always beginning with your mentee's opinion of the lesson
- Always concluding positively
- Always defining future targets (SMART, obviously), probably using Teachers' Standards
- Discussing this agenda itself and whether it needs to change

Developing collaborative practice 69

In particular, the use of numbers (only *two* development points), though mechanistic, is crucial. It is a focusing discipline for you as mentor, it ensures that your mentee has manageable material outcomes and it provides a balance in the conversation. The numbers may also remove emotion from the feedback; the "negatives" (actually development points, becoming targets) are not unexpected because they are a requirement of the system which you have both already agreed to. If, as time goes on, the conversations feel too negative, or (alternatively) too unchallenging, you can return to the numbers and change them.

Task 6.1 Agreeing feedback protocols

At an early stage, reread the example protocol for feedback listed as bullet points above and discuss these points with your mentee.

Set out with your mentee a written, agreed system for lesson feedbacks, discussing each point, including the numbers which you have agreed on.

Agree a meeting date in the near future when you will re-evaluate and possibly change aspects of this protocol to suit your mentee's individual and developing needs.

Collaborative working supports reflection, which is the engine of development (see Chapter 7). Your job as mentor is therefore to create events which will provoke reflection, and then to guide and support that reflection. Let's consider an example of such work and some principles behind it.

Your mentee is struggling with Shakespeare. She lacks confidence. She didn't much like Shakespeare at school; she avoided it when she could in her modular degree; now she faces the fact that, in England at least, Shakespeare is the only compulsory author in the curriculum. She has to teach *Macbeth*, and she doesn't know how to begin.

An *apprenticeship* model of mentoring rests on simple inputs. You talk to your mentee about how to go about starting the play. You explain your own successful approach. She is invited to try this, to emulate it. Perhaps it exists as a scheme of work. This is straightforward and supportive work; you are using your experience to help her development, and your experience is a powerful tool in this relationship. But you are offering her only one single input.

Your mentee needs stimuli which are focused but complex. That is to say, she needs plurality of input. Plurality leads inevitably to comparison, and comparison leads inevitably to reflection. You may be able to arrange for your mentee to:

- Consider your tried and tested approach to *Macbeth*
- Take part in the discussion of approaches to beginning plays at a departmental meeting
- Read some of Rex Gibson's *Teaching Shakespeare*
- Observe another English teacher with a completely different approach to your own
- Observe a drama lesson based on a Shakespeare (or other scripted) play
- Observe a lesson which makes use of film in teaching texts
- Observe a lesson which makes use of opinion and prediction in teaching the beginnings of texts

Of course there are a lot of options here and you can only work with what's happening in your school. But probably you can arrange for three or four of these things to happen. In so doing you have set up events which are bound to generate reflection. The mentee will be considering different approaches, comparing them, relating them to her own preferences and to her perceptions of the students' needs. In making these comparisons she will inevitably be approaching a tentative understanding of some teaching principles. A single input is easier to work with; it offers no contradictions; but it requires no sophisticated thought.

This complexity of input requires collaboration. You (and colleagues) need to work with the mentee throughout such a complex series of experiences. You need to provoke, support and structure collaborative discussions with the observed teachers as well as with yourself. You need to ensure that your mentee's varied observations are guided in subsequent discussions towards creative and purposeful comparison. Without your careful support she may simply flounder amongst this variety. But with it she can begin to understand herself as a teacher.

Task 6.2 Considering and developing experience

Consider the list above of possible experiences in connection with teaching Shakespeare.

    Can you add to this list?
    Write down several developmental questions which you may use with the mentee in various discussions which would happen at different stages in this process.
    Think of another English topic and create a list of varied experiences which might support mentee development. You could be thinking in terms specific to your school or setting.

Collaborative work: The transfer of experience

For developing teachers, most things get better with experience. A beginner will take a week-and-a-half to plan a lesson; a year later he will do this in 20 minutes. A beginner will stare helplessly at assessment level criteria; within six months he is applying them instinctually. Experience is the alchemy of development. It's the one thing you need, and it's the one thing you can't manufacture.

A few years ago I had two experiences with my teacher trainees in one week. On the Monday I was telephoned by a tearful trainee who had been given eighty examination papers to mark. Her mentor was working on the apprenticeship model – teachers have to do it, so training teachers should do it too. I don't know how he expected a trainee to do this work or, more significantly, what he expected the trainee to learn from it. There was nothing remotely collaborative about this arrangement.

Later in the same week, in a different school, I watched a mentor marking a single piece of Year 10 work collaboratively with a trainee. They sat side-by-side, working through the writing, referring to the assessment criteria. The mentor interpreted the criteria in terms of the pupil's writing, and vice versa. The trainee listened and began to make suggestions. They moved to a second script, and the trainee became more active and confident. After quite a short time their conversation about the assessment was an equal, shared conversation between professionals. It was exciting to watch.

You can't buy experience but you can absorb it through focused, collaborative working. I'm suggesting that this is a principle: your mentees need to gather experience as quickly as they can, and focused collaboration is an accelerator.

In this transfer of experience via collaboration, there are a number of participators. Your mentee is a constant but collaboration can be with people other than yourself. As mentor it's often your job to ensure that these collaborators are available and briefed to support reflection. They will include other teachers (because of specific expertise or experience), teaching assistants, peers (such as other beginning teachers) and, perhaps, an offline coach who works to support the mentee without being involved in judging or assessing her progress. (This last is a very useful addition to the team of people around you and your mentee).

Your colleagues at school are a major resource for mentoring. I know of schools that have created mentoring lists which include every member of staff. Each of your colleagues is an expert. They may not always be involved with every beginning teacher. But they could, if necessary, offer their expertise. You are surrounded by experts – lesson objectives experts, lesson beginnings experts, plenary experts, evaluation experts, relationships with difficult Year 10s experts, sense of humour experts, poetry response experts, Shakespeare in the drama room experts, differentiation experts, Year-8 novels experts, gothic experts, persuasive language experts, group discussion experts, marking experts, keeping calm experts, behaviour experts.

The next section contains some suggested collaborative activities, but please bear in mind that the second collaborator need not always be you. In fact the collaborations suggested below often don't even specify which partner is the beginning teacher – it could be participant A or participant B (and of course there may be more than two participants). Sharing experience is growing experience. I'm suggesting that you might (collaboratively) select activities from this list, or others suggested by it, as they seem appropriate to your mentee's needs.

Lesson planning

Sitting beside your mentee and planning a single lesson jointly, explaining decisions which you make, inviting questions and contributions, building a conversation, is a strong model of collaboration, resembling the assessment model described above. It demonstrates the planning process and sets out criteria. Two people focus on a single piece of work. For basic planning experience, simply divide the planning, but work together – it's the conversation that counts. This may be all that's required; but at some stages you may want to divide the work more formally to create focus on specific aspects of mentee development. In particular there are aspects of planning lessons that, when explored through collaborative work and reflection, will support beginning English teachers in making rapid progress.

Focus	A	B
Planning sections of a lesson, based on agreed learning objectives and overview	Plans the starter and plenary	Plans the main activities

Such a division of labour will help a mentee to see how lesson structure might work and how the starter and plenary might combine to effect an evaluative frame. The starter introduces the simile, the plenary evaluates pupils' understanding of the simile. This evaluative function is often neglected but is arguably the most crucial component in building pupils' learning.

Focus	A	B
Using learning objectives	Decides on appropriate objectives	Plans the lesson

Beginning English teachers need to understand the significance of genuine learning objectives. Some see them as mechanistic and uncreative. Some add them to activities as bureaucratic afterthoughts. New English teachers progress exponentially when they begin to understand that planning proceeds from clarity in terms of what pupils are going to learn, as opposed to what they are going to do. Simple collaboration which separates out the objectives may help with this clarification.

Focus	A	B
Questioning in lesson with agreed outline	Devises main activities	Focuses on a range of appropriate questioning

Your mentee's questioning skills may need to develop. She is trying to build her confidence in poetry teaching, and you have discussed how this may be mirrored in building the learners' confidence in their own reactions to poetry. This involves many classroom activities, and whole-class teacher questioning is certainly one of them. Beginning teachers are often limited in their questioning range. A simple planning division like this lifts the pressure of planning the whole lesson and allows focus on questioning skills in particular. Of course the consequent lesson could actually be taught by both of you, allowing either mentor or mentee to focus further on questioning; and then the feedback could focus on questioning as well.

Focus	A	B
Understanding transitions in lesson with agreed outline	Devises key activities	Focuses on key transitions between activities

English lesson plans are usually based on pupil activity. Often lesson-plan blanks have spaces for objectives, pupil tasks, starters, plenaries, but little or no room for the teacher. Many beginning teachers will explain that they don't want teacher talk to dominate the lesson and that they want learners to learn through discovery and experiment. These are, of course, absolutely fine, constructivist attitudes. They can, however, result in lesson plans in which the teacher herself is invisible. One of my trainees once described her need to move from "worksheet administrator" to teacher. If we think we need to limit teacher talk, we need to be all the more assiduous about using it effectively.

Beginning English teachers need help with resolving this. Transitions between activities are often the golden moments of lessons but they are hardly ever planned. We move from activity A - perhaps the starter - to activity B - perhaps the main activity. The moment between the two should be a rich learning period. Many things should happen in this transition. The starter is closed and the learning achieved in it is evaluated and confirmed. Perhaps it's here that the lesson's learning objectives are featured for the first time - the starter having led towards them. The next activity is introduced. Its connection to the previous starter activity is explored. The learners' confidence in taking forward the learning from A to B is confirmed. Their understanding of the next activity is checked. They begin work.

Beginning teachers make strong progress when they recognise the complex potential of lesson transitions. How much they need to plan them will vary from teacher to teacher, but beginning teachers at least need to list the significant events within a transition. Many beginners will need (in the early stages) to script the transitions almost verbatim. This may seem laboured but it may be necessary to draw attention to the richness of the transition and its absolutely essential role in demonstrating the learning to pupils and in joining lesson activities into a single learning narrative.

A collaborative planning exercise in which one partner focuses on the transitions as suggested by the other's lesson activities, and the resulting discussion, will provoke real reflection about transitions and their role in the wider learning.

Focus	A	B
Evaluation of learning	Devises main activities	Focuses on evaluation throughout and on plenary activity

This section offers a series of collaborative lesson planning activities which particularly focus on areas which are crucial to a beginning teacher's development. Grasping these issues will generate real progress, and failing to see them will be a serious hindrance. Another such area is that of evaluating learning. There are many attitudes to this in school, and they range from data-gathering systems to elaborate assessment-for-learning plenary activities. However, sometimes, beginning teachers fail to see that it's vital to check that pupils are learning, and that this probably needs to happen throughout lessons, not just at the end. Sometimes, they employ plenary checks that have little substantial meaning. I have often asked a trainee teacher how she knows that pupils have a chance of retaining their new learning; and often the teacher thinks that decent teaching to a co-operative class is sufficient guarantee.

The teacher needs to know that the pupils are learning. He needs this obviously so that he can support his pupils, by adjusting his practice if he needs to. He also needs it to support his own development. He needs to be able to explain how he knows that learning has happened, and as his mentor you will obviously be asking this question regularly. Relegating the evaluation of learning to a brief final check isn't effective. For example, I was recently observing a Shakespeare lesson. The Year 8 pupils were reading in parts in the traditional way. It was very clear to me that, for the most part, they didn't understand the text. As well as stumbling over odd words, they were making no sense of the sentences. Many of them paused at the end of each line of verse with no sense of the meanings of the speeches. In answer to a brief question in the final moments of the lesson, the pupils assured the teacher that they understood the play perfectly.

We discussed this afterwards. The pupils' reading was an evaluative opportunity. The teacher needed to consider the effectiveness of his lesson in terms of what the reading aloud was telling him about learners' understanding. It hadn't occurred to him that learning could be checked throughout the lesson. It can be checked at the end with a plenary. It can be checked after each activity (as part of transition work). But it can also be checked almost continuously – virtually every exchange with pupils offers evaluative material, revealing the level of their understanding and so, most importantly, the effectiveness of the beginning teacher's practice.

A collaborative planning exercise which sees evaluation not as an afterthought but as a pre-planned series of opportunities will help your beginning teacher to understand that this is itself an important planning focus. With discussion she comes to see the significance of such matters in terms of her own developing practice.

These are pedagogical issues that may profoundly affect the development of a beginning English teacher. In the structured collaborations suggested here, it's the discussions which they provoke that matter most in terms of essential reflection. There are of course many other collaborative planning divisions which will draw attention to issues that matter. A plans a lesson; B approaches this plan with a particular focus on differentiation, on inclusion, on behaviour management. The planning is evaluated and modified in terms of an appropriate theme.

Task 6.3 Considering collaborative planning

Consider a current or recent beginning teacher whom you have mentored. Look back at the collaborative planning suggestions above.

- Choose three or four suggestions which would be appropriate for the mentee you have in mind.
- Add one or two further areas for collaborative planning which would be similarly appropriate.
- Consider which of your colleagues might be involved in any of these activities.
- If there is no mentee available to you for this task, consider which of the collaborative activities you would personally find most rewarding.

Wider collaboration

I have focused above on collaborative *planning* because it's a strong area for development. It allows for structured conversations. It's also pre-emptive and this will help to balance the mentor/mentee relationship which, being based at heart on feedback after observation, is sometimes excessively reactive. It deals after the event; and the beginning teacher needs to learn that success may be planned in advance into the lesson.

Of course, there are activities other than lesson planning which lend themselves to collaboration. "Team teaching" is a hoary notion, but the classroom can offer many opportunities for building confidence and reflection through thematic collaboration. If your beginning teacher needs to learn more about teaching assistants she can do this by becoming one for your lesson. She will need to be briefed on the role and on the pedagogy. The role of TA can be hugely beneficial when a beginning teacher is involved with classroom activities about which she is nervous or inexperienced – such as drama lessons, for example.

She can work on the creation of resources for a lesson which you have planned.
She can observe you teaching and offer feedback, preferably to an agreed focus.
She can work with peers in most of the ways detailed in this chapter.
She can offer training sessions to other staff, within English or across the school. I have known trainee teachers manage this with great success (as well as great trepidation, of course). Sometimes they are more up to date with pedagogy than established staff.

Your beginning teacher may want to focus on an individual pupil or a small group within one of your classes. This selection, and the work that follows – talking to that pupil, marking his work, setting follow-up work – will allow her to see the value of dialogic relationships with learners.

As a mentor you will meet your beginning teacher regularly, probably once a week. This very important meeting may be supplemented by group meetings where several beginning teachers (and perhaps several mentors or staff) meet together to share experiences. Any mechanisms which renders increased experience available to the mentee is likely to generate more reflection and so more progress.

Summary

In drawing towards the close of this chapter, I want to reiterate its basic premise, which is:

teachers make progress by reflecting;
reflection is generated by experiences; and
experience is maximised by collaborative working.

I have emphasised the importance not just of working together but of talking about that work. It's the discussion that counts. As teachers grow they (often implicitly) question themselves. They interrogate their planning and teaching decisions, modifying as they go. This is how they develop in the short, medium and long terms. This internal interrogation is essential to effective professional practice and career development. It is a habit which needs to be kickstarted and developed in new teachers. External collaborative discussions in effect model the internal discussions which good teachers need to adopt.

SECTION 4

Supporting the development of beginning English teachers' knowledge, skills and understanding

7 What knowledge, skills and understanding do beginning English teachers need?

Debbie Hickman and Theresa Gooda

In a recent PGCE session where student teachers were asked to reflect on their experiences in their first placement so far, one student referred to her recent teaching of *Great Expectations* and likened her experience to that of Estella. She compared her own feelings to hers, commenting 'I have been bent and broken, but – I hope – into a better shape' (Dickens, 1861). This student's reflection serves as a useful reminder that the initial training year (and beyond) is not just an opportunity for the gaining of new knowledge but that training to be a teacher of English will likely involve some bending and reshaping of existing knowledge into a form appropriate for teaching. Green observes that although many student teachers of English come to the profession following undergraduate studies in the subject, this knowledge in and of itself is often not sufficient for teaching the subject. He argues that part of beginning teachers' development requires 'reconstructive dialogue with their degree level knowledge' in order to 'establish an understanding of their multi-faceted relationship with their discipline, evaluating their subject knowledge in a variety of different levels' (Green, 2006, p.113). Chapter 3 asked you to reflect upon and consider some of the different types of knowledge involved in teaching and in developing practice, as well as the kinds of knowledge that you might need as a mentor in order to support a beginning teacher. These reflections might have included your revisiting your relationship with the subject of English and with practice in teaching more broadly. This chapter asks you to consider a little more what is meant by subject knowledge and how it might be developed, considering in particular how beginning teachers of English develop their skills in reconstructing and/or reconfiguring their knowledge as part of their emerging teaching practice.

Objectives

At the end of this chapter, you will:

- Have a greater understanding of the nature of subject knowledge and some of the debates thereof;
- Have a greater understanding of subject pedagogical knowledge and some of the theories on which these are built;
- Have reflected on the subject pedagogical knowledge on which your own practice is built and developed;
- Have considered how you might support a beginning teacher in developing their subject pedagogical knowledge.

Outlining subject knowledge

Research conducted on behalf of the Sutton Trust and published by the Education Endowment Fund concluded that teachers' deep subject pedagogical knowledge is one of the key factors of good teaching contributing to good pupil outcomes. This research highlights that it is depth of knowledge, and of subject pedagogical knowledge, which makes the difference to impact and argues, moreover, that 'when teachers' knowledge falls below a certain level it is a significant impediment' (Coe, Aloisi, Higgins & Major, 2014, p2). Thus, mentor support in developing beginning teachers' subject pedagogical knowledge, both breadth and depth, into better shape for practice is a key part of the role. Understanding the complexities of subject pedagogical knowledge will help you and your mentee with this development.

However, Chapters 2 and 3, in discussing subject knowledge, noted that it is often seen to be specific and domain-based. It is commonly identified as academic in form, including that which was gained in educational experience and possibly including the study of a specialist degree. You will know from your own experience and from your experience of working with student teachers that academic subject knowledge alone does not prepare the student teacher explicitly or wholly for teaching. You may also work with colleagues and/or student teachers who have a subject background other than in the domain of English. Subject knowledge in English may therefore be broader than that gained through scholarly, academic activity. It might also include knowledge gained through experience, such as of texts in the context of their use (for instance, texts read for pleasure or writing in a different professional context) and as a result there may be significant overlap with cultural knowledge. Regardless of their own academic background, student teachers will need additional knowledge, including knowledge within the subject domain of Education, so that they can make sense of their own and others' practice.

Muijs and Reynolds (2010) describe that teachers require and use different types of subject knowledge:

1. Subject knowledge (what they know about the subject they are teaching);
2. Pedagogical knowledge (what they know about effective teaching);
3. Pedagogical subject knowledge (what they know about the effective teaching of their specialist subject).

Thus, supporting a beginning English teacher with developing their knowledge will require supporting their growth in understanding and applying a combination of the above in developing the skills needed to plan, teach and evaluate lessons.

Task 7.1 Refelection on own knowledge and practice

Reflect on an individual lesson which you have recently planned and taught.

> Which of the above types of knowledge did you draw upon in the planning and teaching of the lesson?

Were particular types of knowledge easier to identify than others?
Are some forms of knowledge more dominant or significant than others?
From where, and how, did you gain the knowledge that you needed?

Task 7.2 Supporting student teachers' development

You might consider the same prompts when you next review the planning for and/or observe your student teacher teaching. In addition,

When discussing areas for development, what does your student consider their subject knowledge development needs to be?
Do they demonstrate a preference for or prioritise particular types of knowledge?
How might you support them to develop depth and breadth of all of the knowledge above?

You might have found that it is difficult to distinguish between different types of knowledge, or to position certain ideas under particular headings. (Brindley, 2015, p50) argues that subject knowledge development, including the development of professional knowledge 'requires an approach to the subject in ways that demonstrate critical engagement with a network of concepts, rather than discrete "units" of knowledge'.

Thus, we might consider subject knowledge development to be the critical understanding of a range of connected concepts and ideas, for example what it means to be a good reader, rather than just the specifics of particular texts which might be the focus for teaching. As Wright discusses in Chapter 6, development of such knowledge is likely to be ongoing, interconnected and the result of collaboration.

Given that English is primarily concerned with the acquisition, development and application of language in its many forms, there are likely to be significant conceptual connections between subject content and subject pedagogical knowledge. Brindley (2015) describes this as a 'knowledge dichotomy' competing in both content and construct. The tension, in the study of English, between skills and content is well recognised and debated (Green and McIntyre, 2011). The National Curriculum, since inception, has identified the core purpose of English as developing speaking and listening, reading and writing. However, several reconstructions later and the subject is still grappling with its role as both medium and object of study (as described and discussed in Chapter 2). Understanding the case for speaking and listening might help in further exploring the complexities and potential tensions therein.

Developing knowledge about speaking and listening

Brindley (2015) argues that teachers' knowledge is built cumulatively and over time, involving active engagement with ideas. For many practitioners, the explicit prompt for subject knowledge development is usually change, invariably to the frameworks that govern or underpin practice, such as the National Curriculum (NC) (DfE, 2013a) or examination specifications. Such changes often prompt not just engagement with debate about the degree, relevance and impact of change, but may also indicate some need for development of domain knowledge, usually of 'content' when new or additional texts are added to specifications, for example.

However, subject knowledge might also be reconfigured conceptually, such as when aspects of the subject are reframed within a new assessment framework or by new criteria. Such changes are rarely straightforward or uncontested. For example, recent changes to references to speaking and listening in the NC (DfE 2013a) and the way that this is now assessed within GCSE have led to a possible repositioning of its status in the English classroom. Speaking and listening in the current NC is heavily foregrounded as a tool for communication, with emphasis on the teaching of speaking and listening as a skill to be developed for particular purposes. In this context, speaking and listening might be seen as the focus of the subject and the knowledge that teachers might draw upon to inform their practice will include understanding of effective talk in particular contexts such as: knowledge of discourse structures and how these might be matched to purpose and audience, and cultural contexts such as debating conventions. The focus of teaching and learning might well be, therefore, on supporting students in gaining, developing and applying such knowledge: learning to speak and listen.

The NC does make reference, however, to another significant aspect of speaking and listening, in supporting pupils' cognitive, social and linguistic development and that 'spoken language continues to underpin the development of pupils' reading and writing' (DfE, 2013a, p2). This demonstrates, therefore, the role of talk as a pedagogical approach which underpins development in English and as the medium for study: learning through speaking and listening. Talk has long been understood to be at the heart of meaning-making and therefore of learning, as speaking helps and supports children to make sense of their world. The review by Gibbons (2015) of the place of oracy in the English classroom not only charts the research which underpins thinking about the role of talk in learning, but also demonstrates the dual role of talk as both focus of and vehicle for learning.

Understanding the importance of talk to teaching and learning in the classroom is central in all teachers' development and as such might be seen as an example of pedagogical knowledge for all. The various dynamics of talk and ways of developing pupils' responses to teachers and each other are well documented in many generic teaching resources and materials because oracy is key to developing pupils' learning in all subjects. The work of Mercer (2000), for example, is central in supporting understanding of the different connections between talking and thinking and how this might be best practised in the classroom. Similarly, questioning is seen as key for all teachers.

Where the development of knowledge of speaking and listening differs for English teachers is that it serves not only in its role as a medium for learning. Equally important in the English classroom is the development of pupils' abilities to speak and listen well in a variety of contexts and for different purposes, because it is part of the communicative processes that are central to English. Developing subject knowledge of beginning teachers needs, therefore, to consider how pedagogy and pedagogical subject knowledge are related and when they are different.

Consider the following examples:

In planning a lesson focusing on understanding a poem, a student teacher might choose to organise small group work to explore how the text might be reconstructed from its cut-up components. In a different lesson, your student teacher might be supporting his pupils in writing and presenting a speech to the school council arguing for increased access to and use of technology in supporting learning.

In each of the above examples, subject knowledge development will be different, not just because of the needs of the individual student teacher. Alexander observes that:

> Pedagogy is the act of teaching together with its attendant discourse. It is what one needs to know, and the skills one needs to command, in order to make and justify the many kinds of decisions of which teaching is constituted (Alexander, 2004, p11).

In each of the above examples, the student teacher might need support in understanding how and why they have made decisions about the use of speaking and listening in the different contexts. Supporting a beginning teacher to develop their subject knowledge also therefore needs to include developing their understanding not only of effective teaching, but of domain-specific pedagogy, which includes understanding and providing a rationale for the decisions made in the context of practice. This will include understanding knowledge about the importance of speaking and listening, and also the contribution that it makes to pupils' development in English. Such knowledge might become subject-specific pedagogical knowledge when the general pedagogical principles of the place of oracy in pupils' learning is reshaped and refocused in support of the specific learning within the subject domain: for example, in understanding how and why small group work is particularly important in helping pupils to make sense of a text presented for study, or where and how particular questions are posed in order to support pupils' understanding of writing. In this respect, therefore, the use of talk is predicated in pedagogical knowledge, but is enhanced and deepened within an understanding of learning and development specifically in the subject domain.

Task 7.3 Reflecting on the role of talk in the classroom

You might return to the lesson reflections from Tasks 7.1 and 7.2.

> How much speaking and listening was planned for and took place in the lesson?
> Where did your knowledge for this come from?
> What was the impact?

Consider the same prompts and reflect on a recent lesson taught by your student teacher.

> Were there any significant differences?
> What might this reveal about your student teacher's needs?
> How might your student teacher be supported to develop their understanding of and practice in supporting speaking and listening in the English classroom?

Developing understanding of reading

> **Task 7.4 What is reading?**
>
> Reflect on the following:
>
> > What are you currently reading:
> > With your class(es);
> > For professional development;
> > For pleasure?
>
> Are the above three clearly distinguishable or are there overlaps and connections? Consider more broadly, what is reading? Make a note of some of the ideas that occur to you.
>
> From where have these ideas come and how have they developed over time?

Developing pupils' understanding and analysis of literary texts has long been understood as the central domain of English teaching in the secondary context (Dean, 2003), with a particular focus on the study of literature (Giovanelli & Mason, 2015; Yandell & Brady, 2016). Reading matters more broadly than in the study of literature, however, and connections have always been made between reading ability and educational attainment and standards. Indeed, rhetoric about and for improving standards in schools are invariably connected to reading because it is seen as significant in improving educational outcomes (Clark & Cunningham, 2016; Sullivan & Brown, 2015).

Given that it is commonly acknowledged that those who read get better at reading (Cliff Hodges, 2016; Cremin, 2014; Meek, 1988), it is assumed that English teachers are good readers. Subject knowledge development may therefore be viewed as developing breadth and depth in knowledge of texts rather than of reading and reader development. However, in the same way that knowledge about and of speaking and listening might signal the complex relationships between subject, pedagogical and subject pedagogical knowledge, the same may also be true of knowledge about reading.

Bleiman's (2014) blog post about the different knowledges that might be involved in the reading of Dickens' *Great Expectations* (1861) demonstrates the complexity of the concept of reading, and the intricacies of the knowledge involved. She considers the debate about content and skills, commenting on the complexity and significance of knowledge as including:

- Knowledge about and of the text itself – its characters, plots, themes and ideas. In studying a text, readers might be asked to consider the distinctiveness of the text and all that it affords, including in terms of thinking and reflection;
- Knowledge of and about the distinctiveness of the author and their work. The study might be part of a consideration, over time, of a variety of work by the same author. Teachers might find that their pupils, of their own volition or at the teacher's suggestion,

decide to read other works by the same author. In this event, knowledge is likely to include understanding of a particular authorial style and of the unique contribution that a particular author has made, as well as developing understanding of how various works compare and contrast;
- Knowledge of particular historical and social contexts, including how the text might have been received by Dickens' contemporaries as well as comment on the time in which it was produced. Particular knowledge of the context might be valuable in so far as it illuminates aspects of the text for the reader;
- Knowledge about language and writing, of how texts work in attempting to create meaning and effect which might then be applied in pupils' own writing;
- Knowledge of the questions and ideas that are central to English studies at school and beyond, including what it means to study a text. This knowledge allows pupils to learn how to read, think and write critically and with independence, and discover what it means to be a student of English.

In considering developing knowledge of a particular text for the purpose of teaching and studying, therefore, a student teacher might need to consider each of the above, proportionate to their already existing knowledge. It is also the case, however, that for advanced readers such as English teachers, knowledge of texts read is more than the sum of the total. Teachers' understanding of texts (their construction, content, themes, ideas and so on) arises from the accumulative impact of reading, not just of experience of texts. Their understanding of literary study may have been enhanced by academic experience but many teachers of English become effective teachers of texts, both as objects of study and construction, because they are themselves readers. For them reading has been transformative and they want this for their pupils. They are, therefore, teachers of reading, not just of what is being or has been read. Brindley distinguishes between the idea of a 'competent' and 'outstanding' teacher, suggesting that 'the competent teacher can teach about a text or a language theme, but an outstanding teacher uses that text or language theme to demonstrate English as an intellectual mapping of ideas through word and image' (Brindley, 2015, p49).

Your support for your student teacher may begin, therefore, with the identification of texts unknown to the teacher but identified as the focus for teaching, in order to develop their competence. However, developing depth of knowledge as part of the progression of the student teacher ought to move quickly to include much of the above. You are not the teacher of subject knowledge for your student teacher, but rather might signpost or highlight aspects of development which your student teacher might then pursue.

Developing a pedagogy for reading

In the light of Alexander's (2004) idea that pedagogical knowledge requires understanding in order to justify decisions made in the context of practice, development of textual knowledge alone is unlikely to be sufficient for the beginning teacher of reading. Cliff Hodges' (2016) work and research, for example, considers the complexities of the concepts of reading and readership and the role that research plays in supporting understanding and practice. In discussing the development of pedagogy, she suggests the idea of an ecology, comprising the interrelationship of:

- classroom practice (i.e., the acquired craft with which [teachers] develop, and select, from a repertoire of approaches and thereby enact their professional role);
- the values which guide their choice of material, their discourse and their responses to students' learning (often intuitive, but needing to be made explicit);
- the research they read and undertake which deepens their understanding of teaching and hence informs their onward trajectory;
- and their subject knowledge, not only what they have already learnt about the subject, but also their capacity for learning in future and, indeed, the creativity with which they innovate and learn differently, as the need arises (Cliff Hodges, 2016, p25).

Cremin's (2014) work, equally, despite, focusing mainly on primary practice, has significant relevance to and implications for secondary context. In considering reader and reading development, the research foregrounds the need to develop a pedagogy which prioritises motivation and will, alongside skill. This research and pedagogy, with a strong emphasis on promoting reading for pleasure thus positions the teacher as a key role model for pupils, shaping their perceptions of reading and able to engage in discussions about and make recommendations of texts to be read for pleasure.

The two researchers mentioned above hint at the wealth of research available about reading and reader development, some of which your student teacher may be accessing as part of their initial teacher training programme. For some student teachers, grappling with the daily requirements and demands of teaching might surplant their engagement with the theoretical. However, understanding and making connections between theory and practice will help them to move from planning activity to considering learning, as they begin to understand the reasons for the decisions they are making.

Task 7.5 Reflecting on reading

Consider your conversations with your student teacher about reading.
Where have their priorities been focused:

Understanding of text(s)?;
Understanding of reading and readers?;
Both?
Has this emphasis been prompted by anything in particular?
Has your mentee considered, as part of their initial teacher training, aspects of theory about and pedagogy for reading?
How far has this informed their emerging practice?

Both Cliff Hodges' (2016) and Cremin's (2014) work have implications for developing practice and understanding of pedagogy, in part because both acknowledge the significance and impact of taking a position on reading. As discussed in Chapter 2, the position adopted by teachers towards the subject, and an aspect thereof, will impact on the approaches that are selected and preferred. Many current approaches in teaching reading are formulated on and underpinned by theory. For example, Directed Activities Related to Text (DARTS) activities, which build on the work of Lunzer and Gardner from the 1970s and 1980s and propose approaches that support engagement through reconstruction of text, are predicated on a view of reading as social and socially constructed. Similarly, approaches and activities centred around the practice of modelling might be seen as having close connections with Vygotsky's ideas of the expert adult working alongside pupils to support their development. In this context, the teacher might be acting as expert in a number of ways, not just in their knowledge of and about texts, but also as an expert reader. For example, the act of reading aloud to a class might include the teacher modelling a range of aspects of reading, including: fluency, inflection, intonation, rereading, use of punctuation to signal meaning and so on. Practice based on adopting a dialogic approach drawing upon the work of, for example, Alexander (2004), will build on a view of reading as socially constructed, which positions the reader as active in meaning-making and interpretation and therefore draws on the ideas of Iser (1978) and Rosenblatt (1978). Cliff Hodges (2016) thus argues powerfully for teacher engagement in research on the grounds that the complexities of reading and teaching, and therefore the development of pedagogy and practice, are better understood and developed in the light of research activity.

Task 7.6 Reflection on own and mentee's reading knowledge and practice

Reflect on an individual lesson which you have recently planned and taught which focused on the study of a text or on reading.

- Which knowledge did you draw upon in the planning and teaching of the lesson?
- How much attention did you give in the planning to the activity of reading/related to the text?
- How much attention was given to the selection and justification for the pedagogical approaches that you used?
- What does this reflection reveal about your priorities in planning for teaching and learning in reading?

Revisit the prompts above with your mentee.

- Are their responses significantly different from your own?
- From where do their emerging ideas about the teaching of reading come?
- How significant is the contribution of research and scholarly activity in their development?
- How might their needs be further met?

Discuss and review the needs of your student teacher in the light of the ideas of this section of the chapter.

Developing knowledge about writing

Reading comes before writing – for the society and for the individual (Manguel, 1997). In most English subject documentation, writing is also listed last. Though this is an alphabetical as well as historical hierarchy, the relationship – or separation – between reading and writing is complex and frequently contentious. The Bullock Report (1975) insisted that 'reading must be seen as part of a child's general language development and not as a discrete skill which can be considered in isolation from it' (Bullock, 1975, pxxxi). The introduction of the NC had separated reading and writing in terms of programmes of study and assessment. At the end of the second phase of the NC with its focus on Assessing Pupil Progress (APP), reading and writing clearly appeared as discrete skills. Current programmes of study group reading and writing together – and yet, it is through *writing* that our students will ultimately be assessed, both for its own sake and as a measure of reading ability. Its importance cannot be underestimated.

Many English teachers, regardless of the academic and pedagogic route through which they have come into teaching, would identify as 'readers' and could talk freely about the last book that they read and enjoyed. Few would actually identify as 'writers', and very few indeed could identify as published writers. We tend to define teachers as 'people who read, not as people who write' (Elbow, 2000 p9). Indeed, the very word 'writer' is laden with a kind of literary snobbery. And yet, as teachers of English, we ask students all the time to *act* as writers.

Writing is hard, and it is exposing. We are vulnerable once we commit thoughts to the page. New teachers need an awareness of that exposure: an understanding of the formidable nature of the blank page. Perhaps the best way to be inducted into the vagaries of writing is to experience it first hand: 'We simply can't teach writing if we haven't experienced the process as well as the joy of fashioning a text for our peers' (Graves, pviii). and, 'exemplary teachers of writing are themselves writers' (Lieberman & Wood, 2002, p8).

So, writing must be about process rather than product, even though our school assessment systems are primarily concerned with product, or the end result. The product is but a fraction of the experience. 'Writing, like any form of artistic expression, is a very messy operation. There is indeed a general process from beginning to end, but who can predict the intervals?' (Graves, 2003, pxi). As teachers, and mentors, it is important not to shy away from the 'messiness' of writing but confront head on its 'organic, exploratory, muscular' qualities (Smith & Wrigley, 2017, p4).

This can be achieved in a number of ways. Student teachers can be encouraged to write alongside their students whenever writing tasks are set. 'We teach writing by writing' argues Barton (2013, p136). They can practise modelling writing explicitly at every stage of the process, from generating initial ideas to proofreading in the final edit, leading to an important understanding that 'many of our expectations for children's writing are unrealistic' (Smith and Wrigley, 2017), but also so that teachers can demonstrate as well as experience the messiness, and that students 'see that writing is something involving decisions and mistakes'

(Barton, 2013, p136). New and experienced teachers may also wish to join a teachers' writing group to support writing beyond the classroom since, 'teachers who write themselves as well as write with their students offer their students greater flexibility and understanding'(Graves, 2003, pxi).

So, what do student teachers need to know about writing? In essence, they need to know that it is both a craft and a discipline and that the best way to teach it is to *do* it. This helps to form the subject or content knowledge in relation to writing. The pedagogical subject knowledge, the *how* to teach writing is similarly complex.

Developing a writing pedagogy

Locke suggests that there are a number of elements that require 'grappling' with if we are to teach writing:'writer, reader (or audience), text, meaning-making mind, meaning, language (and other sign systems), technological mediation, social context' (Locke, 2015, p119) – and it is how we view these concepts and their inter-relatedness which is central to our writing pedagogy.

Task 7.7 Reflection on writing processes

Take each of Locke's terms, listed above, and reflect on its meaning. Encourage your student teacher to do the same.

Are there any terms on which you have different ideas or disagree?
How significant is your understanding of these terms, and the concepts to which they relate, to your teaching of writing?

If speaking and listening act as tools for thinking, then writing offers similar possibilities as a medium for thought, since it provides occasions to foreground and clarify thinking as well as to generate ideas (NCTE 2004). 'Thinking through writing seems to have been lost in the drive to teach pupils through a strict adherence to genre and the imperative to write to measurable criteria' (Smith & Wrigley, 2017, p18).

Writing is never learned once and for all but is inevitably a recursive process; effective writing teaching involves multiple teaching strategies that 'address both process and product, both form and content' (Nagin, 2006, p16). We should, as mentors, be promoting a rich approach to the teaching of writing, rather than a reductive one. Formulaic rules for writing stifle creativity.

And of course, it is not just *doing* writing that happens in a writing classroom. Teachers also need to find ways of creating a safe space, an environment of mutual trust and collaboration, in order for writing to take place in the first place. Finding ways to share and critique writing is crucial, because this is when students are at their most vulnerable. The first time, as an adult, that I was asked to read a piece of my own writing aloud in front of an audience was the last time I ever asked a student to do it. Student teachers should be encouraged to explore different ways of sharing and responding to writing in the classroom.

Given the complexity and idiosyncratic nature of the writing process itself, it would be difficult to draw any hard and fast rules for the teaching of it; developing a secure writing pedagogy is about exploring ways to 'empower students and help them to like to write' (Nagin, 2006, p18).

Task 7.8 Reflection on own and mentee's writing knowledge and practice

Reflect on an individual lesson which you and/or your mentee have recently planned and taught which focused on writing.

- Which knowledge did you/they draw upon in the planning and teaching of the lesson?
- How much attention did you give in the planning to the process of writing?
- How much attention was given to the selection and justification for the pedagogical approaches that you used?
- How might you further support your mentee to develop their practice in teaching writing?

Supporting your mentee's developing subject knowledge

You might revisit some of the collaborative activities suggested in Chapter 6. As you work through planning together, discuss explicitly the different subject and pedagogical knowledge that you and your mentee draw upon, and indeed might develop, to ensure that your planning and the lesson(s) to which it relates are effective.

How does the explicit attention to subject pedagogical and/or theoretical knowledge change or refigure the process for you both?

Summary

In this chapter we have outlined that:

Subject and pedagogical knowledge are complex concepts. The development of such knowledge for beginning teachers will require careful thought, including engagement with a range of sources and ideas.

Subject knowledge and development are about the *why* as much as the *what* of teaching.

Subject knowledge and development needs to move beyond content development or statutory frameworks if it is to lead to effective decision-making and practice.

Subject knowledge development is iterative and intrinsically connected with reflection and reflexivity.

Further reading

The following offer a range of research informed guidance and advice, including background historical, political and theoretical information, on aspects of pedagogy and practice in English:

Brindley, S. & Marshall, B. (Eds.) (2015). *MasterClass in English Education: Transforming teaching and learning*. London: Bloomsbury.

Davison, J. & Daly, C. (2014). *Learning to Teach English in the Secondary School. A companion to school experience*. (4th ed.) Suffolk: Routledge.

Davison, J., Daly, C. and Moss, J. (Eds.) (2011). *Debates in English Teaching*. London: Routledge.

Fleming, M. and Stevens, D. (2015). *English Teaching in the Secondary School: Linking theory and practice*. London: Routledge.

Subject-specific links

Bibliomania: www.bibliomania.com

British Library: www.bl.uk

The Chartered College of Teaching: https://chartered.college/

Englicious: www.englicious.org

The English Association: www2.le.ac.uk/offices/english-association

The English and Media Centre: www.englishandmedia.co.uk

Folger Shakespeare Library: www.folger.edu

The Globe: www.shakespearesglobe.com

London Association of Teachers of English: https://londonenglishteachers.com/

National Association of Teachers of English: www.nate.org.uk

The Poetry Foundation: www.poetryfoundation.org

Poetry by Heart: www.poetrybyheart.org.uk

Royal Shakespeare Company: www.rsc.org.uk

Subject Knowledge Enhancement courses: https://getintoteaching.education.gov.uk/explore-my-options/teacher-training-routes/subject-knowledge-enhancement-ske-courses

UK Literary Association: https://ukla.org/

The Victorian Web: www.victorianweb.org

8 Supporting beginning English teachers to become reflective practitioners

Julia O'Kelly

Introduction

You are probably familiar with the idea of reflection on practice as a means to work towards improving practice; a means of assessing how well a lesson has gone to help decide whether to repeat that lesson or make changes; what changes might be needed to make learning more successful, what changes are needed to teach that lesson effectively to a different group and so on. You may have heard references to certain mentee teachers as being 'very reflective'.

What do we mean when we use this term? Is it a 'natural' characteristic that some people have, or is it something that can be developed? What role do you have, as a mentor, in helping a mentee teacher reflect in such a way that they are able to improve their practice throughout their career? Indeed, are you a reflective practitioner?

Objectives

By the end of this chapter you will be able to:

- Know what you mean by 'reflective practice';
- Know why reflective practice is fundamental to developing professional practice;
- Understand why reflexivity is an important attribute of a reflective practitioner;
- Be able to identify the types of knowledge that might underpin reflective practice;
- Know how you can support the development of reflective practice through the feedback you give;
- Know how you can support mentee teachers to write effective reflective evaluation.

Task 8.1 Reflecting on your understanding of reflective practice

What do you think about each of these statements?

> I always reflect after every lesson, it's automatic.
> I don't need to write anything down to be reflective.
> I always note What Went Well and Even Better If.

> I ask the person observing me what they think of my lesson and I always take their feedback on board.
>
> I don't need to think about what I'm teaching, I have to follow the scheme of work.

Definitions of reflective practice

Reflective practice is a complex concept for which a number of definitions or models can be found. The title of Schön's key work of 1982, *The Reflective Practitioner: How Professionals Think in Action*, offers a useful starting point. His suggestion is that reflective practice is a characteristic of a professional, as opposed to a technical, way of working and that it reveals the way people think when they are apparently concentrating on 'doing' rather than studying. A teacher might 'perform', or 'deliver', or 'present,' a lesson and succeed in 'getting through' a curriculum, but in order to assess the quality of that practice and thus investigate ways of making that practice more effective, the practitioner needs to understand what they do. If they can show you their thinking, you can work together 'in a process of shared enquiry' (Schön, 1982, p302).

Reference is often made to Kolb's model; his experiential learning cycle (Kolb, 1983). It is sometimes shortened, in the course of busy practice, to 'plan, do, review'. While this can be seen as an adequate summary of the process of reflection, because those are the simple stages in the process which leads to thinking about what you did, considering how it could be better and implementing some amendment, it is limited. There is something important missing from this shortened form, as Figure 8.1 illustrates.

Kolb suggests that some abstract conceptualisation is needed. If the purpose of reflection is to make sense of practice, to understand how and why some aspects may work better or less well for you in your particular context, you need to refer to something other than your own, already formed, understanding. Reflection which relies only on practice is often characterised by practical considerations such as seating plans, resources, and timing of activities rather than by asking questions about what may be affecting learning. As a mentor, you will be involved in the reflective observation stage, at least at the beginning of your mentee's experience. It is possible that your own, already formed, understanding of practice, based on your own experience and context will be significant in your interpretation of what went well and what could be improved. It is quite possible that this type of reflection could lead to replication of existing practice and could even make it difficult for a mentee to develop their own understanding of their professional practice.

So, we need to consider two questions. First, what will affect our individual interpretation of concrete experience in the classroom? Second, what might be useful in ensuring that reflection includes abstract conceptualisation?

Reflexivity

What will affect our individual interpretation of concrete experience?

Reflexivity is fundamental in the process of reflection (Heilbronn, 2011). It is, in simple terms, being aware of and acknowledging what it is that affects your own interpretation

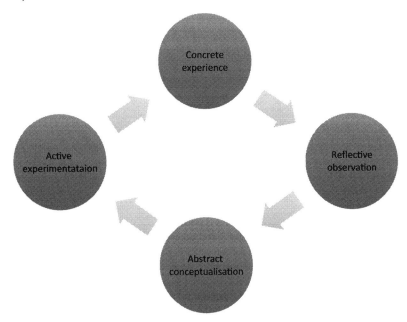

Figure 8.1 Kolb's experiential learning cycle
(Source: Kolb (1983))

and understanding. A person's values and dispositions are crucial to the way in which they reflect (Heilbronn, 2011). For example, I may be Head of English and therefore feel, more than anything else currently, responsible for GCSE results. I may therefore be preoccupied with teaching to the examination specification. I will know whether changes have been made to the specification, what I believe to be more difficult and more straightforward in the current requirements compared with what went before, and I will have my own view of the political context in which changes may have been made. All this will affect the way I view teaching in my department. Your mentee may not know what went before, they may have different political beliefs from you, they may be more keen than you on, for example, the inclusion of canonical texts, and this may be for a variety of reasons. They will have a preconceived idea of what makes a good teacher, and what sort of teacher they would like to be.

Task 8.2 Thinking about reflexivity

How might the following have contributed to your mentee's idea of what makes a good English teacher?

Type of school they went to
Home and family
Social class

> Beliefs – religious or political
> Ethnicity/heritage
>
> How might these differ from your own? (use the same list as a prompt)
> Can you think of other influences?

Thinking about your mentee in this way may help you to understand their view of teaching, but engaging in reflexivity affords more than this. It challenges you and your mentee to consider and acknowledge your preconceptions and assumptions about, for example, expectations affected by gender, social class, and so on (Wilson, 2013, p6). This in turn helps develop the questioning approach required for effective reflective practice. For example, it might cause you to think about some of the statements in the Teachers' Standards that are often seen as unproblematic. For example, commonly, 'high expectations' (DfE, 2013b, Standard 1) is accepted by many mentees as uncontentious; it is through reflexivity that they can start to question what they understand that to mean, and how their understanding may be different from another teacher's, or another school's, understanding.

Making sense of practice

What do you need to draw on to make reflection effective?

Just as you draw on your own experience and context when you try to work out what is happening and how you would like it to be better, you will also draw on a range of 'knowledge' about teaching English. Typically, you and your mentee will need to know the examination specifications when teaching GCSE groups. You will need to be more than familiar with key texts. You will be able to comment specifically on this type of knowledge when you work with your mentee on planning and lesson evaluation. This type of knowledge will be relatively easy to identify and it is very clearly required as part of Standard 3 (DfE, 2013b). There is a range of other knowledge that you and your mentee will draw on to make sense of practice, some of it much less easy to identify. Chapter 3 encouraged you to think about different types of knowledge and how these might inform development and practice. The next section of this chapter expands on these ideas, specifically connecting them with reflective and reflexive practice.

> **Task 8.3 Thinking about the knowledge you use to help you to develop reflective practice**
>
> What sort of knowledge do you draw on to make sense of practice?
>   Which type(s) of knowledge do you think you draw on most often?
>   Where do you expect your mentee to find the knowledge they will need to reflect on practice?

For many mentees it seems obvious that they will learn to teach by practising teaching. They will be in schools, working with teachers who have practical experience: they will watch those teachers, follow their example, and therefore be as successful as those teachers. This view assumes that teaching is a craft and that there are certain ingredients of good teaching. Therefore training to be a teacher is just a matter of learning the techniques that are commonly used and practising until they become embedded in practice. This craft knowledge is often seen as the opposite of theoretical knowledge; typically, craft knowledge being more relevant, or useful, than theoretical knowledge. Furlong argues that this is a 'false dichotomy' (Furlong, 2014, p5) and that a teacher needs to draw on theoretical, or academic, knowledge to understand craft knowledge. This is what provides the abstract conceptualisation that characterises effective reflective practice. It allows teachers to stand back from themselves and to begin to analyse their practice so that they can understand why something may or may not work for them, rather than just that it does or does not work. Without this abstract conceptualisation, they may find that reflection leads to a downward spiral in confidence because they feel that they are required to identify their own shortcomings, rather than use the process to understand what is happening in their classroom.

The practical, craft knowledge that experienced teachers use is, of course, very significant for a beginning teacher. They will learn a great deal from watching other teachers and talking to them about their practice, but there are limits to its value for developing reflective practice. A mentee will work with a limited number of teachers, who may or may not be enthusiastic about working with mentees. Many established teachers have, understandably, become reliant on repeating what works for them in their teaching and, although not necessarily unwilling to reflect critically on their own practice, may not have the time to prioritise interrogating their own knowledge about teaching over the day-to-day demands of a highly pressurised job. Schön goes so far as to suggest that for some successful, established teachers, questions about why they do certain things in lessons, why they think that works, and whether it could be done differently is threatening: 'Many practitioners, locked into a view of themselves as technical experts, find nothing in the world of practice to occasion reflection ... For them uncertainty is a threat; its admission is a sign of weakness'. He also recognises 'Others, more inclined toward and adept at reflection-in-action, nevertheless feel profoundly uneasy because they cannot say what they know how to do, cannot justify its quality or rigor' (Schön, 1983, p63).

Eraut (2004) describes the sort of knowledge that established teachers use routinely, but cannot identify, as tacit knowledge. This is knowledge built up from their own experience: they know what works for them and can say what they do, but may not know themselves, or be able to explain to somebody learning to teach, why they do what they do and why it is successful. Mentees can sometimes observe very good lessons without seeing overt evidence of what the teacher has established over time to make that lesson work. One purpose of reflective practice is to unearth this tacit knowledge.

Task 8.4 Starting to make tacit knowledge overt

What do you think you do 'automatically'?

When and how did you learn those techniques/practices?

What is it about your practice that a mentee would not see when they observe one of your lessons?

Tacit knowledge is explained further by Hargreaves (2000) as embodied knowledge, being knowledge that has become part of the person. To this Hargreaves adds the categories of encoded knowledge and embrained knowledge. Codified knowledge includes all procedural, imposed knowledge such as policy (national or school specific), curriculum specifications and the Teachers' Standards. This type of knowledge can be part of craft knowledge if it is used uncritically, presented as a requirement and accepted at face value, or it can be used as a framework for developing critical reflection. Embrained knowledge may be knowledge of English, or knowledge of Education, which are the academic disciplines underpinning professional English teaching. Mentees need to draw on embrained knowledge to question encoded knowledge; for example, why this text, who devised this curriculum, what was their view of English?

Eraut (2004) also identifies further categories of knowledge used in workplace learning. He includes codified academic knowledge and also personal knowledge and cultural knowledge. Cultural knowledge is knowledge specific to the culture of the specific workplace in which the mentee is learning. Each school has its particular culture, as any teacher moving to a new school can testify, to the extent that what works in one school may not work in another. Policies and practice can be quite different in a similar social and geographical area, let alone in different local authorities, academy chains or socially contrasting locations. In many or most initial training routes a mentee spends a very large amount of time in one school. Sometimes they will be in one school for the whole year with only a brief visit to a second school. Sometimes they will even train to teach in the school in which they were a pupil themselves. Eraut (2004) argues that the mentee needs to be able to draw on academic knowledge to question and begin to understand how an accepted practice might operate differently in a different school culture. Personal knowledge can be thought of as the basis of reflexivity. If a mentee has experience of working in a different school, or as a Learning Support Assistant, or went to the school in which they are training, their personal knowledge will affect the way they interpret their experience.

Thinking about the type of knowledge that a mentee may draw on can therefore provide the abstract conceptualisation needed to prevent reflection becoming a process of identifying personal weakness by dwelling on perceived failings. It can provide a framework in which to work towards understanding that teaching is not simply a question of replicating established practice. There may be factors to do with something other than your own aptitude for teaching that affect your success as a beginning teacher. It can help a mentee begin to understand why something may or may not work in practice for them in that context. It can move them away from concentrating on the practical, technical changes they could make to seating plans, timing of tasks, managing resources, and so on.

Task 8.5 Thinking about the knowledge your mentee can use to make sense of practice

Think of a lesson you have seen your mentee teach:

> How could your mentee use observations of an experienced English teacher (craft knowledge)?

> How could your mentee use observations of an experienced teacher in a different subject (cultural knowledge)?
> How could they use the Standards (encoded knowledge) as a starting point for their evaluation of that lesson?
> How could they use the work of Mercer or Gibson (academic knowledge) to reflect on their pedagogical choices and impact thereof?
> How could they use knowledge of other works of fiction (academic knowledge) to reflect on the impact of their text choices?

Reflection in verbal feedback: How can you help your mentee to develop reflective practice?

One of the ways in which you find out about your mentee's understanding of their teaching is through the conversations you will have with them as part of your feedback to them. The way you organise these discussions, and particularly the questions you ask, can help them develop reflective practice. You can reinforce a mentee's expectation that you, as their mentor and an experienced teacher, will be able to tell them what they need to do next to improve, or you can move them towards becoming a reflective practitioner who is able to see how to develop their own practice. These ideas are considered in more detail in Chapters 10 and 11.

In the first chapter, models of mentoring were considered, including the stages of mentoring as a mentee develops from survival to maturity (Katz, 1995) or from support to challenge (Daloz, 2012). This is not necessarily a linear development (Clutterbuck, 2004). Underlying these models is the concept of progression moving from you, as the mentor who is the fountain of knowledge, guiding the mentee with clear, practical advice, to the mature mentee becoming able, through reflective practice, to identify not only what they might do next but how and why that will have an impact on their practice.

A model proposed by Davis, Little and Thornton (1997) offers a helpful summary of how different approaches may be experienced or interpreted by learners, as shown in Figure 8.2.

This model is particularly relevant for developing reflective practice because it suggests that your attempts to develop your mentee to be an autonomous professional may be seen in different ways at different stages of their development. When your mentee is ready to move below the line in the diagram, you will be developing their capacity to reflect critically. If you were to start asking your mentee too many questions about why they used a particular technique, or reacted in a particular way in a lesson, at the beginning of their training you are likely to be seen as hyperspeculative, critical, and unsupportive because, at this stage, your mentee needs the security of knowing that they are following procedures correctly and are being supported with specific instructions about what they could do next. However, as your mentee develops reflective practice they will begin to respond to the challenge of being asked questions about their practice and become confident that they are developing into an autonomous professional capable of innovation and creativity. Until your mentee is aware of and is able to draw upon the knowledge they are using, they will not be able to respond positively to your questioning. As they develop their knowledge they will become more able to tell you how they understand their practice. You will need to tell them less, and listen more.

Beginning Students' Interpretation	Teaching Interventions	Advanced Students' Interpretation
Nurturing	Exposure to basic rules	Infantalizing
Helpful	Specific Instruction	Rule Chanting
Structuring	Directive	Authoritative
Hyperspeculative	Questioning	Challenging
Passive	Searching Quality	Curious
Abandoning	Undisruptive of the Process	Supporting Autonomy

Figure 8.2 Davis, Little and Thornton's Spectrum of teaching interventions and possible interpretations by students
(Source: Davis, Little and Thornton (1997))

Ways of developing reflective practice in written evaluation

If you are mentoring a beginning teacher, you are likely to be following a programme which will have its own requirements for written tasks, including lesson evaluation/reflection. There may be a form to complete after each lesson, short and long evaluations, a continuing reflective journal, or any combination of formats. While the conversations you have with your mentee may be used to develop their reflective practice, you are still the guide in the process. Written reflection or evaluation is your mentee's independent work. It can therefore be highly reflexive, revealing the writer's 'grounded perception' (Turvey and Anderson, 2011, p62), and it allows them to refer to various forms of knowledge to support their evaluation.

Written reflection is therefore a source of knowledge for you about how your mentee's thinking is developing, what they understand about teaching English, what sort of English teacher they aspire to become. You may encounter mentees who complain about having to complete written evaluations, typically saying that the process is repetitive. This suggests that they are not using abstract conceptualisation but instead are 'reflecting' that the lesson went well, or not, with little reference to the specifics of the lesson or to the types of knowledge discussed above.

Task 8.6 Considering the value of written evaluations

Choose one of the evaluation forms that your mentee is required to complete:

What prompt questions could you ask/add to support the process?
How would these help your mentee to develop their reflective practice?
Is there an advantage to encouraging 'free writing' with no formal report?
What might be the advantages and disadvantages of this?

Finally, Task 8.7 asks you to reflect again on how you can help your mentee to develop reflective practice so that they can become an autonomous professional, able to analyse their practice and develop into effective and creative English teachers.

> **Task 8.7 Reviewing our understanding of reflective practice**
>
> Having read this chapter, reflect again on your understanding of reflective practice:
>
> What will you expect from your mentee?
> How will their reflection help them to develop into better English teachers?
> How will their reflection help you to help them develop into better English teachers?

Summary and key points

The way that your mentee reflects on their practice may challenge you. It may cause you to think reflexively, to consider your own tacit knowledge, the impact of your school or department's culture on practice, the extent and type of academic knowledge required to teach English effectively, and to consider how far encoded knowledge is accepted or analysed in your context. The challenge should also be invigorating, providing you with an opportunity to think in different ways about the practice of teaching English.

In this chapter you have considered the importance of:

- Developing reflective practice, beyond practical considerations, as a way of thinking that will enable your mentee to become an autonomous professional;
- Using different types of knowledge as a framework for analysing practice;
- Thinking about how the different ways of developing and presenting critical reflection might help your mentee develop reflective practice but also might help you to understand your mentee's thinking.

Further reading

Eraut, M. (1994). *Developing Professional Knowledge and Competence*. London: Routledge.
Michael Eraut is an authority on workplace learning. This book is very readable and will help you understand how your mentee makes sense of what they do in the classroom.

Heilbron, R. & Yandell, J. (Eds.) (2010). *Critical Practice in Teacher Education. A study of professional learning*. London: IOE.
This book has several chapters that will be useful, particularly Chapter 1, The nature of practice-based knowledge and understanding and Chapter 3, The reflective practitioner.

9 Supporting beginning English teachers to support pupils' learning

Louise Beattie

Introduction

Having considered how the mentor supports the development of knowledge required for the effective teaching of English for beginning teachers, it is now time to think about how this can be applied to the planning of lessons. This section will cover how to support mentees with planning good lessons, evaluating the effectiveness of the lessons they have taught and moving towards planning and teaching sequences of learning. Whilst acknowledging the experience that the mentor can bring to this collaboration, a degree of reflection upon these experiences will strengthen your approach and thereby the learning experience for the beginning teacher.

This chapter will go through the stages of planning, teaching, reflecting and developing and draw on several approaches to mentoring which will be applicable at different points. You will be encouraged to draw on your own pedagogical understanding as well as considering differing beliefs.

Objectives

By the end of this chapter, you will be able to:

- Reflect on the process that underpins effective lesson planning;
- Consider how the mentor supports the mentee by adopting planning approaches and internalising the processes;
- Understand how to develop the mentee's evaluative reflections over time.

Task 9.1 Mentor reflection: Why plan?

Why do you plan?

> How do you plan for a half term or for a unit of work?
> How do you use shared units of work and personalise them for specific ability groups?
> What are your key considerations when teaching a new scheme or text for the first time?

Thinking about the processes in Task 9.1 will enable you to start considering your rationale for and understanding of how a pedagogical understanding of planning, teaching and learning is paramount. At this stage, the process for us as experienced teachers will be internalised. As mentors, we need to bring this tacit knowledge to the foreground in order to crystalise these with and for the trainee teacher.

Supporting the planning process: Starting out

To the beginning teacher, the thought of planning can be overwhelming. Despite the excitement of the first school experience and their anticipation of using their knowledge in the classroom, the mammoth task of tailoring this for a particular class for a particular period of learning can seem an unrealistic goal. Equally, there may be some trainees who have the additional anxiety of teaching a text or area of English language with which they are less familiar or confident. Whether following a university-led, School Direct or School-Centred Initial Teacher Training route, the beginning teacher should have had some initial input on planning. This might have included developing an understanding of differences between a long-term plan, medium-term plan or a lesson plan (short-term plan). It will almost certainly have included some 'versions' of lesson plans or perhaps a template that they are expected to use whilst on school placement. Even with effective discussions with their peers and tutors about how to plan and the rationale for each stage, beginning teachers are inevitably going to feel some trepidation as they embark on the process for the first time. Many, poised behind their laptop and filled with a variety of creative ideas, will be both capable of and anxious about honing these into an acceptable and useful professional document for the first time.

As noted by John (2006), the approach of planning a single lesson at a time offers a linear and rational sequence based on Tyler's model of planning (1949) and its veracity depends on its use by trainee teachers. Used ineffectively, such plans can become segmented and compartmentalised opportunities to learn where there is little overview or real understanding of the learning by either pupil or teacher. As a starting point, however, the sense of structure offered by this model allows for a rational way of approaching planning. Enow and Goodwyn (2018) suggest this initial stage in a long process is necessary to developing expertise. So, what is it that we actually mean by 'planning'?

Task 9.2 Mentor reflection: What does planning mean?

From your previous reflections, what key 'ingredients' does the beginning teacher need when beginning the planning process?

What questions would you offer to support them with understanding lesson structure or a planning format?

How could you help your mentee to make sense of and utilise 'in-house' schemes of work?

The experienced teacher may describe planning as spontaneous, juggling aspects of subject content knowledge, awareness of pedagogy, knowledge of pupils and a myriad of other considerations (John, 2006). Given this, in order to support the planning of a novice teacher, the mentor needs to step away from an almost natural and intuitive approach to planning and reflect on how *she* approaches planning in a methodical way. The commentary that she ascribes to these stages and the rationale behind them will be helpful in the initial discussions with the beginning teacher and thus contribute to the mentoring conversations. John (2006) notes that at this point, the dialogical model can act as a powerful descriptive tool to familiarise trainee teachers with the various modes of planning and the complexities therein.

Maynard and Furlong's (1995a) approach to mentoring discusses how dialogue such as this may include: sharing and modelling how the mentor would plan (the apprentice model); looking at the requirements and key skills behind the planning as cited in the Teachers' Standards and the National Curriculum requirements (the competence model); and discussing how the mentor's plan worked in the classroom (the reflective model). It will also mirror the belief that interactive teaching requires planning that is flexible and practical from the start and that a dialogical model which includes the mentee in this process will give them a better insight into lesson planning (John, 2000).

In their early discussions, mentees may focus on their observations during an induction period and a review of the timetable as a whole. Honing in on and encouraging focused observations of particular classes will afford the mentor the opportunity of guiding the mentee towards some specific areas as preparation for their first planning experience. McCann comments:

> A mentor can help beginners to interrogate what they see, labeling the elements in an instructional sequence and recognizing the purpose for each instructional move. This can lead to attempts at similar practice and reflection on its efficacy
>
> (McCann, 2013, p 90)

You might structure this early experience in any number of ways and student teachers may need some significant support with understanding how to use and capture observational learning. One possibility is suggested in Task 9.3.

Task 9.3 Reconstructing planning

Ask your student teacher to reconstruct the plan for a lesson of yours that they are observing. Reconstructing the plan as they observe might encourage them to make connections between the what, how and why, as well as impact on learners.

Following the observation, you might discuss their notes and ideas and compare this with your original plan.

- What differences do you both note?
- Where has the student teacher focused their ideas? What does this signal about their understanding of planning?
- How does this compare with your priorities?

Prerequisites and additional things to consider are:

- It can be helpful for the beginning teacher to have access to the teachers' plans when observing lessons (this need not be a formal plan but might be a reference to the medium-term plan or an overview of the intended learning).
- The mentee might be supported, during initial observations, by having something specific to focus on. For example, did the teacher thread the learning objective through the lesson and if so, how? Did the pupils achieve the teacher's expectations and how can she tell? The school or initial training provider might offer induction booklets or key questions for focused observation. During your discussion with your mentee following observation, you will need to ascertain how much these observations are contributing to your student teacher's understanding of the classroom and the significance of planning.
- Time can often be difficult to find. Although five minutes whilst walking to the staff room or at the end of the day can allow the mentor to elicit some initial views, it might be that, in the initial stages of the training and placement especially, time will need to be found beyond that afforded by the formal mentor meeting that you will have. Chapter 6 offers some useful ideas for focusing and supporting particular aspects of planning.
- Having been introduced to their timetable, the staff they will be working alongside, their classes and departmental schemes, the beginning teacher may be ready to lead part of a lesson. Although at this stage the student teacher may not yet be planning independently, for their induction to the classroom to be a meaningful activity it is important that she has been part of the planning process for this particular lesson or at least had a conversation with the teacher about rationale and intended learning. As above, see Chapter 6 for some ideas about how this might be scaffolded.

The planning process: The bigger picture

Expert-novice studies have shown that whereas the experienced teacher can see the 'bigger picture' and can use this to help them plan, the trainee will be more engaged with the short term (John, 2006). The beginning teacher has so many things to learn, filter and undertake during the induction period, before they start teaching. Occasionally, as a mentor, we might worry about overloading them with 'paperwork'. However, it is worth noting the value of different documents and deciding which ones are imperative to the trainee's initial understanding. Knowing 'what texts they are teaching' is inevitably at the forefront of their minds; particularly if this requires peripheral reading or familiarisation with literary works. However, the trainee also needs to consider the bigger picture. Are they really 'doing Frankenstein' with Year 9? Whilst this might be teacher language for the staff room it is unhelpful for the trainee teacher. Firstly, it sounds overwhelming and secondly, there is not a hint of learning in this phraseology.

How the mentor manages this dichotomy can often depend upon the particular department and the schemes of work and resources available. Whilst both the mentor and the beginning teacher will have the lesson plan template at hand, it will be important to have the conversation about why gothic literature is on the Year 9 long-term plan and what aspects of literature and language are going to be taught. Ideally, a medium-term plan or unit of work will show the direction of learning or intended outcome and will give the beginning teacher an idea of the context in which they are working (what they are aiming for).

Quigley (2014) describes this process of having a clear destination and plotting an appropriate route. Similarly, the idea of planning backwards (Griffith and Burns, 2014) can allow the trainee to have some overview of the learning and the period of time which is allocated to it. Setting these ideas as foundations will help both the mentor and the mentee to hone in on individual weeks and lessons as they move towards planning their first lesson. Jerome and Bhargarva describe the process as having 'some conceptual coherence underpinning the decision to consider the content as a single entity' (Jerome and Bhargarva, 2015, p 2). In some instances, the conceptual coherence might be masked by a simplistic idea – for example, study of a novel. However, in order to understand how planning might support pupils' learning and progression, a student teacher must understand not only the nature and focus of the novel study but also have some conceptual understanding of the development and progress that the study will afford the pupils. In the initial stages of planning and development, it is the mentor who will help with this conceptual understanding and how it is represented in the departmental schemes of work.

The planning process: Individual lessons

It is important that the beginning teacher has some specific questions to consider when starting the planning process. These will enable them to manage their own thoughts and understanding while attempting to 'fill in' the lesson plan template. We know that the beginning teacher will spend disproportionate amounts of time planning in these early months but the mentor can rationalise this for them as a fellow teacher who also used to take two hours to plan a one-hour lesson. The questions that you consider for guidance, therefore, will be particularly important as they will not only guide them through this part of their training but will lead them towards a way of thinking about planning and, in time, internalising the process so that it is more efficient and effective.

Task 9.4 Supporting the planning through focused questions

Consider the following questions – to what extent will they support the beginning teacher in the planning process? Your training provider's template may frame these slightly differently and you may have other ideas that you would want to include. However, the central questions are likely to be very similar.

Who am I teaching? *What is the year group, class size and ability of the pupils? What are the varying learning needs? Are there any pupils I need to focus on today?*

What aspect of language and/or literature am I teaching them? *What is the objective of the learning? How does it follow on from the last lesson's learning?*

How am I teaching it? *Are there specific teaching approaches or learning activities which will lend themselves particularly well to this lesson and the learning objective?*

> How will I assess learning during the lesson? *How will I monitor the pupils' access to the learning and their progress with it? How will I know when to intervene to support or challenge to move the learning on or develop key points? Can I plan for this transition (movement) through learning?*
>
> How do I measure the learning after the lesson and how does this inform my next lesson plan? *How can I use today's learning and experiences to help me to plan ahead? Does the marking of written work affect this process and how? Is the learning taking place over time?*

As a mentor, thinking about these questions as you model or collaboratively plan, will allow you to articulate a thoughtful commentary for the mentee. The speed at which you would ordinarily plan in your head needs to be slowed down for the beginning teacher so that they can see and hear the process. This will be a powerful learning experience for your mentee and validates the thinking that you undertake even if your planner cites, 'Macbeth – continue with Act 2'. It is at this point that joint planning with the dialogical element layered on top of the practical plan will enable the trainee to understand your planning process and how you have become adept at internalising much of this (John, 2006). The ability to share this with your mentee will ensure that this is crystallised in their thinking.

At this stage, the mentor is *supporting* the beginning teacher in the process. You will be helping your mentee, using collaborative experiences in order to support them to gain an insight into English teaching and how experienced teachers plan (McCann, 2013). McCann argues that regularly using collaboration as a learning experience for the mentee will not only avoid them struggling in isolation but will also give them confidence and the opportunity to thrive (McCann, 2013, p 89). You will have read about the importance of collaboration in Chapter 6.

Table 9.1 shows a suggested structure for lesson planning. The example includes some key ideas that you might develop and questions you might pose for the beginning teacher when discussing and evaluating lesson plans.

Teaching and evaluating lessons

Of course, the planning is only part of the process. Standard 4 of the Teachers' Standards (DfE, 2013b) highlights the connection between planning and teaching lessons, and therefore part of the evaluation of the lesson will include reflecting on how well the plan supported the teaching and contributed to pupils' learning. The challenge here will be to ask how the student teacher knows this. If the trainee focused on how she would facilitate learning at the planning stage, this will inevitably be easier. Rather than honing in on what she did or didn't complete in the plan, the discussion should centre on the pupils' learning and how well this was supported, including as a result of the planning. At the early stages of their school experience, this may invariably focus on the perceived success of the activities that featured in the lesson plan. Over time, however, with your support and encouragement, the focus should shift to consider the impact on learning. Your discussions will move to more

Table 9.1 Thinking about the process behind the lesson plan

Lesson Stage	Objective	Activity (indicate differentiation)	Evaluation Methods
Starter *You may want to include timings in this column*	Each part of your lesson should have a clear learning purpose. Ideally these will connect vertically through the lesson stages, building towards the overall learning outcomes.	Note here what you and the pupils will be doing through the stage. You may want to script your introduction to the lesson here. You should show how you are varying your teaching to suit the range of pupils.	How will you know that the starter has achieved its learning objective? Will there be key questions to record here or a list of pupils you would like to focus on?
Transition	Indicate here how you will move the lesson from the previous stage to the next. **Consider how you are making the learning explicit to the pupils. This will be an important part of the teacher commentary.**		
Main Stage	Each part of your lesson should have a clear learning purpose. Ideally these will connect vertically through the lesson stages, building towards the overall learning outcomes.	How does this stage move the pupils towards achieving the learning objective? Is it focused, relevant and meaningful for this particular lesson?	How will you know that the approaches have supported the pupils to achieve the learning objective? Is there an opportunity for you to reflect and review before you move into the next transition? Are the pupils ready and able to move on?
Transition	Indicate here how you will move the lesson from the previous stage to the next one. **Consider how you are making the learning explicit to the pupils. This will be an important part of the teacher commentary.**		
Developmental Stage	Each part of your lesson should have a clear learning purpose. Ideally these will connect vertically through the lesson stage, building towards the overall learning outcomes.	How does this stage further develop the learning? Is there opportunity for the pupils to showcase what they have learned and apply it independently or in pairs/groups?	How might your observations or key questions elicit the pupils' progress here? How are you using your knowledge and information about pupils to inform this part of the assessment of learning?

(continued)

Table 9.1 (Cont.)

Lesson Stage	Objective	Activity (indicate differentiation)	Evaluation Methods
Transition		Indicate here how you will move the lesson from the previous stage to final reflection. **Consider how you might encourage your learners to elicit their learning from the lesson overall. This will be an important part of the teacher commentary as you move into an effective plenary. There should be a clear sense of the 'shape' of today's learning in both your mind and the learners'.**	
Plenary	Evaluation of lesson objectives	Show how you will create opportunities from which you can judge the extent of pupils' learning and thus the achievement of the lesson objectives, as demonstrated through the outcomes. Are there opportunities for the pupils to reflect upon what they have **learned** as opposed to what they have **done**?	

evaluative reflection of *how* the student teacher first developed then implemented their plan and the extent to which this *facilitated* the intended learning.

It will be important for the mentor to ensure that the trainee understands the difference between the planned lesson and the taught lesson (Fautley and Savage, 2013). A number of hours may have gone into the lesson plan with well-intentioned objectives but circumstances in the lesson itself might have thwarted this plan. The beginning teacher might have encountered behaviour or timing issues which affected the planned timeline. How they reacted to this in the lesson will obviously be worthy of exploration with them. In many instances they may begin their post-lesson observations with the aspects of the lesson that went 'wrong'. From an early stage, how the mentor manages this perspective will affect how the trainee views their practice. Therefore the mentor should model an open and reflective approach to post-lesson thinking and a positive outlook on the next lesson (previous chapters have offered some ideas on how this might be achieved).

As mentor, you might plan some key questions for the post-lesson discussion in order to focus the trainee teacher's mind on the learning and pupil progress, as underpinned (or not!) by the planning. As a subject-specialist mentor, you will want to develop an effective post-lesson discussion that will naturally lead into the next planning phase for the trainee and ensure that they are making clear and purposeful steps towards developing their practice. This will model the cyclical process that is planning, teaching and reflection/evaluation.

As a mentor, it is worth remembering that the effectiveness of the discussion in enabling greater depth of reflective thought and evaluation will depend in some part on your feedback. As we observe lessons, we are also engaging with the plan and formulating ways of structuring the discussion afterwards. Are there key questions or prompts that you might note down as they occur to you during the observation?

As discussed in Chapter 8, different routes into teaching will have varying methods for the beginning teacher to capture their evaluations of lessons. These, together with the modelling provided during the post-lesson discussions, should enable the student teacher to develop effective reflection. They may have a certain number of lesson evaluations to complete in a week or have a weekly review in which they focus on some aspect of their practice. It will be important to remind the student teacher of the value of these activities in that effective and thoughtful engagement with them will increase their capacity to improve their practice. Although these activities will be time consuming in the beginning, reiteration of them will embed a professional practice that will support them throughout their teaching career. The degree to which the mentor in the post-lesson discussion encourages the trainee to reflect will affect their responsivity to future planning and teaching, reaffirming that they are both interrelated and dynamic (John, 2006). Chapter 10 deals in detail with lesson observations and post-lesson discussions as part of mentor support for beginning teachers.

Using data and assessment to inform planning and teaching

Didau (2014) offers some key considerations when planning: marking is planning; focus on learning not activities; and know your pupils. Interestingly, this takes us straight to the heart of what data really is. The beginning teacher in the modern world can be overwhelmed with a plethora of data, particularly in numerical form. How they manage this and use it effectively will be modelled by mentors and developed during their working relationships with mentors on teaching practice.

Most departments will have developed assessments which will give a focal point to the planning or require 'planning backwards'. Even if this is not the case, as we explored earlier, this often offers a transparent view of the learning and will enable the beginning teacher to consider why aspects of the lesson are necessary or valid. Ongoing discussions about planning and teaching will enable you to ensure, however, that the teaching sequences devised are not driven entirely by or primarily towards a particular assessment outcome. Numerous studies warn of the limitations that this can impose on teaching and learning.

Whilst schools will have their own marking policies and protocols, the mentor can model how marking becomes meaningful data which feeds directly into the next lesson plan. You can show how many seemingly disparate parts of the role of being an English teacher are interlinked and mutually dependent. For example, a student teacher may list marking, assessment, planning and teaching as a variety of tasks that a teacher undertakes. Rather your role will be to constantly show how one affects the other: how the next lesson plan needs to be refined after marking a set of books is a valuable lesson for the student teacher in managing data and ongoing assessment.

Likewise, how you engage with some of the data in order to arrange classes, plan for a variety of learning activities and interact with pupils will be significant aspects of your practice to focus on in your discussions with your mentee. Once again, you will crystalising the many aspects of practice, being explicit about how these permeate every aspect of your day and therefore inform a 'lesson plan'. Without this guidance in situ, the mentee may still perceive planning as completion of the lesson plan template as opposed to an intricate skill which they are hoping to develop. It is this 'relational authenticity' (Ragins, 2016) which compounds much of the learning that the beginning teacher is processing. They will listen to and absorb your own real-time commentary. Being honest and open about what has worked (or not worked) in some of your planning and lessons will be a way of conveying a real sense of how your role as a mentor is informed by your practice as a teacher. Chapter 6 offers some useful guidance on managing the workload of planning and dealing with data so that the focus remains on effective practice rather than task completion.

Moving from individual lessons to planning sequences of lessons

The concept of the beginning teacher moving towards planning a sequence of lessons is one which mentors can often worry about. There is an irony here in that the trainee can only begin to understand how to plan an individual lesson if she understands how it fits into the overall plan for learning. Just as we began this process with considering the interaction with the department's schemes of work or medium-term plans, there comes a point at which the beginning teacher will be best able to meet the needs of the pupils if she has a clear overview of the learning over a sequence of lessons. This may happen quickly for some while others may take longer to begin to see the links and fusion between lessons and learning.

From the mentor's point of view, there is no fixed time in the training year when this will become the next step in the student teacher's thinking and therefore practice. As noted by Maynard and Furlong (1995a), the professional learning of beginning teachers will progress at different speeds. This next step, however, is more likely to occur during the second placement or at some point in the spring term. The key to this transition will be the mentor's knowledge of her mentee and the rate of their progression. The weekly review meetings will give a clear indication and there are some signs to look for such as: a greater degree of ownership of the classes; a more proactive approach to the planning and marking cycle; and a more confident and thorough exploration of this in evaluations and reflections, including in the review meeting. You will need to think about managing this progression carefully, challenging where appropriate and supporting when student teacher understanding and practice needs further consolidation.

How can beginning teachers promote learning over time on school placements?

Keeping the beginning teacher focused on getting to know their pupils and planning effective lessons will be key in considering how they are able to contribute to pupils' learning on school placements. Although student teachers will usually have a phased start to their teaching timetable on both school experiences, they will inevitably move towards spending a considerable amount of teaching and learning time with classes and they will therefore invariably be contributing to pupils' learning over time.

Therefore, it is timely for the mentor to consider how their own practice promotes learning over time.

Task 9.5   Reflection on promoting learning over time

Think about one of your classes that is currently midway through a unit of work. Identify the intended learning outcome(s) at the end of the unit and consider how you will assess progress, perhaps through a formalised assessment.

Now, consider how this class and certain individuals are making progress towards this **at this point in time**. If there was an impromptu parents' evening, what overview and evidence of their progress would you be able to highlight for the parents/carers at this point in the term?

Think ahead to the end of unit assessment. How does the information provided by this opportunity contribute to the picture that you already have of the class's learning and progress? How does it inform the next steps of your work with the pupils?

Do these considerations prompt you to think differently about your planning?

Useful additional points to check for learning over time

Thinking about your own practice, consider the following prompts:

How well do I know my pupils and how do I build this picture over time?
How do I assess prior knowledge and understanding? Is my starting point right? Are my expectations appropriate?
How will I know if the pupils have learned? Do I rely on more formal assessment opportunities (both for and of learning)? How significant are the less formal opportunities? How much notice do I pay to a pupil's explanation, comment to a peer, thoughtful analogy or link to relevant learning?
Do I understand the continuum for learning in this medium-term plan? Starting point ›noticing learning taking place › assessing learning over time › achieving intended outcomes?
How do I use written and oral feedback to build an effective dialogue with my pupils?
How do I plan time to allow pupils to respond and take part in this dialogue?

How do these points reflect your current practice and thinking about pupils' learning and progress? Are there any others that you might add? How might your reflection on these support your work with your student teacher?

Summary and key points

We have reflected on the complex task of planning and how we can break this down for beginning teachers, underpinned by the dialogic model of planning as proposed by John (2006). The fluidity of this approach will have clarified our own understanding of planning and how we can best support the beginning teacher through the different phases of their training year. In so doing we have considered:

- The processes that teachers engage in when planning lessons and sequences of lessons;
- How we might articulate and model these processes for beginning teachers;
- The centrality of reflection in effective practice.

Further reading

Savage, J. (2015). *Lesson Planning: Key concepts and skills for teachers*. Abingdon: Routledge. A useful book on lesson planning.

10 Observing beginning teachers' lessons

Rachel Roberts

Introduction

This chapter considers the place of observation as part of teacher training, as a central part of how beginning teachers learn. The chapter explores the role that mentors have when observing teachers and its relationship with feedback, both spoken and written. Practical suggestions are provided for each section so that observation and feedback are effective in supporting beginning teachers' progress.

Objectives

By the end of this chapter, you will be able to:

- Reflect on the place and purpose of observation in supporting student teacher development;
- Consider how the mentor supports the student teacher in and through observation and subsequent feedback and discussion;
- Understand a range of approaches and strategies in developing effective observation and feedback.

Student teachers observing teaching

All student teachers need to observe others teaching; it is built into all Initial Teacher Education (ITE) programmes and often the main occupation of the trainee teacher in the initial days of their school placement. It is therefore worth considering *why* it is such a fundamental element of teaching practice. Lortie's (1975, p. 61) seminal sociological study of the schoolteacher described teaching as an 'apprenticeship of observation'; observation is conceived as a vital way to learn. This suggests that, as a mentor, you should be able to organise opportunities for your trainee to observe some excellent teaching and that they'll learn directly from it: *teacher see, teacher do*.

Unfortunately, it isn't quite as straightforward as it might appear. Of course, it is likely that a novice will learn *something* by observing some lessons, but without structure it may not be very effective. This is partly because teaching itself is highly complex and, because of the familiarity of the classroom environment, teaching well can appear easy to the untrained eye. Teaching's complexity is partly to do with its contextual nature; it is helpful to think of teaching as being 'dilemma based' (Loughran, 2010, p.13). Consider the number of decisions that you make (many of them unconsciously) within a ten-minute segment of a lesson. This could range from reinforcing your classroom routines (reminding pupils to line up outside the classroom), to the type of question you ask an individual pupil during whole-class discussion, to dropping an activity that you had planned.

An inexperienced observer in a classroom may not notice some of the more nuanced decisions that are being made because they don't know *what* they are looking for (Goodwyn, 1997). This is nicely illustrated in Chabris and Simons' now-famous 'Invisible Gorilla' experiment, which demonstrates selective attention (see the link at the end of this chapter to their website and video clips of the experiment). If you haven't come across this before, stop reading and take a minute to watch the original video. The experiment asks the viewer to count the number of times a ball is passed between basketball players wearing white. However, in the middle of the clip someone in a gorilla suit walks across the screen. Chabris and Simons reported that around 50 per cent of viewers did not see the gorilla, because they were so focused on the ball. The point is that it is impossible to see *everything*, particularly if you are tasked with a very specific focus.

Because everyone has been a student in a classroom, there is an assumption that an observer will understand everything that she sees. Classrooms are complex, dynamic places and even experienced observers are likely to notice different things in the same lesson. It is not surprising, therefore, that Jegede, Taplin and Chan's (2000) research found that trainees are less able to see the moment-by-moment decisions made by the teacher who they are observing.

Task 10.1 The purpose of observation

Think about the most recent lesson that you observed. What was the purpose of the observation? Was it for performance management or part of a professional learning activity? What difference did the purpose of the observation make to how you observed?

Did you have a school proforma to complete or particular things on which you wanted to focus? Did you 'just' observe, or periodically walk around the classroom interacting with the students? How were the notes you took influenced?

Other reasons why learning from observing can be problematic include the Hawthorne effect (Cohen, Manion & Morrison, 2011): the presence of another person in the classroom will affect the events to some degree and the potential negative connotations that may be associated with the process of being observed (and therefore judged). We'll think more about this later in the chapter.

There is also a problem with what might be termed 'teacher knowledge', much of which is tacit. According to Polanyi (1958), tacit knowledge, like an iceberg, is the stuff that the teacher is doing that can't be easily seen on the surface. Imagine you're observing a Year

7 lesson about film genres. The teacher displays a variety of film posters, asking the class to identify who they think are the target audiences for each. Following feedback from the class that classifies each film, the teacher develops the discussion to consider stereotyping, making the point that marketing draws directly on assumed stereotyping (such as 'Rom-Coms' being principally aimed at women). A link is therefore made between the conventions of genre and how the film industry perpetuates genre. The teacher asks one pupil, a keen superhero-movie fan, if he can think of examples of films that flout the convention and an interesting and somewhat heated debate develops on the representation of female superheroes such as Wonder Woman. An inexperienced observer may assume that, in planning terms, this was an 'easy' lesson: show some film posters, point out what they depict and identify genres. They might also comment on the engaged nature of the class discussion. An experienced observer might notice the scaffolding of critical thinking that enabled the class to think beyond the micro discourse of individual film genres to the macro discourse of stereotyping and its relationship with media. The latter is rooted in deep subject knowledge but also pedagogical content knowledge (as the teacher moves from the familiar 'little picture' ideas to the less familiar 'big picture' ideas) *and* knowledge of the class in managing discussion and drawing on pupils' prior knowledge and interests.

There is something of a double-bind to the development of expertise in teaching, as more experienced or expert teachers may be better at noticing (Mason, 2002) and recognising the tacit knowledge of person they are observing, but they may find it difficult in explaining their own decision making; they have become 'unconsciously competent' (Howell, 1982). It is here that you, as mentor, can make a real impact on deconstructing the process of your student teacher learning from observing. You can:

- Articulate expertise for your trainee (Goodwyn, 1997);
- Use modelling (i.e. demonstrate for your student teacher in a lesson that they observe), but ensure it is analysed as part of a process of your mentee's learning (Hattie & Yates, 2014);
- Help your mentee shift their perspective from that of a pupil to that of a teacher (Walker & Adelman, 1975);
- Enable discussion between your student teacher and others that they observe, to potentially allow access to otherwise tacit knowledge (Roberts, 2014).

In effect, this means that you will need to think carefully about how you: set up observations for your student teacher; discuss with them what they have observed; identify and agree areas of focus; and consider what has been learnt.

Task 10.2   Joint observation

Set up a joint observation, so that you can observe alongside your mentee. As you are observing the lesson, talk about what you 'notice' and what your student teacher can see. This will unlock some of the 'tacit knowledge' that may be otherwise hidden from them. If you can, schedule some time for you both to talk to the class teacher.

Being observed

An inevitable aspect of mentoring is that you will be observed by your mentee, probably a number of times if they will be taking some of your classes. Being under such scrutiny may make you uncomfortable; after all, this is likely to be the most often that you will have been observed since your own training. There are a number of reasons why you may not be filled with joy at the prospect of being observed so frequently. Observation within teaching in England has become burdened with negative connotations, not least because of the punitive culture that has grown up around Ofsted inspections (Day, 1999; Goodwyn, 2010; O'Leary, 2014). Your more recent experiences of being observed may be tied to high-stakes performance management or, depending on the culture of your school and its approach to professional learning, it could be based around sharing of ideas or collaborative planning.

Task 10.3 Being observed

How do you feel about being observed? Consider the reason for your feelings.

Are you worried about being judged or making a mistake in front of your trainee? If you're worried about being judged, think about the purpose and nature of the observations: they are for your trainee to learn and for you to demonstrate aspects of teaching that you can discuss with your trainee. That doesn't mean that your lessons all have to be perfect! It would actually be beneficial to discuss with your trainee things that you might change for the next lesson; you are then modelling some of the process of reflection for your trainee.

It is worth thinking about how to organise the lessons that your mentee will observe. Consider the range of different classes you teach (it is helpful for them to see your most challenging classes as well as your most productive!) and the conversations that you are going to have pre- and post-observation. If you provide a focus, it will stimulate discussion after the lesson; it will allow your trainee to consider the decisions you've made in planning and execution. For example, you might ask your trainee to observe your Year 11 lesson revising poetry, focusing on lesson structure. Your intention for the lesson is for pupils to recall their knowledge of the poems, reactivate connections between them and revisit some of their interpretations. In your discussion after the lesson, you can then deconstruct the sequence of activities, their purpose and how successful you felt they were in enabling the class to revise.

Observing beginning English teachers

Whichever pathway into teaching your student teacher may be following, they will need to demonstrate that they are 'meeting' the Teachers' Standards at a certain level in order to achieve Qualified Teacher Status (QTS). They will therefore need to gather evidence. Whilst the collection and organisation of evidence is the responsibility of the beginning teacher, your role will include observing and feeding back. Be clear about the purpose of observing: primarily it should enable you to have a conversation with your mentee about the teaching and learning in which they have been engaging. Ideally, this will stimulate and facilitate reflection and development on the student teacher's part. In addition, your written feedback might provide 'evidence'; this aspect will be covered in more depth in the section 'The purpose of written feedback' later in this chapter.

Observation of your trainee should not be used as a means of control; all teachers have their preferred ways of doing things, their own teaching style, but when working with a beginning teacher it is important to be aware of your own bias (O'Leary, 2014). It is instinctive when watching a novice to think: 'I wouldn't have done it like that.' Whilst this may be intuitive, it wouldn't be very helpful to fill your feedback notes with what *you* would have done; this is about *their* development and practice, after all. It is more helpful to be open-minded about different approaches, so that your beginning teacher can have the freedom to experiment.

As noted earlier, lessons are dynamic, changing environments and it is impossible to see everything that is going on. When you are observing, consider the focus. In the same way that you plan for your pupils' progression, you will want to plan observations in such a way that they support your mentee's progress. A suitable focus could be identified in consultation with your mentee as part of their weekly training. For instance, if a target from the previous week was to develop a greater range of questioning strategies, this should form one of your focuses.

The following is a (by no means exhaustive) list of different aspects of a lesson on which you might focus:

- Questioning
- Body language and use of voice
- Subject knowledge
- Whole-class management
- Managing discussion
- Transitions between activities
- Starting and finishing a lesson
- Timing and pace
- Quality of explanations
- Relationships with pupils (including use of language and tone of voice)
- The engagement/progress of individual pupils
- Checking for understanding
- Use of differentiation

Many of these are explicit in the Teachers' Standards, such as Standard 5: 'Adapt teaching to respond to the strengths and needs of all pupils' (DfE, 2013b, p. 11). However, refrain from using them as a 'checklist'.

For your observations to be more than evaluations, they need to be part of a cycle of training. One way of ensuring this would be to use a form of 'deliberate practice'. This century has seen an explosion in interest in the development of expertise. Anders Ericsson, one of the most prominent figures in expertise research, identified 'deliberate practice' as a primary function of expertise development. Deliberate practice, according to Ericsson, is the time devoted to practice plus the sophistication of the practice strategies.

The principles of deliberate practice include:

- Development of specific skills
- Outside 'comfort zone'
- Well-designed, specific goals
- Requires full attention and conscious actions
- Feedback and response to feedback
- Both produces and depends on effective mental representations (Ericsson & Pool, 2016)

Task 10.4 Using deliberate practice as part of training

In consultation with your mentee, choose a specific part of their classroom practice that needs developing. Spend some time discussing different approaches, then demonstrate one or two of them in your own lessons, with your mentee observing. Discuss what you did and how it worked. Plan a similar approach or activity with your mentee and observe them deploying it within a lesson. Review it together and then give your mentee the opportunity to try again.

Here is an example of what this might look like:

Yasmeen is working with Year 10 on descriptive writing. You are keen for her to use modelling as part of her approach, although she doesn't feel confident in this. You discuss how 'live' modelling of writing on the board, whilst providing a commentary about your options, enables pupils to see that writing is about choices and that they need to see you choose words deliberately, including changing your mind and crossing out. You recommend that Yasmeen looks up the Talk 4 Writing approach, which is highly successful in the primary sector (see link at the end of this chapter).

Yasmeen observes you teaching Year 7, where you are improving a piece of creative writing using a visualiser. You articulate your thinking to the class, such as 'hmm, that's not quite the right word I'm looking for. I think "skittered" would work better here because it reflects the sound of the mice's feet...'. After the lesson you discuss the process, identifying specific techniques that Yasmeen can use herself, such as taking suggestions from the class.

Yasmeen then plans her lesson for Year 10 and you observe her developing the approach and employing these techniques. Following the lesson, you ask Yasmeen to reflect on how effective her modelling was; she was still a little unsure of herself in the 'moment' of writing publicly. You suggest that she can semi-prepare a short paragraph, to build her confidence in 'live' writing.

Other ways of using observation to support training include the use of video technology: videoing your student teacher and watching extracts back with them during feedback can facilitate reflection. It is also useful for your mentee to see how they come across in the classroom, particularly if you are working on aspects such as classroom management or rapport with pupils. If possible, do try to co-observe your mentee with the other members of staff with whom they are working. Not only can this provide you with the opportunity to discuss your mentee's progress with another member of staff, it can be a point of professional development, particularly if the other member of staff has not worked with student teachers before.

One innovative activity you might want to try as your trainee moves towards teaching independently, is 'unseen' observation (O'Leary, 2014). This consists of discussions between yourself and your mentee before a lesson, so you can explore the rationale and intended learning of a lesson, the trainee teaching the lesson (without you observing), then a post-lesson conversation in which your discussion will enable your mentee to lead on their reflection of it. This can be a particularly powerful strategy, as your presence in a classroom *will* affect the behaviour of the pupils and your trainee. This alternative will move the focus away from your evaluation to the mentee's reflection. Whichever approach you use, what is most important is that your observation enables you to have a developmental discussion.

Effective feedback

Providing feedback to your beginning teacher is a vital aspect of your role, because it is part of their learning. However, the nature of feedback in ITE is often 'high-stakes' (Donaghue, 2015; Mercado & Mann, 2015) *because* it is linked to assessment and, ultimately, whether or not the student teacher will achieve their teaching qualification.

Feedback should not just be evaluative: for your trainee to learn from it, it does need to be formative; that is to say, it must enable the learner to make progress (Ramaprasad, 1983). Hattie and Timperley suggest that effective formative feedback should answer the following questions:

- **Where** am I going? (What are the goals?);
- **How** am I going? (What progress is being made toward the goal?);
- **Where to** next? (What activities need to be undertaken to make better progress?) (Hattie & Timperley, 2007, p. 86).

This can only happen if there is dialogue between yourself and your mentee. Rather than feedback occurring in isolation following each lesson observed, try to incorporate it into a training process, as illustrated in Figure 10.1.

Positioning feedback as a dialogue between mentor and mentee means that your beginning teacher should have the opportunity to 'reflect-on-action' and articulate, with your input, what was effective about the lesson. My own research (Roberts, 2019) suggests that trainees appreciate feedback that is specific and constructive: it *describes* as well as evaluates. An example would be: 'Using the starter to recall what happened in Act 2, Scene 1 and reducing it to three key events was a really good way of recapping prior learning.'

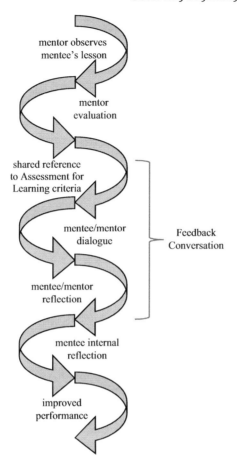

Figure 10.1 Positioning feedback into a training process

The following sections will consider how to give feedback, how mentees might react to feedback and how to write up feedback.

Verbal feedback

When and how you conduct the feedback conversation is important. If it is done in the corridor hurriedly, before racing off to the next lesson, it diminishes the learning opportunity the conversation would afford. Arrange a time to sit down, at a point in the day where you are less likely to be interrupted, so that you can properly talk through the lesson with your mentee. Try to do it as soon as you can following the lesson (if it is more than a day or so later, then the immediacy of being able to reflect fully is likely to be lost). Allow sufficient time, at least 20 minutes, for the conversation; this will enable you to talk it through properly. Don't wait until you have your designated meeting to do lesson observation feedback, particularly as this will then take up most of your session (especially if trainees are teaching more than one lesson a week!).

In Chapter 4, we considered the nature of the mentor–trainee relationship: it is a complex one and for the relationship to work, both parties need to show that the other is important, competent and likeable (Schutz, 1994). If you've set aside time to provide feedback for your mentee, then you are showing them that they are important. What you *say* in the feedback conversation matters and it is more than just being positive. Teachers, and beginning teachers especially, are vulnerable to criticism *because* they want to do their best for the children that they are teaching (Kelchtermans, 2009); they can therefore perceive criticism as an attack on their ethical intentions – see Chapter 4. When you're discussing a lesson with your beginning teacher, you do need to be aware of their *affective* or emotional response: receiving feedback can be painful (Roberts, 2019), particularly if mentees feel that it is being 'done' to them.

Task 10.5   The feedback conversation

Think about feedback that you have received following a lesson observation. What can you remember about it? Were there particular words or phrases that stick in your mind? How did they make you feel? Did you feel that you learned from the conversation? What enabled or prevented you learning from it?

Things to think about when providing feedback include:

- **Structure** – how to begin the conversation; how to move things on; how to conclude
- **Specific language use** – what kind of language is used, particularly evaluative language
- **Tone** – *how* the language is spoken
- **Body language** – what is being communicated non-verbally

Watch a colleague (from your department, from another department in school or from elsewhere, perhaps from the ITT provider) giving feedback. Consider how effective the discussion is and the impact, or otherwise, of the above.

The pivotal nature of developmental feedback recurs in the literature and research around mentoring (Hobson, Ashby, Malderez & Tomlinson, 2009; Hudson & Hudson, 2014; Mercado & Mann, 2015). Mentors who focus solely on what needs to be improved (which is likely to be a lot at the beginning of anyone's professional career) are in danger of 'Judgementoring' (Hobson & Malderez, 2013), which can be a highly negative experience for a novice.

There are a number of ways in which you can structure the feedback conversation so that it is of benefit to your student teacher and which should lessen any awkwardness you might feel in taking on the role of arbiter of teaching quality. First, try to avoid beginning the conversation with an emotional response (either yours or theirs!). It is common for those giving feedback to begin by asking 'How do you think/feel it went?' (Iyer-O'Sullivan, 2015); whilst starting this question is less immediately judgemental or evaluative than 'I thought that lesson was good/great/messy etc.' and is intended to provoke reflection in the trainee, it can lead to quite limited responses. Trainees may fall back on saying something like: 'Well, it was okay' and then begin to list all of the elements of the lesson they felt were 'wrong' or things that they didn't do very well. A better starting point would be to move away from a generic 'what went well' question, to a more focused 'What did you want the pupils to *learn*?' Immediately, this question will mean that your trainee's reflection focuses on the learning of the pupils, rather than their own performance. This has two benefits: it means that they are less likely to fall into a cycle of self-flagellation by criticising their own capabilities and it should open up a deeper conversation about the strategies and decisions that took place in the lesson, including their impact on pupils' learning. The ensuing discussion is therefore less likely to feel judgemental, as you are both critiquing the dynamic interaction between learning activities and pupils' engagement and reaction to them.

The literature on mentor feedback identifies a number of features which make it effective, including: being supportive (Martinez Agudo, 2016); showing empathy (Akcan & Tatar, 2010); recognising trainees' efforts through using praise, which will encourage and motivate them (Rhodes, Stokes & Hampton, 2004); being sensitive and balanced (Parsloe & Wray, 2000); being goal-oriented (Brandt, 2008). At the University of Reading, we advocate using the REVIEW structure for feedback conversations, as illustrated in Table 10.1:

Response to feedback

The other, perhaps more significant, half of the equation in feedback conversations is your mentee's response. It is helpful to put yourself in their shoes: you are an experienced, qualified teacher and will ultimately be assessing them. This makes you quite a powerful figure and your student teacher may be especially nervous in hearing your opinion of their teaching; they will want to make you proud, after all.

O'Leary (2014) suggest a series of prompts that would be useful for trainees to use when reflecting on their teaching:

1. What do I think I achieved during the lesson?
2. What am I most proud of?
3. Did my learners learn what I intended?
4. Were my learners productively engaged in the activities?
5. Was I satisfied with my planning, selection of resources, teaching and assessment?
6. What have I learnt about the learners and my chosen teaching and assessment strategies?
7. What worked/didn't work? Why? Why not?
8. What have I discovered about myself as a teacher?
9. What happened that I didn't expect to happen?
10. If I could teach this lesson again, what would I do differently and why?
11. What is the key thing that I want to improve in my next lesson/when I next teach this class?
12. What do I need to do to enable this to happen? (Adapted from O'Leary, 2014, p. 87.)

These could be useful to stimulate independent reflection in your student teacher before discussing the lesson with an observer.

Table 10.1 The REVIEW Process for structuring feedback conversations

Stages		Comments	Sample Statements/Questions
R	Reassure and re-integrate	Reassure without letting mentee know your thoughts; even if they know you thought some teaching was effective, they still have to work out what!	Thank you. There was some really effective work there …
E	Establish focus on objectives	Personal goals may be relevant at the start of the programme; as teacher grows, focus must fall on pupil learning	What did you want to achieve yourself? What was your personal goal? What did you want the group to learn?
V	Visit through questions	Get the mentee to think about importance of lesson plan to success or otherwise of lesson Link questions to specific Q Standards, particularly those that were a focus of the lesson and part of the mentee's targets OR depending on the mentee a much more open-ended approach can be used and they can set the agenda Note strength of answers – assessment	In trying to achieve your outcomes how helpful was your lesson plan? What went well with regard to …? What else went well? What about… How did that go? If you had the opportunity to do it again, what would you do differently? What didn't go to plan? What were you less happy about?
I	Input – your own contribution	If the mentee has run out of ideas (frustrated at questioning) move to more direct 'leading' (telling)	Questioning What about …? What else …? How else …? How could that have been achieved?
E	Emphasise and summarise key points raised		Lots of useful points there – Let me try to summarise them for you… (briefly pick out the key issues)
W	'What have you learnt?' 'What will you do now?'		Ask the mentee the questions and try to identify precisely what they will do with what they have learnt to take them forward.

Studies have shown that people tend to use more positive than negative language in general conversation, commonly known as the Pollyanna principle (Dodds et al., 2015). Negative language, however, has a stronger effect. This means that, even if feedback consists of more positive than negative comments, the negative comments will have greater impact on the recipient. Jing-Schmidt (2007) argues that the negativity bias operates on a biological level (therefore negative language invokes a kind of 'fight-or-flight' response), rather than a linguistic level. This could impact on learning (Nicols, Schutz, Rodgers & Bilica, 2017) and could be detrimental to the progress of a trainee. Beginning teachers sometimes have a tendency to be over-critical of themselves and may internalise negative judgements, affecting their self-efficacy (Roberts, 2019). In the heightened situation of a feedback conversation, consideration of the evaluative language used is therefore important.

You could consider your choice of words, particularly vocabulary that is directly associated with grading, for example for the PGCE. This might imply grading of individual lessons, a practice now abandoned by the majority of schools. You could also consider the amount and type of praise that you use; think about how you might use it to reward and motivate.

Task 10.6   Framing feedback

Read the following pen portraits of English trainee teachers. Decide how you would frame feedback on a lesson to each of them:

Jamilla
Jamilla is keen to get everything right. She is very hardworking, although she doesn't always work 'smartly' and can get quite stressed if she feels she hasn't done the right thing and feels under pressure. When asked how she feels about her progress, she will automatically list all of the things she can't do or hasn't done very well.

Mindy
Mindy is disorganised, which means that she often misses deadlines and the beginning of lessons can be messy. She is passionate about English and is proud of her good subject knowledge. Her self-confidence is low and she has a tendency to 'put her head in the sand' when things become difficult; she doesn't readily ask for help. You suspect that her home-life is troubled in some way.

Omar
Omar is a confident young man and really enjoys being in the classroom. He has been praised for his positive relationships with students, particularly those seen as challenging. His planning can be minimal, although his classroom presence is strong. You have mentioned to him before about the importance of planning, and he agreed, but his practice did not seem to change in light of your comments.

Occasionally, you may encounter resistance to feedback. This can be difficult to address. It is worth trying to identify what trainees are resisting: is it linked to a fear of failure or another insecurity? If they are having trouble recognising where things are going wrong in their lessons, then using video clips of their teaching as part of their regular training conversations can help them to see elements of their practice that they find difficult to pinpoint. It may be the case that they become defensive, which could be linked to prior experiences; early conversations about the nature of the training course and how your relationship with them functions (as discussed in Chapter 5) are helpful at this point. Discuss with them how they have dealt with criticism or points for development in their past professional roles or academic courses. Do they have difficulty accepting criticism from other members of staff? Is it connected to the *way* in which feedback is conveyed? Again, if feedback is a conversation, rather than something imposed upon them, it is more likely to be accepted by the trainee as they will have some ownership of it. If you find that there are ongoing issues around listening to feedback, enlist the help of your in-school ITT coordinator or university tutor, who may be able to offer a fresh perspective. Further guidance for having difficult conversations is provided in Chapter 11.

The purpose of written feedback

Writing feedback for your beginning teacher can feel like an additional burden, particularly if you have spent some time discussing the lesson with them already. However, written feedback is an important form of evidence and it can be done with minimal additional work for yourself. Take time to familiarise yourself with your ITT provider's documentation, as they are likely to be quite different from your school's observation proforma. Although these vary from provider to provider, it is likely to contain boxes with information regarding the class, content of the lesson, where you feel you have seen evidence of elements of a Teachers' Standard having been met and targets for development. It is helpful to have a specific focus.

It is probably easier to write a running commentary of the lesson as you go (personally, I type it directly onto the observation form on my laptop, as this saves the job of translating scribbled notes onto a computer screen at a later point), making notes as to particularly effective aspects of the lesson (e.g. 'Effective use of questioning to draw out Abigail's answer') or questions to draw attention to elements you want the student teacher to reflect on (e.g. 'How might you change the order of the group activities, so that they all have a clear understanding of the events of this scene?'). As the lesson nears its end, you are likely to have a clear idea of the key elements that you felt were effective and areas for development (try to keep the latter to two or three targets at the most). If you aren't going to have your feedback conversation immediately after the lesson, you can take some time to consider the evidence towards the Standards demonstrated in the lesson, although, try not to use it as a 'checklist': if trainees don't evidence every Standard in the lesson it doesn't mean the lesson wasn't any good!

If you want to try recording notes for feedback conversations in a different format, you could experiment with using question boxes (illustrated in Figure 10.2). The questions in each box can relate directly to a Standard and can change from observation to observation to reflect a different focus in your beginning teacher's changing training needs.

Framing your feedback as comments in answer to pre-agreed questions is a good way of developing a reflective cycle in training.

Summary

Observation is a fundamental element of learning how to teach, although it is not a straightforward process. This is partly because it is impossible to 'see' everything that goes on in

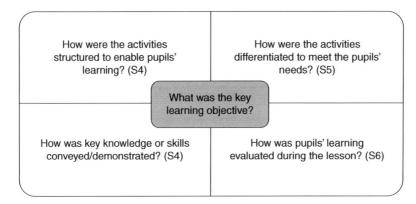

Figure 10.2 Question boxes for written lesson observation feedback

a lesson – beginning teachers often don't know what to look *for* and 'teacher knowledge' is largely tacit and therefore difficult to access. This difficulty can be addressed through the mentor modelling specific skills and discussing decisions that they made during a lesson.

Mentors are likely to be observed quite frequently by their mentees; this can be effective if the student teacher has a specific focus and if a discussion takes place following the lesson. Mentors should be confident when being observed, as they are experienced in their practice and should remember that their lessons don't need to be faultless for trainees to learn from them. Providing mentees with a specific focus for observation should be tied to their cycle of training – the use of Deliberate Practice, video capture and 'unseen' observations can be helpful.

Feedback is high stakes for student teachers, because it is linked to assessment. For it to be useful it should be specific and descriptive, not *just* evaluative. The 'when' and 'how' of providing lesson feedback is important: relatively soon after the lesson, so that it is not forgotten, and with enough time to properly discuss the lesson, so that issues and learning can be aired. It may be helpful for mentors to move away from beginning feedback conversations with 'How do you think/feel that went?' to 'What did you want the children to learn?'; the focus then becomes the pupils' learning, rather than the (more personal and therefore more emotive) performance of the trainee. Language is important in feedback, as evaluative language imbues power. If your trainee appears resistant to feedback, try to work out *why*. Written feedback is a format for highlighting success, providing evidence of meeting the Teachers' Standards and recording targets for progress.

At the heart of observation is an understanding of its purpose and respect for the intention behind the effort put into teaching.

Further reading/links

The Invisible Gorilla experiment: http://theinvisiblegorilla.com/gorilla_experiment.html

Iris, video-capture technology for the classroom: www.irisconnect.com/uk/

The Talk 4 Writing approach: www.talk4writing.co.uk

11 Holding weekly debriefs

Rachel Roberts

Introduction

This chapter explores the nature of the weekly debrief meetings - or mentoring conversations - that occur in most Initial Teacher Education (ITE) programmes. The conversation is considered as part of a reflective cycle that provides support for beginning teachers' progression, for, as Sadler (1989) commented, 'Research into human learning shows there is only so much a person typically learns purely from being told'. Topics for discussion at different points in the training year are suggested; how to deal with emotions and difficult conversations are also considered and a range of strategies provided.

Objectives

By the end of this chapter, you will be able to:

- Reflect on the place and purpose of the weekly mentor meeting in supporting student teacher development;
- Consider how the meetings can provide support for the development of the student teacher;
- Understand various topics for discussion and how these might be staged across the training year;
- Consider strategies for dealing with difficult conversations and emotional situations.

The reflective conversation

It is a common feature for ITE programmes to have weekly meetings between mentor and trainee scheduled during the school placements. The name for this meeting varies from 'mentoring sessions' (Franke & Dahlgren, 1996) to 'mentor-protégé-conferences' (Evertson & Smithey, 2000). Whatever your training programme terms this meeting, it should be a designated time for you to talk to your mentee about their learning and development over the course of the week. Try to make this time sacrosanct as it is the point at which you are able to both monitor *and* promote progress: it provides a space for discussion of concepts that are vital for your mentee's understanding (Aderibigbe, Colucci-Gray & Gray, 2016). It is also the point in the week that you are facilitating deep reflection for your mentee; the key aim

Holding weekly debriefs 127

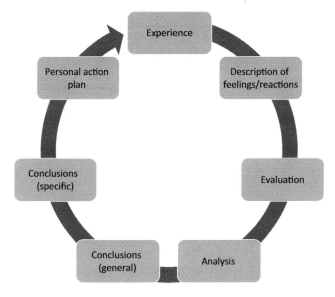

Figure 11.1 The reflective cycle
(Source: Adapted from Gibbs (1988, p. 50))

of these conversations is to take stock of their learning and consider how to approach their development in the coming week. Some possible areas that will be covered are listed here:

- Discussing the mentee's key learning over the last week
- Discussing the highs and lows/successes and failures of their teaching
- Addressing targets as part of their training plan
- Explaining pedagogical approaches or strategies
- Discussing possible solutions to problems the mentee is facing
- Talking through school systems/policies
- Planning and discussing opportunities for the coming week

Gibbs' (1988) reflective cycle (Figure 11.1), based on Kolb's (1983) model of experiential learning (also discussed in Chapter 8), is helpful in understanding the function of your mentoring conversation as part of your mentee's learning.

It is the process of the conversation that allows learning to take place, through its structured reflection. As your discussion is going to centre around their experience, considering how you structure the conversation will clarify the purpose and important learning points for that week. Gibbs (1988) suggests using questions for the stages of the cycle, adapted in Table 11.1 with some examples.

From this model, it would seem that the main feature of a mentoring conversation would be a dialogue between the mentor and trainee, where questions are used to scaffold the reflection of the mentee. Talk that is dialogic should be collective, reciprocal, supportive, cumulative, and purposeful (Alexander, 2005), an approach familiar to teachers of English. However, some research suggests that conversations between mentors and mentees can be overly focused on performance (Orland-Barak & Klein, 2005; Timperley,

Table 11.1 Suggested questions to facilitate reflection, adapted from Gibbs (1988, p. 54)

Step in Gibbs' reflective cycle	Example questions/prompts
Description	Tell me what happened in your lesson on Tuesday.
	Can you describe the incident with Jamal in more detail?
	What were you thinking/feeling at that point?
Evaluation	Thinking about what you wanted the pupils to learn, how effective did you think that activity was?
	What did you find easy/difficult?
Analysis	Why do you think your poetry lesson with Year 10 was difficult? How was it different from the previous lesson with that class?
Conclusions	If you were to teach that lesson again, what would you change?
Action plan	As you've suggested that most of the class found the first activity too easy, let's think about pitch and pace at the beginning of lessons …

2001) and that, although mentors professed to use dialogic talk, in reality they were much more directive. In the busy day-to-day working of a school, it is perhaps not surprising that time can become squeezed and, as a mentor, you may feel under pressure to get through your meeting as quickly as possible. This can mean that the discussion can be overly focused on targets – and whether or not they've been met. Of course targets are important, but be wary of them driving the learning or overloading the student teacher (Wright, 2018).

Knowing how to help

For many, the essence of teaching is *knowing how to help*. By this I mean being able to anticipate things that children might struggle with (conveying the effect of sentence structures in a piece of non-fiction writing, for example), planning a series of steps that explain and demonstrate (such as: sharing two versions of the same piece of writing, one with short sentences and one with complex sentences with lots of subordinate clauses) and presenting this in an accessible way in a classroom. There is also the *knowing how to help* in the moment – when you get an unexpected question, or you need to break things down further for individual pupils. Because such a lot of this is tacit knowledge, multi-layered and text or topic specific, it can be difficult to move between 'big' teaching concepts (such as those set out by the Teachers' Standards), specific subject pedagogical knowledge and then specific strategies in a way that mentees are able to understand and then practice themselves.

Chapter 9 discussed the relationship between planning, teaching and assessment. Sharing the cyclical nature of this relationship can be a good starting point for discussion with your student. At first, trainees often struggle to see the connection between assessment and planning (partly because their initial focus in the first few weeks of their school placement tends to be the planning and teaching of individual lessons); your conversations with your trainee, coupled with observations of your practice, will demonstrate how this cycle operates. In essence, you need to be explicit about what you do and *why*, so that you can allow the trainee access to your otherwise tacit professional knowledge (Wright, 2018).

Let's consider how this might work in practice. Planning is often the most time-consuming part of student teachers' practice, particularly at the beginning. For a novice, planning lessons *is* hard because it can be difficult to identify where the pupils are in terms of attainment, where their learning is going and how they are going to get there. Once beginning teachers have a fair grasp of the structure of individual lessons, it is helpful to move them towards medium- or long-term planning. Practically, this means more than providing them with a PowerPoint; if you are able to talk through the rationale of a scheme of work, they will begin to see the connection between lessons and how anticipated progress 'looks' – at least in theory. This will also allow you to explain how assessment feeds into your planning. As you are unlikely to be planning individual lessons at the level of detail required from trainees, it may also be easier for you to show how you use medium- to long-term planning. Some strategies that you might use to help your trainee understand planning in English include:

- Discussing the relationship between the 'big picture' of National Curriculum requirements or examination board specifications and the 'little picture' of individual lessons
- Explicit demonstration of the difference between objectives and outcomes, as illustrated in Table 11.2
- Deconstructing the decisions you have made in planning and how this worked in practice; discussing your own teaching after your trainee observes you is helpful
- Joint planning (this might include you planning and the trainee teaching or vice versa)

If planning and teaching are seen as joint endeavours, at least to begin with, your mentee is likely to feel more confident as they move from observer to participant in the classroom. Chapter 6 discussed collaborative activities such as these in more detail.

Barriers to progress

You may find that your student teacher struggles at different points in their training. They may have more fundamental barriers that are preventing them from making progress.

Task 11.1 explores some possible scenarios and solutions.

Table 11.2 Examples of lesson objectives and outcomes

Lesson (or Learning) Objectives What the teacher intends pupils to learn	Learning Outcomes How achievement will be demonstrated by pupils (sometimes expressed as all/most/some)
For example: • To identify the persuasive features of a political speech; • To evaluate the effectiveness of these for a specific audience	For example: • Pupils will be able to pick out and comment on rhetorical devices such as hyperbole, anecdote, repetition and apply them in their own writing

Task 11.1 Barriers to progress

Below are four different scenarios, with beginning teachers presenting quite different issues. Consider how you might support them so that they are able to overcome their 'barrier' to progress. Some possible approaches are suggested at the bottom.

The scenarios

> **Scenario A**: *Your mentee appears to be quite disorganised; they are sometimes late and frequently don't send you documentation when it is due.*
> What can you do?
> **Scenario B**: *Despite feedback from you and other colleagues, your mentee seems to keep repeating the same basic mistakes in lessons.*
> What can you do?
> **Scenario C**: *Although your mentee is making progress, you notice that they are very anxious and tend to take criticism very personally.*
> What can you do?
> **Scenario D**: *You feel that there are some elements of your mentee's conduct that aren't professional (but not in such a way as to be obviously not meeting Part 2 of the Standards).*
> What can you do?

Some possible solutions

> **Scenario A**: *Sit down with your mentee and try to find out if there are reasons for their disorganisation. (Could there be issues at home preventing them from working effectively?) If they are struggling with meeting deadlines, they may need help in prioritising their workload. You could help them put together a timetable of working patterns. There may be something fundamental that is preventing them from fully engaging with the course; if this is the case, you may need to enlist help from SLT or your programme provider. If the training programme is linked to a university, it is likely that the trainee will have access to their student support services, including counselling. (Chapter 5 discusses in detail supporting student teacher well-being and managing workload).*
> **Scenario B**: *Try to identify if there is an issue with an aspect of teaching that they are not 'getting', such as differentiation, in which case you could put an intervention strategy in place. This might include a couple of weeks of focused work on differentiation (the mentee reading about and researching it, observing specific differentiation in lessons, practising using some of these in their own lessons). If you feel that the student teacher is struggling to understand or 'hear' feedback in general, a conversation about the nature of reflection as a learning process might help.*
> **Scenario C**: *Discuss with them what specifically is making them anxious; if it is connected with subject knowledge, then you can support by suggesting some*

> reading and share resources with them to exemplify pedagogical approaches to a text or topic. If they are anxious about lots of aspects of the training, try using some of the CBT techniques discussed in Chapter 5.
>
> **Scenario D:** This can be difficult and you will need to have specific examples of what you consider to be less than professional conduct. You could approach it from a generic training perspective, by spending some time discussing what behaving professionally means in the context of your school. It would also be worth highlighting how this is connected to safeguarding: for example, trainees may not be aware of how their social media profiles can be seen by others (including pupils) and therefore positing images of themselves on a night out may convey an unprofessional image to the school community.

Topics for mentoring conversations

Once your trainee is settled in, the topics for your conversations are likely to be forthcoming from the experiences (successes and failures) of their teaching. You may be working with an ITE provider that suggests topics or aspects of training to cover at different points in the school placement. Listed below are some suggestions for different phases of training that you may want to cover:

The first phase of training

- Subject knowledge and prior experience;
- Learning from observing others;
- Their timetable (including details of classes;,
- Micro teaching or team-teaching experiences;
- Discovering what resources are available, where they are kept and how they are used;
- Planning and finding resources (including programmes of study and schemes of work);
- Reviewing how the work of the department addresses the National Curriculum, KS3 assessment and examination requirements at KS 4 and 5;
- Finding out about which examination specifications the department adopts for GCSE and A Level;
- Acquiring knowledge of pupils with special needs and pupils who have EAL and are G&T, school policies on Pupil Premium and understanding what approaches and support best suit these pupils;
- Developing an understanding of the various components and requirements of lesson planning;
- Evaluating lessons and units of work;
- Finding out about and evaluating different strategies for teaching English and managing behaviour for learning in the classroom;
- Becoming familiar with the school's policy on Behaviour for Learning;

The second phase of training

Once the induction phase has been completed, tasks and discussions in mentoring meetings should become more challenging. Topics for discussion at this stage might include:

- Differentiating tasks to suit different ages and abilities;
- Finding appropriate ways of assessing English work, especially demanding elements like speaking and listening;
- Developing knowledge, understanding and use of assessment, both of and for learning, in the classroom;
- Developing an understanding of the department's approach to assessing pupil progress across the key stages;
- Evaluating the effectiveness of a range of approaches to both formative and summative assessment;
- Writing formative and summative evaluations of their work and recording the progress made by individual pupils and whole classes;
- Contributing to report writing and reporting directly to parents;
- Participating in and contributing to moderation/standardisation activities;
- Focusing on how students learn and how teachers know they are learning;
- Exploring the department's contribution to cross-curricular issues and to extra-curricular activities.

Table 11.3 displays possible topics specific to English that might be addressed in the different phases of school placement.

Beginning teachers will need to gain experience of the department's approach to summative and formative assessment, and to understand the role and importance of assessment in informing their planning and teaching and in enhancing pupils' learning. With your help, they will also begin to learn about recording and reporting on assessment for a range of audiences.

However, this should be seen as a gradual training process, during which student teachers work alongside you and your colleagues. For example, in November or December, beginning teachers may be asked to mark a **small** sample of work and then be given the opportunity to discuss their marking with yourself and the class teacher. A similar approach may be taken in relation to report writing. As their confidence grows, student teachers will be able to take on greater responsibility in this area.

We will all recall how long it took us, as beginning teachers, to read, comment on and perhaps grade one piece of work or to write one report. Beginning teachers can find the responsibility overwhelming if they are required to do too much too soon, but they can also think that they *should* be able to cope, leading to feelings of frustration and inadequacy. With your support, they can be helped to gain experience and confidence in this area as their practice progresses.

Evaluative language and praise

As discussed in Chapter 4, the mentor-trainee relationship is not an equal one, because of the requirement to assess beginning teachers' progress in meeting the Teachers' Standards. This aspect of the relationship can be the source of conflict, or at least shift the emphasis

Table 11.3 Topics for discussion in mentoring conversations

First school placement topics	Second school placement topics
Professional attributes	
• What do we mean by 'high expectations' and how do we achieve and maintain them? • What statutory frameworks and professional duties are particularly pertinent to the English teacher?	• What issues are involved in communicating effectively with parents, carers and other outside agencies? • What is the best way to demonstrate a commitment to collaborative and co-operative working?
Subject and curriculum knowledge and understanding	
• What specific areas of your existing subject knowledge do you need to develop? • How is the transition from KS 2 to KS 3 managed? What knowledge and experiences do Year 7 pupils arrive with? How is this discovered and built upon? • What is the school's literacy policy? How have you implemented literacy across the curriculum? • What are the requirements of the GCSE, AS and A Level specifications and what alternative routes are there through which pupils can progress in English from 14-19?	• How does English contribute to the PSHE and Citizenship programme? (This is connected to Part 2: Personal and Professional Conduct of the Teachers' Standards.) • How are pupils with diverse needs, including EAL, SEND, and G&T, accommodated, included and supported in the school and the department? • What provision is made for Pupil Premium pupils in your department and across the school? • What links exist between the English and other departments? Are there opportunities for cross-curricular learning?
Skills – planning	
• What are appropriate learning objectives in English? How do learning objectives differ from learning outcomes? • What sort of strategies are commonly used for planning in the English department? • How do you make the best use of the available resources to enhance teaching and learning in English?	• What are effective ways to differentiate work in English? • How best can we plan for progression across the age and ability range? • What processes and requirements are needed to organise a trip to the theatre or similar opportunities to learn in out-of-class contexts?
Skills – assessment and feedback	
• What constitutes constructive oral feedback? • How does knowledge of pupils' achievements in English inform future planning?	• How can progress be monitored effectively in English? • What are appropriate ways to set, mark and give feedback on written work? • What are appropriate ways to report on pupils' progress in English? • How is GCSE and A Level examined and moderated? • What happens at parents' evenings?
Skills – the learning environment	
• What are effective ways of motivating pupils and promoting independent and personalised learning in English? • How are health and safety issues addressed in the teaching of English and Drama?	• What are effective ways of establishing a purposeful classroom environment, conducive to learning and to promoting learners' self-control and independence? • How are issues of equal opportunity addressed in English?

(continued)

Table 9.1 (Cont.)

First school placement topics	Second school placement topics
Other issues • How close are the links between the English and Drama departments? How are school productions organised? • What role does Media/Film have in your department?	• How does English contribute to the wider school community? • What makes an effective letter of application? • What constitutes effective interview techniques? • What might be appropriate personal targets for the start of the NQT year?

from support to judgement. Evaluative vocabulary and phrases connected with authoritative bodies, such as Ofsted, can have powerful effects and the balance of negative to positive words is something of which mentors should be aware. Even praise should be considered carefully, particularly if it can be more difficult to 'hear', as suggested by the negativity bias, discussed earlier.

Given the imbalance in the relationship, praise may be construed as a form of approval and people both use and receive praise differently (Chapman & White, 2012). My own research (Roberts, 2019) found that praise was linked to motivation and self-efficacy on the part of the student teacher. This is connected to a fundamental aspect of the mentor-trainee relationship: your belief in their *competence* (Schutz, 1994), as argued in Chapter 4. If you don't show that you have faith in their ability to progress, then it is likely that progress will be impeded. Should you find yourself in the position of a mismatch of praise (either you feel you are not providing enough or the right kind, or your mentee is not 'hearing' it) then you could try recording your conversations and playing them back. In written feedback, your student teacher could highlight the praise – this may physically represent how well they're doing and counterbalance their tendency to focus on criticism.

Criticism that 'hurts' is likely to be that which is most *judgemental*: this kind of evaluative language appraises the person's capability, rather than their performance (Martin & White, 2005).

The role of emotions in mentoring conversations

In Chapter 4 I argued that mentoring is a kind of *affective practice* and that it involves emotional labour (Hochschild, 2012). As a mentor you will need to accommodate your emotions *and* your mentee's, to an extent. Look again at Gibbs' (1988) reflective cycle (Figure 11.1): notice that before any evaluation or analysis can take place, the process requires a description of feelings or reactions. Beginning teachers typically experience a wide range of emotions during their training year (Yuan & Lee, 2016) and this can be particularly evident when they are discussing lessons or experiences that they felt were negative.

Sometimes your mentee will need to have the space to vent their emotional reaction to experience before you are able to discuss what might be done differently next time. You can help this process by using 'reappraisal'. Reappraisal is the process of 'modifying one's appraisal of a situation ... to alter its emotional impact' (Gross, 2015, p. 9) – this is similar to the CBT approach discussed in Chapter 5. Mentors can help mentees reappraise, or reframe, experiences they feel to be very negative so that they are able to take some positives from it (Roberts, 2019).

Task 11.2 Using reappraisal

Read the following conversation between mentor and trainee and identify how the trainee (Viktor) is feeling, why he may be feeling this way and how the mentor (Amy) reframes his negative experience.

Amy: Shall we talk about Year 10?

Viktor: Um, I guess.

Amy: Can you tell me about the lesson - maybe start with what you planned?

Viktor: You know that class is really difficult. I don't think I've had a lesson with them where they've just got on with the work.

Amy: Mmm.

Viktor: And last lesson on a Friday... I thought that we'd do something fun, and we've finished looking at all of the poems now, so I spent ages organising a carousel activity where they had to move from table to table and write up their notes on each poem - each one was on a petal, so that they would join together to make a flower (like the poem 'Poppies') and they'd see how they all sort of fitted together. I even went in a break to rearrange all of the tables and set up all of the resources. And I thought 'Oh, I need to be really positive'.

Amy: Ok.

Viktor: It started ok, but when they had to move tables they all just started mucking about.

Amy: What did you do?

Viktor: I gave them a warning, but they didn't listen and I was going to send Kayleigh out. But nothing worked and I got really annoyed, as I'd started really positively and spent ages planning the lesson and in the end I just had to stop the whole thing and the lesson was ruined.

Amy: You still sound angry.

Viktor: I am a bit - I spent the whole weekend brooding.

Amy: That's not good!

Viktor: No. I know.

Amy: Do you want to continue to talk about it now?

Viktor: Um, I might need some more time.

Amy: Ok, we can discuss it tomorrow. You see them again on Wednesday, I think?

Viktor: Yeah.

Amy: All right. Although you said they *all* started mucking about - was it all of them?

Viktor: Well, no, but a few.

Amy: And they must have got something from the lesson?

Viktor: I think Alice and her group did - they actually made some really insightful connections between the poems.

> Amy: So it wasn't a complete disaster!
> Viktor: I guess not.
> Amy: But I understand why you feel annoyed; we'll think about how we can deal with this behaviour issue together – remember that you're not on your own. Let's talk again tomorrow.
> Steve: Ok, thanks.

Turner and Braine's (2016, p. 68) research in how to address well-being and emotional resilience in student teachers suggests that developing 'resilience relies on trainee teachers knowing and believing in themselves and how to respond to their inward, daily emotions. In order for trainee teachers to be honest about their learning and experiences, a safe space needs to be provided for them to have the time and opportunity to explore their feelings and thoughts'. The mentoring conversation provides that space.

Having difficult conversations

Sometimes you will have to have a conversation with your mentee that is difficult, such as a conversation about unprofessional conduct or a relationship breakdown with a colleague. Most people, particularly in professional settings, will try to avoid conflict *because* disagreement can affect working relationships. The nature of the mentor–trainee relationship is close yet hierarchical, so if there is conflict between you it can make the experience very uncomfortable for both parties.

As mentor, you may find yourself as the broker between colleagues if there are issues between your trainee and another member of staff, and you may feel torn between supporting your mentee and showing solidarity with your colleague. It is important, in these instances, to see the situation from all points of view. Stone, Patton and Heen's (2010) book *Difficult Conversations* suggests that there are actually three conversations going on in a difficult conversation: *what happened, feelings and identity*. They argue that both parties will have their own perspective of events, so unpicking *what happened* can be challenging. Those in a difficult conversation will have individual *feelings* and responses to *what happened*, which can make the conversation difficult because they may feel angry or hurt and this may threaten their sense of self, their *identity*. Stone et al. recommend the following step-by-step process for having a difficult conversation with a positive outcome:

1. Prepare by walking through the three conversations (sort out *what happened*; understand *feelings*; ground your *identity*).
2. Check your purposes and decide whether to raise the issue (consider what you would like to achieve, emphasising problem-solving; consider if this is the right time/way to raise the issue).
3. Start from the third story (describe the *difference* between your two stories; share your *purposes*; *invite* them to participate in resolving the situation).

4. Explore their story and yours (*listen to understand* their perspective, acknowledging feelings behind the issues; paraphrase to check that you've understood; try to work out how the circumstance came about; *share your point of view*; *reframe* – move away from judgement and blame to understanding).
5. Problem-solving (Agree on *options* on which both parties can agree; consider *standards* or expectations of what should happen; discuss how to keep open *communication* in the future) (Stone et al., 2010, pp. 233-234)

Essentially, you need to 'have a dialogue about the dialogue' (Wright, 2018, p. 20), being direct but understanding. In her TedX talk (link at the end of this chapter), Joy Baldridge (2018) suggests some useful 'ways in' to starting difficult conversations, such as using the words 'noticed' and 'wondering': '*I noticed* that … and I was *wondering* …'. These can be used to structure feedback (both positive and negative) and then followed up with 'likelihood' and 'when' to close the conversation: 'What's the *likelihood* that you can … and *when* might that be?'

Task 11.3 Having a difficult conversation

Samina, a mentor, knows that she will have to have a difficult conversation with her trainee, Harriet, as she did not attend a lesson that Samina had arranged especially for her to observe. This lesson observation was tied to a specific target that Harriet had (the managing of transition points in a lesson) and had asked a favour of a colleague who had rearranged their planning to accommodate this request. Samina's colleague, a very experienced teacher, remonstrated with her at the end of the day, commenting on Harriet's unprofessional behaviour and mentioned that he had sent an email to Harriet with words to that effect. Although Samina has not yet seen Harriet, she knows that she is upset as she was reportedly in tears in the staffroom.

Read the following conversation and identify where Samina structures the conversation so that she is able to communicate why her colleague was annoyed and her expectations of professionalism, and identify steps to repair the relationship with her colleague and prevent the same situation recurring.

Samina: Harriet, I noticed that there has been some friction between you and Jonathan and wondered how I could help?
Harriet: I'm not sure; I don't think he likes me much.
Samina: Well, why don't you tell me what happened, then I'll share his perspective.
Harriet: Ok. I knew that I was supposed to observe him at some point on Tuesday, I definitely wrote it down but I left my planner at home so I thought I'd check with him. But when I came in I remembered that I was supposed to take part in rolling tutor period and I had to go and prepare for that 'cos I was teaching it. I wasn't confident about this at all, as it was on voting rights so that took up period 2. And I was over the other side of the school, so I didn't see Jonathan

Samina: *at all and by the time I got back here I realised that I had missed the lesson completely. I'd thought it was period 3, but I was wrong.*

Samina: *Ok; thanks. So, you had a busy morning and were feeling anxious about teaching your tutor group a topic that you weren't confident in and you thought you had the right lesson, but by the time you realised, it was too late?*

Harriet: *Yes, that's right.*

Samina: *Ok, let's think about Jonathan's point of view. He was going to be doing an assessment with Year 7 on Tuesday, but was happy to reorganise things so that you could see him and his way of managing the class transitioning between activities. This was a favour for me, really. He said that he even wrote out a lesson plan for you. This made him feel put out, as he had gone out of his way to be helpful. He said that he would have expected at least an email to say you weren't going to be there or an apology for not showing up.*

Harriet: *I did try! But I was teaching period 4 and then had our training meeting, so I didn't have time.*

Samina: *Let's summarise the two perspectives of what happened: Jonathan changed his lesson so that you could observe, he expected you to show up, but you didn't and didn't let him know why or apologise. You were fully intending to observe but had to change your morning plans because you were asked to teach your tutor group and you had to prepare for that. You sound like you were quite anxious about the whole thing – is that right?*

Harriet: *Yes, I didn't want to let the tutor down and I was also worried about my lesson in the afternoon. I'm sorry I didn't get around to emailing Jonathan.*

Samina: *Let's think about how we can resolve the situation with Jonathan and prevent this kind of thing from happening again. Would you like to speak to Jonathan?*

Harriet: *Yes, I think I need to explain why I didn't show up and apologise – I realise that he changed his lesson for me.*

Samina: *When would you like to speak to him?*

Harriet: *Can I email him?*

Samina: *You can, but it might be better to do it in person – perhaps first thing tomorrow.*

Harriet: *Ok.*

Samina: *What about the future; how can we prevent this from happening again?*

Harriet   *I'll try to be more organised (and not forget my planner!) and speak to people as soon as I can if I have missed something.*

Samina: *Ok, that's great.*

Values and the problem with progress

I would like to end this chapter with a final comment about the nature of progress in teaching. Reflective practice is a fundamental way of thinking about how we can continue to improve as teachers. However, there is a danger that this could be interpreted by student teachers as never being good *enough* (Roberts, 2019). Most aspiring teachers enter the profession with the desire to help young people achieve their potential; to give something back. This is quite an altruistic motivation. Mentees may feel that criticism (including constructive criticism) is a form of judgment of them as a person, rather than their capabilities as a teacher at a given point. When discussing progress, therefore, it can be helpful to frame it as evaluation of aspects of their *performance* rather than them as a *person,* so 'That was an excellent, engaging lesson' rather than 'You're a great teacher' or 'The resource was less effective than the one you used last lesson' rather than 'Your planning wasn't effective'.

Summary

The weekly slot that you have with your mentee is a really important part of their training; it therefore needs time and consideration as a learning opportunity that is part of a reflective cycle. Try to make your conversations dialogic: a more equal balance between yourself and the trainee will enable them to take ownership of their learning but still be steered by your experience and expertise.

The starting point for your conversations needs to be the fundamentals of pedagogy – the *knowing how to help*; your discussions with your trainee can unlock what might appear to be the mysterious process of planning, teaching and assessment. Moving from individual lesson planning to medium-term planning is an important step; talking through the rationale for a scheme of work, for example, can be helpful.

As your trainee gains greater experience of being in the classroom, your focus in conversations will need to change to reflect their progression, and these experiences should inform your topics of discussion. Where barriers appear in their progress, try to keep communication open with them, so that you can investigate what might be preventing them from developing.

Don't underestimate the power that you have and can wield through evaluative language: praise and motivation are connected and if you find difficulties in conveying praise (or your trainee 'hearing it') you can try recording your conversations or highlighting written feedback, so that it is balanced against criticism.

Try to deal with emotions or feelings first; reappraisal – reframing experiences to focus on the positives – can be a helpful tool to enable your trainee to acknowledge their successes. When you have to have a difficult conversation, try to see the other person's point of view and articulate this (remember the three conversations: *what happened, feelings, identity*).

Remember that your meeting with your trainee is a vital part of their training experience and it provides a much-needed space for them to grow and learn. For this to happen, it needs to be valued.

12 Developing the wider, professional role of the teacher

Debbie Hickman

Introduction

In order to consider what is meant by the wider, professional role of the teacher, and therefore to support your student teacher in their induction into the role, it might be helpful to ask yourself some questions:

- What is the role and purpose of school in society?
- What is the role of the teacher in school?
- In what ways is teaching a profession?
- How is teaching similar to of different from other professions?

Your answers to these questions will reveal a lot about your values as a teacher and your position on the purpose and place of education in children's lives and society more broadly. As discussed in Chapter 2, the values that you hold are not arrived at in a vacuum: they will have developed over time in response to a number of factors. This chapter therefore elaborates on some of the ideas of previous chapters but with particular reference to ideas of professionalism and the teacher's wider professional role.

Objectives

At the end of this chapter, you will be able to:

- Have a greater understanding of some of the debates about professionalism and how this might relate to teaching;
- Have a greater understanding of the role of the teacher as a professional, and how this might be manifested in different tasks and requirements;
- Use your understanding to support a beginning teacher in understanding and developing their professionalism.

What does it mean to be a professional and how does this relate to the role of a teacher?

> **Task 12.1 Reflection on roles and responsibilities**
>
> Reflect on a typical week in school. Consider the various roles and duties that you have as a teacher. These might range from specific activity to broad areas of responsibility.
>   In what ways are these roles and duties part of being professional?
>   What does it mean, therefore, to be unprofessional?

Allen and Toplis (2013) suggest that, in the initial training year, the roles and responsibilities of a student teacher relate largely to teaching particular classes. Although they may have experience of some of the wider roles and responsibilities of teachers, this is usually for familiarisation so that the successful beginning teacher can become further involved after completing their ITE. Allen and Toplis point out, however, that the concept of professionalism underpins the role and responsibilities for all, including student teachers (p.32). This concept is referenced particularly and specifically in Standard 8 and Part 2 of the Teachers' Standards through repeated use of the words 'profession' and 'professional'. It is worth, therefore, spending some time exploring what is meant by 'professionalism' and what it means to be 'professional'.

Allen and Toplis (2013, p.33) argue that the main attributes of professions, shared across many, including teaching, are:

A specialised body of knowledge;
A substantial period of training before acceptance into the profession;
Commitment to meeting the needs of clients;
A collective identity;
A level of professional autonomy;
Self-governing as well as publicly accountable.

How do these ideas about the profession compare to your reflections at the outset of this chapter?

Allen and Toplis (2013) argue, too, that teachers' work is shaped and changed often because of government initiatives and policies. The influence of the state in education, including the reshaping of the professional identify of the teacher, is much debated (Ball, 2003; Cunningham, 2008; Hargreaves, 2000; Sachs, 2016). Hoyle & John (1995) argue that the increasing intervention of the state in education has led to a reshaping of teaching from one of an autonomous community of a profession to reconceptualisation of and focus on individuals as professionals. They suggest that there is a change of emphasis and that to be a professional, rather than member of a profession, refocuses on the individual rather than on a collective identity. This is seen as negative and the shift in focus has implications for professional practice as well as identity:

From:	To:
Profession	Professional
Knowledge	Skill
Education	Training
Effectiveness	Efficiency
Conception	Delivery
Status	Contract
Clients	Consumers
Influence	Compliance
Responsibility	Accountability
Leadership	Management

(Hoyle & John, 1995, p.61)

For example, in this model, the collective knowledge of the English teaching community would contribute to the development and conceptualisation of an English curriculum. However, the individual teacher as a professional is compliant in and accountable for delivery, rather than conceptualisation, of a centralised curriculum. In the context of secondary teaching of English, this 'delivered' product might be seen to be the statutory orders for English, which prescribe the requirements for the curriculum. It is a curriculum shaped primarily by government policy than by collective professional knowledge. Viewed through the lens of Hoyle's model, teacher development becomes focused therefore on compliance with the statutory contract. Teacher development within this model means acquiring and honing skills of delivery through training, rather than conceptualisation of knowledge through education.

Task 12.2 Considering Hoyle and John's model

Consider Hoyle & John's model.

- Reflect on the roles and responsibilities from Task 12.1 in the light of these. Which of the various activities do you consider to be part of your membership of a professional community and which are related to individual professional behaviours?
- How do the ideas of professionalism compare with those that you listed?
- How do the ideas of previous chapters sit within the different ideas of professionalism and the professional as discussed in this model? For example, in supporting your student teacher development with planning, have you been focused on supporting their knowledge and conceptualisation, or on skill and efficiency in delivery?

You might find that some of these questions are not easily answered, or that the response is complex and variable. You might find that some aspects of your role as a teacher fit more easily into one category and that others are more ambiguous and open to interpretation. You might find that you have a preference for working in one way but that your school or institution requires that you work differently. Lunt (2008), in discussing teacher professionalism and ethics, argues that:

The diverse origins of professionals' attitudes, beliefs and values result in a complex and multifaceted situation where an individual professional may experience conflicts and tensions between personal and professional values, and between personal beliefs and professional duties.

(Lunt, 2008, p. 82)

The conflict between personal and professional values and beliefs is commonly described as cognitive dissonance (Muijs & Reynolds, 2010). There may be times in your career when you have experienced such tension or dissonance. You might, for example, have been uncomfortable with aspects of recent curriculum reform, such as the changes to GCSE examination requirements for English, or the prioritisation of certain types of literature over others in the National Curriculum. You (and/or your pupils) might be bored of certain aspects of your department's practice, such as the pedagogy and practice for teaching analytical writing. However, because it is well established and leads to good examination results, you might feel unable to debate or challenge the practice because you do not want to upset staff or established protocols or because you doubt your own experitise. You might have felt uneasy about recent developments in school policy, for behaviour management for instance, but feel unable to comment for similar reasons or because you feel it is not your place to do so.

More importantly, in your role as mentor, you may experience aspects of tension for your student teacher as they grapple with the various challenges and expectations of becoming a teacher. Although this has been referenced already in a number of chapters, it is useful to reflect on when this might have happened and why.

Task 12.3   Reflection on cognitive dissonance

Reflect on your experiences with your student teacher:

> Have there been any aspects of teaching and learning about which you have disagreed or debated?
> What was the root of the difference? How and why was there a difference in view and from where did each of you draw your ideas?
> How was the difference resolved?
> Did the experience support the student teacher to make autonomous professional decisions or to comply with institutional norms?

Lunt argues that the concept of professionalism includes values and ethics that enable an individual to act with integrity, such as 'self-awareness and the realisation of our own values, prejudices, beliefs, limitations and fallibility. An extended understanding of professional integrity involves the development of reflexivity' (Lunt, 2008, p. 92).

The development of professionalism is therefore intrinsically linked to the ideas of reflection and reflexivity referenced in many of the chapters so far.

Professional Studies and the wider role of the teacher

The discussion and development of the professionalism of your student teacher may also be addressed as part of their understanding of their role in school. This understanding might therefore be developed as part of a wider package of support for your student teacher, provided both within your school and by their ITT provider, under the heading of 'Professional Studies' (PS) or 'Professional Themes'. You might be fully engaged in the programme and contribute to some of the sessions, or you might be aware of this as a programme which students complete regularly but the content of which is unknown to you. Commonly these sessions are organised by a lead teacher, usually a Professional Tutor or Professional Mentor who has overall responsibility for the ITT programme in your school. They are typically a senior member of staff who will liaise most regularly with members of the ITT provider to ensure that the programme requirements are being met and that the school is in compliance with the ITT's Partnership agreement. They will meet the student teachers on placement at your school for regular sessions and monitor their progress overall. During these PS sessions, student teachers will consider and discuss a range of concepts, ideas and issues related to the place and role of the teacher, regardless of subject specialisms. They will consider the range of policies and practices in the educational field and the extent to which they inform, form and shape teachers' practice. These sessions might be led by a number of members of staff within the school with particular areas of expertise. The benefit of these sessions is that they will expose your mentee to a range of ideas and opinions, not only of staff, but also of other student teachers in similar positions but from different subject areas and with sometimes contrasting ideas and beliefs. These sessions will support your mentee in understanding some of the issues facing teachers in other curriculum areas (for example, the differences in managing behaviour in PE, Dance and Drama when compared to traditional classroom-based subjects) as well as considering themes and ideas which are central for all.

Some of the indicative themes and ideas of a Professional Studies programme might include (this is not an exhaustive list):

Behaviour management and the promotion of positive pupil behaviour;
Safe-guarding and child protection;
The pastoral system and role of the tutor;
Developing a teacher identity and presence;
Equality, diversity and inclusion;
SEND provision;
Personal, Social, Health and Economic (PSHE) education and Citizenship;
Promoting Fundamental British Values;
Communicating with parents and parents' evenings;
Ofsted;
Primary liaison;
Literacy and numeracy across the curriculum;
Working with data and data management;
14-19 provision;
Organising a school trip.

You might find that your student teacher has varying degrees of confidence with aspects of the programme and that their engagement with the programme will also impact on their practice in your department. Being aware of the concepts covered and advice offered will enable you to support your mentee in incorporating some of the principles and ideas into their subject-based practice.

Task 12.4 Professional Studies programme

Consider:

- Who is responsible for organising the Professional Studies programme within your school?
- Which concepts and ideas are considered in the programme?
- How will you ensure that your mentee knows and can work within the various policies which inform practice in your school?
- What other Professional Studies experience has your mentee had as part of their ITT provision (with their ITT provider, for example)?
- How might their experience of the above be of value to you in your mentoring role and in their development?
- How might you incorporate or reference some of the ideas as part of your mentoring discussions?

Pastoral care and the role of the form tutor

Hramiak and Hudson remind us that 'It is important to remember that the curriculum was intended to be, and should be, more than simply gathering facts, forming opinions, and passing exams' (Hramiak & Hudson, 2011, p.238). They continue that 'Schools have a responsibility to prepare students for the 'opportunities, responsibilities and experiences of adult life', and this involves more than ensuring that students leave with a list of academic qualifications. They remind us that the concept of pastoral care is a particular feature of the British education system and it is not commonly found in education systems around the world. The use of the word 'care' is significant in that it distinguishes this particular aspect of schooling as something other than the 'formal' curriculum. We will focus, in this part of the chapter, on the role of the teacher as 'caring' for pupils, and how the systems and structures of the school might support this, so that you can further help your beginning teacher in this aspect of their development.

Almost all teaching staff in a school will be involved in a pastoral role of one kind or another. However, schools organise their pastoral systems differently (Hramiak & Hudson, 2011) and each structure has its own rationale and benefits. Regardless of the structural differences, each system is designed to support pupils' care and well-being with key, identified members of staff designated to particular roles within the structure. In some schools, key pastoral roles are carried out by non-teaching specialists, whereas in others pastoral leaders are seen as central, senior members of staff. Regardless of the hierarchy and organisation of the system, central to these structures is the form tutor. Your student teacher is likely to become involved with the pastoral system of your school via the role of the form tutor. It is possible that this is a role which might excite and enthuse your student teacher, or cause them some significant anxiety.

The role of the form tutor can be seen as both challenging and rewarding in equal measure. Nonetheless, it is seen by some as 'a fundamental part of the experience of being a teacher' (Hramiak & Hudson, 2011, p.288). The tutor is certainly a significant person in the daily lives of pupils. For one, the form tutor may well be the important, consistent and constant adult in the pupil's daily school life. The role and responsibilities of a form tutor may differ from school to school. Other than the legal requirement to take a register, your student teacher will need to be aware that they could be asked to take on responsibility for all or some of the following:

Administration - including taking of the register, handing out notices etc;

Home-school liaison - the form tutor may be the first port of call for communication between parents or carers and school;

Academic monitoring – because they see the pupils every day and may be aware of their concerns and difficulties as well as strengths, the tutor may be asked to take responsibility for monitoring the academic progress of their tutees, particularly when patterns emerge which may require intervention;

Behaviour monitoring – as above, the form tutor may be expected to have an overview of how their tutees are behaving and when this may be impacting on progress in school. Monitoring of academic performance and behaviour can be an important part of keeping children safe and in identifying changes which are a cause for concern;

Providing support - in carrying out various duties related to the above responsibilities, tutors may find themselves supporting their tutees with difficult or sensitive issues, including bullying, personal, emotional experiences and issues of safeguarding. Schools have clear policies about each of these and your beginning teacher will need to have access to and a clear understanding of how these operate. It is expected that your beginning teacher will have had access to and have read *Keeping Children Safe in Education* (DfE, 2018b), which outlines the statutory safeguarding requirements for all adults working with children in schools;

PSHE, Citizenship, Fundamental British Values, spiritual, moral, social and cultural (SMSC) development- there may be a 'pastoral' curriculum which sits alongside or instead of a more formally taught curriculum to support pupils' wider development. This may include but is not exclusive to the school's assembly programme. As a form tutor, your beginning teacher may be required to participate in teaching this programme and may therefore find themselves teaching or leading sessions on topics or subjects with which they are less familiar. As with other aspects of their subject knowledge development, they may come to you to ask for support and advice.

Task 12.5 Reflection on the pastoral structure and the role of the form tutor

How is your pastoral system structured?
   Why is it organised this way?
   What are the key roles of the form tutor within this structure?
   How will your student teacher become involved in this role?
   How is PSHE and Citizenship taught in your school? What will be the extent of your mentee's involvement? Who might support them?
   How are Fundamental British Values promoted in your school? How might this impact on your student teacher's practice in English?
   How is pupils' SMSC development promoted in your school? How might this impact on your student teacher's practice in English?

It may be that you have little to no involvement in your student teacher's induction into the pastoral role: they may be co-tutoring with a different member of staff outside your department. They might, however, be co-tutoring with you in order to understand the differences and similarities in this role and their main, teaching role. Whichever situation you find yourself in, your beginning teacher will come to see that their role and relationship with their pupils as a tutor will be very different from those as a subject teacher. The value and importance that they attach to both may affect their ability to balance their work and their development accordingly. Therefore it is important for you to have at least some knowledge of their position and development.

Task 12.6 Reflecting on relationships

Part 2 of the Teachers' Standards (DfE, 2013b) requires that teachers 'develop appropriate professional relationships with colleagues and pupils'. Consider the following, and if appropriate, discuss with your mentee:

   What is an appropriate professional relationship?
   How might the relationship between a form tutor and their group be different from that between a subject teacher and their class?
   Should it be different?
   How might you support your mentee in negotiating and developing appropriate relationships with their tutees?

Working with others

As part of their development in understanding the wider role of the teacher, your student teacher will need to understand the importance and significance of working with others in school. Hramiak and Hudson (2011, p.50) describe 'the team that is a school'. There is a variety of different staff with whom your student teacher may have contact and with whom they will need to forge and manage professional working relationships (Capel, Leask and Turner, 2013).

They will include members of different teams, as Hramiak and Hudson, (2011, p.50) list, such as:

Administration staff – finance or business managers, receptionists, for example;
Examination staff – including the exams office, various invigilators, members of different examination boards, etc.;
Site management staff – caretakers, cleaners, etc.;
Medical staff – this may be a trained specialist, such as a school nurse or counsellor. However, there may be named personnel in school who should be the first point of contact in a first aid incident or emergency;
Catering staff – including lunchtime supervisors, etc.;
Cover staff – your school may use external supply agencies and internally employed cover supervisors as well as teaching staff to cover staff absence;
Technical support staff – ICT technicians, resources managers, etc.;
Support staff – led by the SENCo, there may be a team of teaching assistants or learning support assistants with whom your student teacher will work closely;
Governing body – the executive group with strategic oversight and accountability for the school;
Community staff – there may be members of staff from different community organisations who regularly contribute to the school, such as in running after-school clubs or activities, working with particular groups of students or in addressing a particular aspect of the school's business.

Task 12.7   Introduction to others

How will your student teacher be introduced to the various members of the school community?

Does the school have particular protocols for requesting assistance and support? How will your mentee be made aware of and use these?

Making a positive contribution to the wider life of the school

Many beginning teachers, at interview or in the early stages of their training, when asked about their motivation for being a teacher, will explain that they want to make a difference.

Although their ideas of how this might be achieved will vary, beginning teachers are usually united in seeing joining the profession as an opportunity to make a positive contribution to society and to improve the life chances of children and young people. This might, too, be what is meant in the Teachers' Standards by 'maintain high standards of ethics and behaviour' (DfE, 2013b). Capel, Leask and Turner (2013, p.552) argue that, therefore, 'it is incumbent ... to ensure that every pupil is given the very best opportunity to fulfil his or her potential' and that this is dependent on the teacher's belief that every child is capable of achieving their best. This fundamental idea that education can serve as a form of social justice to address disadvantage and inequality, as manifested in many forms, is central, therefore, to the development of the ethical practice of a professional teacher. The ideas of reflection and reflexivity, as well as personal beliefs and values, have been discussed in other chapters already. However, it is worth recapping here the role that you, the mentor, can play in supporting your mentee in grappling with some of their (sometimes unconscious) ideas and beliefs about young people. This might result in the need for some sensitive and probing questions about attitudes to inequality and/or vulnerable groups in society and possible causes and solutions. Engaging in such conversation and discussion as part of your programme for the student teacher's professional development may be where you, the mentor, have the opportunity to make the greatest difference.

Summary

In this chapter we have considered:

The nature of professionalism and how this might be manifested in teaching;
Some of the roles and responsibilities of the professional teacher;
Some of the ways in which you might support your beginning teacher to develop their professional identity.

Further reading

Dymoke, S. (Ed.) (2013). *Reflective Teaching and Learning*. London: SAGE.

13 Continuing the mentoring of beginning English teachers beyond their intitial teacher training

Yvonne Williams

Introduction

At this point in your career you may be just about to embark on the mentoring of a newly qualified teacher (NQT) having never officially been a mentor before. The role may be filling you with some trepidation – after all, it is usually a conscious choice that leads teachers towards mentoring teachers completely new to the profession. No one can predict when a post in your department will fall vacant or the level of experience of the person who fills it.

Therefore, you would probably benefit from reading some or all of the preceding chapters to get the overview and detail that comprises the mentoring process in general. In addition, picking up on the administrative details such as details of form-filling and ways of structuring mentor meetings will be very helpful because such activities are common across the professional stages. What differs of course is the type of detail and the expectations you should have of your mentee.

If you are taking up the mantle of the NQT mentor and have experience of mentoring the PGCE student, then welcome back. The big questions on your mind will be how you can link what you already know and how you will adapt this to the NQT process.

Objectives

By the end of this chapter, you will be able to:

- Have a full understanding of the process of mentoring an NQT, including statutory requirements and documentation;
- Know what roles others involved in the process should play;
- Have a greater understanding of how the performance of an NQT will be judged against the teaching standards and in the context of the first year in a full-time (or equivalent part-time) post with reference to some pedagogical theory about teacher development;
- Have reflected on the ways in which your own learning can be useful in directing the experience of your NQT;
- Have gathered useful contacts for NQT lesson observations;
- Ensure that your records are kept up to date to track the progress of your NQT;
- Know how to proceed should there be any shortfall in performance;

- Know how to proceed in the very rare event of an NQT failing to complete the year satisfactorily, including the appeals process;
- Have a wider understanding of how to signpost your NQT to significant learning and professional development opportunities beyond qualification.

So where to start?

The practicalities

Before you even meet your mentee you will need to ensure that you are compliant with the NQT guidance: DfE (2018c) *Induction for Newly Qualified Teachers (England)*.

Even though the initial set-up may not fall within your remit it is helpful to review this from your own perspective and that of the mentee.

Meeting with the induction tutor

In my school I was very well supported in my role as mentor because the school's deputy head in charge of professional development was the link with our university PGCE provider and very much accustomed to ensuring that the rules were followed in spirit and to the letter. She met with me to explain how we would be meeting the requirements.

> **Case study: The initial set-up**
>
> The set-up process established how our school would be able to support an NQT and meet the statutory requirements by checking the following points:
>
> A relevant body was overseeing our work - in this case the Independent Schools Teacher Induction Panel (IStip).
> All relevant documentation had been read and understood over the holidays before the term began.
> The governing body/multi-academy trust (MAT), etc. were satisfied that the school had the capacity to support the NQT. Whilst I was not party to this discussion, it was clear that as a school we had previous, successful experience of mentoring PGCE and GTP students on placements and had mentored new teachers in the past, and that there were a number of subject mentors in the school.
> Our head and deputy were able to oversee and make the final recommendation.
> The necessary paperwork had been received to show that the inductee was suitably qualified, permitted to work in a British school and eligible for the role.
> The post was suitable - in this case it covered classes in Key Stages 3-5 for which the mentee was wholly responsible that academic year, so offered a range of experience. As Head of English I am responsible for making recommendations for teachers and teaching groups, which will be followed as far as possible (there are always other factors in the writing of the timetable). These classes required similar planning, teaching and assessment processes as those covered by other

full-time teachers. A level classes were shared so that ideas and approaches could be shared.

The mentee was to have support in place for non-teaching responsibilities – thus the mentee was able to share a form and have mentor support in form periods, for example.

Eighty per cent of a normal timetable was in place.

In addition, as required by IStip, I as mentor had an hour of protected time each week for a formal, minuted meeting to review progress and modify existing targets or set new targets.

Task 13.1 Setting up the NQT induction

Getting the right things in place from the start may seem onerous at the end of an exhausting school year, but time spent on this will be time well spent. You can thus ensure that everything is in place for the start of the new placement.

Questions you need to ask yourself at the outset (see p.6 of the statutory guidance document) are:

Have you met with the Induction Tutor?

Who is going to induct the mentee into the policies, procedures and practices of the whole school at the first opportunity and how will your departmental protocols fit into that introduction?

Have you ensured that all the meeting dates are scheduled and that the relevant personnel are available and noted in your own calendar?

Have you familiarised yourself with the standards and the requirements?

Is the timetable appropriate in terms of the spread of ability and range of Key Stage experience?

Are the classes appropriately selected? (Ensure that the mentee has not been given all low or high ability classes, that the classes do not consist of larger than usual numbers of students who are potentially disruptive and that appropriate pastoral support is available if need be.

Data storage and access

The institution must ensure that all personal data is safely stored and accessed only by those who need to see it. If the governing body has concerns about the NQT, it is not automatically entitled to see all assessment and feedback forms. It must contact the relevant body overseeing the school induction. The mentee has control of the documents in the sense that he or she should always know who has access to their records and the use that is being made of them.

All the usual rules governing staff and student data apply here: you may already be using software platforms for pupil data. All data associated with the NQT induction process should be kept for six years and then destroyed.

What will be the demands on the mentor's time?

Although institutions following good practice will timetable a dedicated one-hour slot each week so that the review can take place regularly, there will be rather more demands on mentor time. Initially on an almost daily basis there will be questions about protocols and practical issues such as stationery and books. This input will reduce quite rapidly as the mentee settles in.

Time will be needed for twice-termly lesson observations, evenly spaced to see development and progress, that fulfil the normal requirements of quality assurance and professional development as well as the need to ensure the NQT is well supported in developing pedagogical practice. Observation time may need to be taken from your own planning time or you may need cover to observe your mentee's lesson. Either way, you will need to plan for work beyond your normal class responsibilities.

As the placement progresses there will be demands on time as the mentee takes on more responsibility for examination classes so is required to know and understand how specifications work for KS4 and 5 classes.

Documentation

It is possible that you will find completion of the documentation for weekly NQT meetings more time-consuming than that for a student teacher (depending on the ITT provider's requirements). In my case, for IStip, it is the mentee who minutes the weekly meetings and the mentor who minutes the half-termly reviews. The intention in the words of IStip is to "funnel all the accrued evidence", thus avoiding a last-minute flurry of evidence collection. Lesson observations had to be scanned in as did any other associated paperwork.

Each term there was a meeting with either the head or the deputy head to comment on progress and ensure everything was on track. At the end there was the final report to write.

Task 13.2   Reflection on time management

Put together the knowledge you have of the mentee's timetable and meeting schedule and the school calendar of events. Reflecting on the varying demands of the school year, can you identify the pinch-points where you might anticipate the NQT feeling the pressure adversely?

Create an overview, using the following headings and consider any tips you might give to help manage the time:

Date   Combination of events   Coping strategy

Have you realised any important issues for your own ability to support your NQT in these times? Consider the implications and how these might be resolved.

Establishing expectations

The DfE Statutory Guidance (2018c) indicates that the NQTs' performance will be judged against the "relevant standards". Because an NQT has only one chance to complete the year the conditions and expectations need to be finely and appropriately tuned to match their experience in your institution against the national standards (DfE, 2013b). So it's worth stopping briefly at this point to assess the way in which expectations are set out in the guidance. The exercise in Task 13.3 will enable you to pitch your mentoring and judgements most effectively to provide the appropriate support. This can also act as a modifier of targets that you will set at the start of the induction period and of the ways in which you monitor and adjust them as the mentee moves on.

Task 13.3 Reflecting on the language and expectations of the DfE's Statutory Guidance

How would you define and exemplify the following key terms within paragraph 1.5 (p.6) of the Guidelines:

"**Satisfactory**" upon completion of induction: What would satisfactory look like? What is not satisfactory?

"Taking into account the NQT's **work context**". The Guidance provides for a range of establishments from British independent overseas schools to MATs to Pupil referral units (PRUs). How would you define your context and what are the opportunities for and possible barriers to success?

What can be "**reasonably expected**" of an NQT"? In what ways might this be less stringent than for other more experienced teachers?

"**Effectively consolidated** their initial teacher training". How might you understand the prior training and experience of your NQT, particularly if they did not train or complete an experience in your school? How might you use the targets identified at the end of the ITT year as the starting point for your support?

"Ability to meet the relevant standards **consistently**" – what is meant by "consistently"? How will you and your mentee monitor this?

"Over a **sustained period** in their practice" – what is meant by "sustained"? How will you and your mentee monitor this?

Having considered all these aspects in advance you will want to find out more about your mentee. You may have met at interview or you may have been the mentor for the PGCE placement. In such cases you will already have formed an impression of the person you will be supporting for the year. You may have had access to their references and curriculum vitae from the interview. Although these early impressions are very important, it is a good idea to remember that this information comes from a different context and that it is now your job to help map previous successes onto future gains and to help the mentee cope with areas of development.

At your first meeting to set the overall objectives you may want to refer to a guide for the induction year. For example, IStip have provided a Teachers' Standards – Evidence Tracker to help the NQT track their efforts and note down the evidence to support their entry.

Another requirement that you might want to discuss early is for the NQT to use their time not allocated to teaching as an opportunity to set up observations of colleagues to see different and exemplary practice. As a mentor you might wish to make recommendations as to which teachers would be good role models, provide varied practice and have something to offer to an NQT who might be struggling with one aspect of the job or another.

Considering the expertise in your school

It is highly likely that your school asks its teachers to do peer observations to reflect on and improve their own practice as well as offer advice and encouragement to each other. You might also solicit advice from experienced colleagues who have particularly strong teachers in their departments, or your school may already have a published list of the areas in which school staff are comfortable to be observed. You might think about producing a list for your NQT, as having these recommendations to hand to refer to will make life easier for a busy NQT. You might also want to keep an overview of the pattern of observations from which the NQT is benefiting when you observe a lesson. Most teachers are glad to help and will often donate some more time to discuss any issues arising from the lesson. As not every lesson is perfect – in fact very few are – it will be useful to see that even the best teachers have concerns and continue to evaluate their performance after a lesson.

The observed practice of other teachers may also help in the problem-solving stages of your regular meeting to set new strategies with which to experiment or refine.

Conducting meetings

You may well be an experienced PGCE mentor so are used to conducting discussions about performance and target setting. What will be very different is the level of experience from which the NQT is speaking. So whilst there will be much in the early stages of this book to guide you in your questions and evaluations, you might like to consider how the differences between initial teacher training and ongoing teacher induction will play themselves out in discussion.

Therefore your conversation will likely address issues with core activities of planning and teaching, with an increasing focus on monitoring pupil progress and analysis of data. The following sections consider how you might support the continuing developing reflection of your NQT in core areas.

Planning

In the earliest stages the mentee will be most concerned about planning, so your weekly meetings are likely to be devoted to strategies for effective planning and what constitutes a good lesson plan. There is advice offered already in this book.

There is a lot of information and material available on the internet from groups such as Team English, Teachit, the TES teaching resources and exam board materials, which may fill a small gap. It varies in quality and will take some experience on the part of the mentee to tease out what is most appropriate for the context of the school, the class and the curriculum. Particularly in the early stages of your relationship with your NQT, you may find yourself needing to 'curate' these available sources. The old Chinese proverb, attributed by some to Confucius: "Give a man a fish and you'll feed him for a day: Teach a man how to fish and you will feed him for a lifetime" holds true here and not just for lesson-planning skills. In the short term, using pre-designed plans and materials and customising them to suit the class and the teacher may ensure consistency, but it may not support the NQT to develop skills to sustain them during a long-term career. At this stage you may put your own learning to good use by sharing the various stages of planning, the setting of objectives and differentiation strategies. This may require revisiting some of the ideas of some of the relevant chapters in this book.

More importantly, at this stage you will be seeking to embed an understanding of planning as a sequence of learning as opposed to discrete lesson plans. Teaching Standard 6 can only be properly addressed by modifying plans in the light of what has gone well and what could be improved in the previous lesson. Weekly plans leave little room for manoeuvre and can encourage the thinking that unswerving adherence to the lesson plan is most important, whatever the evidence from the lesson.

A really useful model is the Dreyfus Model of skill acquisition, which has been applied to the process of lesson planning by Enow and Goodwyn (2018). This model, used to inform teacher development, has five stages: Novice, Advanced beginner, Competent, Proficient, Expert . Goodwyn asserts that it "provides a focus on holistic quality of teaching and not the reductive view so often featured in models of 'mechanistic performance management'" (Enow & Goodwyn, 2018, p.123).

In identifying characteristics of the novice stage and the advanced beginner, Enow and Goodwyn make it easier to pick out the characteristics which mentors might be seeking to embed in the advanced beginner.

The advice on moving on the approach to lesson planning is particularly helpful, comparing a script from which the novice will hardly deviate with a plan that is a statement of intent with spaces for pupil response. The induction period may be an ideal time to focus on fostering independence and the ability to react more flexibly to pupils' responses.

It is highly likely that NQTs will be accustomed to planning for smaller incremental stages of pupil development, ensuring secure understanding and comfort in the classroom, but they will be less secure with planning for pupils to take bigger steps in their learning. Risk-taking is hard when so much rides on the final results in examinations. Therefore time built in at this stage could be well spent reading more deeply into articles on planning in journals compiled by the subject associations for English, The National Association for the Teaching of English and The English Association. Membership may be needed to access their materials and in-depth research, but some schools do have membership of these organisations.

Realistically it is likely to take more than just one year to move on most mentees via the Advanced beginner stage to the Competent stage. The official advice in the Guidance (DfE, 2018c) is to consolidate practice and enable the trainee to meet the satisfactory standard over a sustained period. This does not mean that the mentee should be standing still. After all, what is satisfactory for the end of ITT is not the same as it should be for NQT stage.

In the light of these ideas, it might be a good opportunity to review your progress and that of your mentee so far.

Task 13.4 Supporting planning

In your meetings on planning, initial lesson observation and reflection after observation what are the signs that:

- Your mentee is reflecting on the planning?
- Your mentee is aware of the sequencing of tasks and its effectiveness?
- Your mentee knows the difference between a plan and script and has the confidence to start letting go of the script?

What support is needed now?

You might at this stage dispatch your mentee to the best planner in the department or even the deputy head in charge of the academic side of the school for a discussion on creating effective plans and adapting them. One word of caution, though: Enow and Goodwyn (2018) do tell us that the expert may well not commit plans to paper and may be able, even at a split second's notice, to alter a plan completely. It may be better to involve a teacher closer in experience, perhaps a couple of years on, who can share their craft and the developments they have made.

These activities and associated thinking will help you to address all strands of Standard 4: Plan and teach well-structured lessons at the level required to make satisfactory progress as an NQT.

Marking and assessment

The ITT year may have been a time in which the beginning teacher gets to grips with a number of assessment systems. This could cover anything from spoken feedback in the lesson to the triple marking or deep marking whereby there is teacher marking, feedback and pupil response to be marked again by the teacher. In previous chapters attention has been drawn to the DfE workload reports and the advice to schools cautioning against this practice as it has no greater impact on pupil learning than normal marking.

As your mentee progresses through the induction year the continued practice of marking across abilities and key stages will embed a greater understanding of the standards. This growing understanding is unlikely to be fully consolidated as expertise by the end of the year, but it will certainly become more accurate at least within the standards prevailing in the English department.

This is no mean feat and it is well to draw attention again to the guidance, which sets reasonable expectations and sustainable workload. One way in which to enlarge the mentee's experience is to use departmental time and mentor time for standardising work across the year groups to show the best work, middling standard and that of students who struggle more with writing for a number of reasons. In pitching the learning for the NQT you might take into account the following:

- How typical is the work of the level of achievement you are exemplifying?
- The length
- Is there a clear path to improvement that you can demonstrate in how to pitch feedback to the student?
- Are there places where marginal annotation can signal achievement?

These activities can contribute to the strand relevant to accurate assessment in Standard 6.

Considering the use of assessment in monitoring learning and progress over time will require more preparation from you than usual. You might prefer about halfway through the year to deal with marking and feedback whilst observing a lesson and check on books in situ, then selecting some books from the class to discuss progress over time with your NQT. PGCE students are unlikely to have seen a long period of work with the same class so this is where the concept of sustainable over time comes in.

You and they should not expect to see a perfect incline in the students' achievements. Progress will go up and down, especially in English. Most often the main form of assessment is via the essay, which requires a whole armoury of skills. Thus it is extremely difficult to get consistency when all skills are required at once. English is not like some other subjects where the addition of one piece of knowledge or improvement of one skill allows a student to make a significant advance in performance. This may be a point at which you provide the reassurance that this is what the subject is like.

However, it is very useful to undertake an audit of the types of assessment to see what long-term advice could be given to the student. By this middling stage of the year it is likely that there will have been some whole school data harvest to which your NQT will have contributed.

Task 13.5 Considering assessment of progress over time

How could you have a productive conversation and use it to consider in more detail Standard 6 - Make accurate and productive use of assessment, and Standard 2 - Promote good progress and outcomes by pupils?

- By considering the pattern of marks and data outcomes?
- By seeing trends in the work across the class which might be addressed in subsequent planning and assessment opportunities?
- By identifying achievements and the thinking and planning behind them?

This last is an important question, not just in getting the mentee to teach positively but also in recognising the progress made by the mentee. Such positive feedback is necessary encouragement and helpful in identifying progress against the relevant standards to be recorded.

NQTs will likely have done some assessment of examination papers in their placements so should be reasonably prepared to play their role in the mock and other more formal examinations in your school. You may need to have to consolidate understanding of and exemplify the standards for external examinations via exam board materials. Now that the specifications for English Language and English Literature at A level and GCSE are beyond the early stages, there is plenty of exemplar material available. You could include some papers from your school to enable your mentee to understand the application of the mark schemes. In this way they will get the picture of how they are contributing to the department's work in preparing students for external qualifications.

Lesson observation feedback

Mentees are well versed in reacting to lesson observations. However, this is the stage at which you can sharpen their insights into the impact of their practice in the classroom by asking them about how specific students are reacting. This means that they will move more quickly beyond the delivery of a scripted lesson and become more attuned to the effects of their approaches and strategies. This could be followed up by further observation of other staff.

What can be most tricky for any teacher is effective differentiation. This is what Standard 5 is there to tease out. It is not enough to input differentiated tasks – the standard requires knowledge of how and when to use them. Planning and teaching should have given the students an opportunity to embed their knowledge of inhibiting factors.

Other key strands will come into play and it is worth noting some down when undertaking Task 13.6.

Task 13.6 Some prompts for focused observations

You might consider the following in the context of the key phrases discussed at the outset of this chapter:

'Satisfactory'
'Reasonably expected of an NQT'
'Effectively consolidated their initial teacher training'
'Ability to meet the relevant standards consistently'
'Over a sustained period'

How does the mentee create a positive learning space for the class whilst you are observing? Is the set-up more subtle than might be expected in the early stages of teaching experience?

What role did behaviour of students play in the success or otherwise of the lesson? How did your mentee respond? Was there behaviour that impeded progress that was not picked up?

How did your mentee engage students positively?
Were the approaches and activities appropriately pitched?

> Were there signs that the needs of all students were addressed?
> Were there signs of stretch and challenge?

These questions are fairly usual and based on the Teaching Standards. To develop further, would it be helpful to supply the NQT with this list to help focus on self-direction which can be addressed in the subsequent mentor meetings? Thus the teacher could be less reactive to what the mentor has to say and more proactive in developing their practice.

The wider professional role

As the school year progresses you will be seeing your mentee meeting parents to enable them to see how their children are progressing. This may have been done in partnership with their PGCE mentor but will be initially daunting when the mentee has to "fly solo".

It may be hard to observe anything at all if you too are dealing with a long line of parents so it is well to brief your senior team about the expectations you have of your mentee so that they can intervene or support if necessary. A debrief in the next mentor meeting will help put into context for the mentee how knowledge of the background at home has an impact and so could go towards the successful implementation of Standard 5 – Adapting to the strengths and needs of students. It is not always a negative that has to be addressed, but can be a positive to help the student move on.

Cross-curricular involvement

Even though a mentee is in the induction year there will be scope for them to make a contribution, whether through accompanying a trip or assisting with lunchtime or after-school clubs. It is tempting to expect that there will be considerable involvement but as a mentor you will probably be looking more for quality of involvement and the learning experience for the mentee when encouraging participation.

Supporting a weaker NQT

What happens if you have doubts that your mentee will pass the NQT year?

It goes without say that you should already be supporting your mentee in two very crucial ways. Firstly you will have kept them up to date with their progress. Should there be concern that the standards are not being met, you will have already set targets and provided the necessary support to enable a teacher at this stage of their career to meet the expectations of the NQT year. The DfE guidance (2018c, p.27) makes it clear that the response to inadequate performance should be immediate. Mentors should not wait until the next assessment point. Usually the support programme will be sufficient to put the mentee back on track.

Secondly, you will have been diligently completing the forms, having relevant discussions about what is being recorded and ensuring that the professional journey is mapped in sufficient detail. In this way the mentee, the mentor and the Induction Tutor, together with the headteacher and the NQT providers will know where the shortfall lies, the attempts to improve and the reasons for the judgements being made. This is so important because there is only one chance for an NQT to pass the year and all concerned in the process will want to be certain that everything that could have been done was done.

At this stage it should be stressed that failure is an extremely rare outcome. It may happen for a number of reasons, not all to do with the competence and motivation of the NQT. If you suspect that other factors to do with health and family life are having a detrimental effect on the NQT then it would be best to seek further help and advice from outside agencies – please see Chapter 5 on well-being.

What next?

If there are further concerns at the next assessment point and this is not the last stage then the headteacher will explain to the NQT the consequences of failure to complete the induction year. The details of the format for this conversation can be found on p.27 of the DfE guidance (2018c). Your next assessment report will reflect the brief details of the issues and the remedial action against which progress to the next assessment point will be judged.

Capability procedure

The full details can be found on p.28 of the guidance and, if necessary, further guidance on the appeals process. Where the capability procedure is instigated the mentoring process will run alongside it. It is worth noting that dismissal before the end of the induction period does not prevent the NQT completing the induction at another institution: 'all NQTs must complete a full induction process before they can be judged to have failed induction.' (DfE, 2018c, p.28).

Mentoring an NQT to adapt beyond the induction year

In many of the mentoring activities used to address the task of successfully inducting an NQT into the profession you will have been balancing the need to consolidate learning and ensure that the experience is sustainable to meet the grading of at least satisfactory. This is enough to pass. But is good mentoring simply getting someone from A to B? It should not be a route march through the standards for the second time, but a widening of experience in spite of the enormous and often daunting drain upon the time of both mentor and mentee.

There is no doubt for me that mentoring is a privileged and rewarding role, one that carries with it a heavy responsibility. This is the last formal stage and the last fully supported year for the mentee. In this year, then, you may be hoping to offer further experiences and contacts that will move the teacher from advanced beginner to competent stage. Beyond that stage will come a greater understanding of how the art of teaching can be improved.

Becoming a member of the professional community

The obvious first port of call will be subject associations. Getting involved initially as a member will provide useful contacts and put the members in touch with key debates. Subject associations usually have regular publications. The NATE classroom magazine contains some excellent articles on elements of teaching, on the different aspects of the subject such as film and media studies and the ways in which assessment shapes or distorts the teaching of English. The journal, *English in Education*, from which the referenced article by Enow and Goodwyn (2018) on planning and five stages of teaching comes, is a thrice-yearly publication which is more research focused. Much is new thinking that can be adapted and used in deeper reflection. It is a journal that addresses some of the deeper debates about English. The English Association journal is a halfway house containing articles on how to teach some writers, in-depth reviews of recent books related to practice and to criticism. The association offers chartered teaching status for a teacher putting together a portfolio.

There are a number of associations and other providers of material (such as the TES website, TEACHIT and TeamEnglish). A teacher can enhance his or her professional development by contributing ideas and activities to any of these. The internet provides a vast range of bloggers, vbloggers, TEDtalks and so on, all willing to share their ideas and insights.

How else can you signpost your mentee to other experiences and sources of inspiration and knowledge?

Exam boards are always on the lookout for good examiners. Most examining is online which means that standardisation can take place at home. It is claimed that examining is a very good form of CPD which brings examiners into contact with a range of responses and thus enables them to develop a better idea of different teaching strategies and of the national standards. It is argued, by exam boards in particular, that every teacher should become an examiner at some stage of their career. It is a worthwhile job, but the pay is low and the hours are long. If mentees do undertake this task then you would do well to support them in their time management. Few institutions have an easy rundown into the summer. Most marking happens from half term break in the summer right up to the summer holidays.

Government departments such as Ofsted and Ofqual publish subject-specific reports and reports on marking each examination season.

Some PGCE courses have contained Masters-level elements and provide credits towards the final qualification. These are very useful to provide deeper insights and are probably the best support for further independent research. Cliff Hodges (2016, p.26) argues that:

> teachers learning from being research-active themselves is different from finding out information or extending knowledge based on other people's findings. Doing research for oneself steers skill and knowledge towards understanding and thus has potentially an even more profound impact on teaching and learning.

You might, then, consider how you might support a newly or recently qualified teacher who is interested in continuing or furthering their own academic studies.

Signposting them towards any number of these valuable sources will help them to become members of the English teaching community beyond your school.

REFERENCES

Aderibigbe, S., Colucci-Gray, L. & Gray, D. (2016). Conceptions and expectations of mentoring relationships in a teacher education reform context. *Mentoring & Tutoring: Partnership in Learning, 24*(1), 8-29.

AITSL (Australian Institute for Teaching and School Leadership) (2011). *The Australian Professional Standards for Teachers*. Melbourne: AITSL. Available at: www.aitsl.edu.au/teach/standards

Akcan, S. & Tatar, S. (2010). An investigation of the nature of feedback given to pre-service English teachers during their practice teaching experience. *Teacher Development, 14*(2), 153-172.

Alexander, R. (2004). Still no pedagogy? Principle, pragmatism and compliance in primary education. *Cambridge Journal of Education, 34*(1), 7-33.

Alexander, R. (2005). Culture, Dialogue and Learning: Notes on an Emerging Pedagogy. Paper presented at the Education, Culture and Cognition: Intervening for Growth Conference, Durham, UK. Available at: www.learnlab.org/research/wiki/images/c/cf/Robinalexander_IACEP_2005.pdf

Allen, M. & Toplis, R. (2013). Student teacher roles and responsibilities. In S. Capel, M. Leask & Turner, T. (Eds.), *Learning To Teach in the Secondary School* (pp. 25-41). Oxon: Routledge.

Anderson, E. & Shannon, A. (1995). Toward a conception of mentoring. In T. Kerry & A. Mayes (Eds.), *Issues in Mentoring* (pp. 25-34). London: Routledge.

Aristotle (2014). *Nicomachean Ethics* (H. Rackman, Trans.). Cambridge, MA: Harvard University Press.

Baldridge, J. (Producer) (2018). Difficult Conversations Made Easy. Available at: https://youtu.be/4TkbHLD5Mnw

Ball, S. J. (2003). The teacher's soul and the terrors of performativity. *Journal of Education Policy, 18*(2), 215-228.

Ballantyne, R., Packer, J. & Hansford, B. (1995). *The Crisis in Teacher Education: A European Concern?* London: Falmer Press.

Barton, G. (2013). *Don't Call it Literacy*. Abingdon: Routledge.

Bleiman, B. (2014). Knowledge about literature at Key Stage 3: What's significant knowledge? www.englishandmedia.co.uk/blog/knowledge-about- literature-at-ks3-whats-significant-knowledge

Brandt, C. (2008). Integrating feedback and reflection in teacher preparation. *ELT Journal, 62*(1), 37-46.

Brindley, S. (2015). Knowledge in English teaching – the naming of parts? In S. Brindley & B. Marshall (Eds.), *MasterClass in English Education: Transforming teaching and learning* (pp. 45-57). London: Bloomsbury Academic.

References

Brindley, S. & Marshall, B. (Eds.) (2015). *MasterClass in English Education: Transforming teaching and learning* (pp. 45-57). London: Bloomsbury Academic.

Brooks, V., Abbot, I. & Duddleson, P. (2012). *Preparing To Teach in Secondary Schools: A student teacher's guide to professional issues in secondary education*. Maidenhead: Oxford University Press.

Bullock, A. (1975). *The Bullock Report: A language for life*. Report of the Committee of Enquiry appointed by the Secretary of State for Education and Science under the Chairmanship of Sir Alan Bullock FBA. London: Her Majesty's Stationery Office.

Capel, S., Leask, M. & Turner, T. (2013). *Learning To Teach in the Secondary School*. (6th ed.) Oxon: Routledge.

Chapman, G. & White, P. (2012). *The 5 Languages of Appreciation in the Workplace*. Chicago, IL: Northfield Publishing.

Child, A. & Merrill, S. (2005). *Developing as a Secondary School Mentor: A Case Study Approach for Trainee Mentors and their Tutors*. Exeter: Learning Matters.

Cho, C., Ramanan, R. & Feldman, M. (2011). Defining the ideal qualities of mentorship: A qualitative analysis of the characteristics of outstanding mentors. *The American Journal of Medicine*, 124(5), 453-458.

CIPD (Chartered Institute of Personnel and Development) (2012). *Coaching and Mentoring Fact Sheet*. Available at: www.cipd.ae/knowledge/factsheets/coaching-mentoring

Clark, C. & Cunningham, A. (2016). *Reading Enjoyment, Behaviour and Attitudes in Pupils who Use Accelerated Reader*. London: National Literacy Trust.

Clarke, S., Westbrook, J. & Dickinson, P. (2010). *The Complete Guide to Becoming an English Teacher* (2nd ed.). London: SAGE.

Cliff Hodges, G. (2016). *Researching and Teaching Reading: Developing pedagogy through critical enquiry*. London: Routledge.

Clutterbuck, D. (2004). *Everyone Needs a Mentor: Fostering Talent in Your Organisation* (4th ed.). London: CIPD.

Clutterbuck, D. & Lane, G. (2004). *The Situational Mentor: An international review of competencies and capabilities in mentoring*. Hants: Gower.

Coe, R., Aloisi, C., Higgins, S. & Major, L. E. (2014). *What Makes Great Teaching. Review of the underpinning research*. Durham: Centre for Evaluation and Monitoring/The Sutton Trust.

Cohen, L., Manion, L. & Morrison, K. (2011). *Research Methods in Education*. Abingdon: Routledge.

Connelly, F. M. & Clandinin, D. J. (1999). *Shaping a Professional Identity: Stories of Educational Practice*. New York: Teachers College Press.

Cox, B. (1991). *Cox on Cox. An English curriculum for the 1990s*. Sevenoaks, Kent: Hodder & Stoughton Ltd.

Cremin, T. (2014). *Building Communities of Engaged Readers: Reading for pleasure*. London: Routledge.

Cunningham, B. (2008). *Exploring Professionalism*. London: Institute of Education, University of London.

CUREE (2005). *National Framework for Mentoring and Coaching*. Available at: www.curee.co.uk/resources/publications/national-framework-mentoring-and-coaching

Daloz, L. A. (2012). *Mentor: Guiding the Journey of Adult Learners*. New York: Wiley.

Davis, L., Little, M. & Thornton, W. (1997). The art and angst of the mentoring relationship. *Academic Psychiatry*, 21(2), 61-71.

Davison, J. & Daly, C. (2014). *Learning to Teach English in the Secondary School. A companion to school experience* (4th ed.). Suffolk: Routledge.

Davison, J., Daly C., & Moss, J. (2010). *Debates in English Teaching*, London: Routledge.

Day, C. (1999). *Developing Teachers: The challenges of lifelong learning*. London: Falmer Press.

Day, C. & Leitch, R. (2001). Teachers' and teacher educators' lives: The role of emotion. *Teaching and Teacher Education*, 12, 403-415.

Dean, G. (2003). *Teaching Reading in Secondary Schools*. (2nd ed.). London: David Fulton.
Department of Education and Science and the Welsh Office (1989). *The Cox Report: English for ages 5 to 16*.
DfE (2013a). *Statutory Guidance. National Curriculum in England: English programmes of study*. Available at: www.gov.uk/government/publications/national-curriculum-in-england-english-programmes-of-study
DfE (2013b). *Teachers' Standards. Guidance for school leaders, school staff and governing bodies*. London: HMSO.
DfE (2016a). *A Framework of Core Content for Initial Teacher Training (ITT)*. London: Crown. Available at: https://assets.publishing.service.gov.uk/government/uploads/system/uploads/attachment_data/file/536890/Framework_Report_11_July_2016_Final.pdf
DfE (2016b). *National Standards for School-based Initial Teacher Training (ITT) Mentors*. London: HM Government. Available at: https://assets.publishing.service.gov.uk/government/uploads/system/uploads/attachment_data/file/536891/Mentor_standards_report_Final.pdf
DfE (2016c). *Standard for Teachers' Professional Development*. London: HMSO.
DfE (2016d). *Eliminating Unnecessary Workload Around Marking. Report of the Independent Teacher Workload Review Group*. London: HMSO.
DfE (2016e). *Eliminating Unnecessary Workload Around Planning and Teaching Resources. Report of the Independent Teacher Workload Review Group*. London: HMSO.
DfE (2016f). *Eliminating Unnecessary Workload Associated with Data Management. Report of the Independent Teacher Workload Review Group*. London: HMSO.
DfE (2017). *Evidence-informed Teaching: An evaluation of progress in England. Research report*. Available at: www.gov.uk/government/publications/evidence-informed-teaching-evaluation-of-progress-in-england
DfE (2018a). *Reducing Workload in Your School*. London: HMSO.
DfE (2018b). *Keeping Children Safe in Education. Statutory guidance for schools and colleges*. London: HMSO.
DfE (2018c). *Induction for Newly Qualified Teachers (England). Statutory guidance for appropriate bodies, headteachers, school staff and governing bodies*. London: HMSO.
Dickens, C. (1861). *Great Expectations*. London: Chapman and Hall.
Didau, D. (2014). *The Secret of Literacy*. Carmarthen: Independent Thinking Press.
Dixon, J. (1967). *Growth Through English*. London: NATE and Oxford University Press.
Dodds, P., Clark, E., Desu, S., Frank, M., Reagan, A., Williams, J., ... Danforth, C. (2015). Human language reveals a universal positivity bias. *Proceedings of the National Academy of Science*, 112(8), 2389–2394.
Doecke, B. (2016). What I 'know': Literary studies and the teaching of English. *Changing English*, 23(3), 292–308.
Donaghue, H. (2015). Differences between supervisors' espoused feedback styles and their discourse in post-observation meetings. In A. Howard & H. Donaghue (Eds.), *Teacher Evaluation in Second Language Education* (pp. 117–134). London: Bloomsbury.
Driscoll, L. G., Parkes, K. A., Tilley-Lubbs, G. A., Brill, J. M. & Pitts Bannister, V. R. (2009). Navigating the lonely sea: Peer mentoring and collaboration among aspiring women scholars. *Mentoring and Tutoring: Partnership in Learning*, 17, 5–21.
Eagelton, T. (1975). *Literary Theory: An Introduction*. Oxford: Blackwells.
Elbow, P. (2000). *Everyone Can Write: Essays Toward a Hopeful Theory of Writing and Teaching Writing*. Oxford: Oxford University Press.
Elliott, V., Baird, J, Hopfenbeck, T. & Ingram, J. (2016). A Marked Improvement? A review of the evidence on written marking. Available at: www.researchgate.net/publication/301749224_A_marked_improvement_A_review_of_the_evidence_on_written_marking

Enow, L. & Goodwyn, A. (2018). The Invisible Plan: How English teachers develop their expertise and the special place of adapting the skills of lesson planning. *English in Education*, 52(2), 120-134.

Eraut, M. (2004). Transfer of knowledge between education and workplace settings. In H. Rainbird, A. Fuller & A. Munro (Eds.), *Workplace Learning in Context*. London: Routledge.

Ericsson, A. & Pool, R. (2016). *Peak: Secrets from the new science of expertise*. London: The Bodley Head.

Evertson, C. M. & Smithey, M. W. (2000). Mentoring effects on protégés' classroom practice: An experimental field study. *Journal of Educational Research*, 93(5), 294-304.

Fautley, M. & Savage, J. (2013). *Lesson Planning for Effective Learning*. Maidenhead: Open University Press.

Ferrier-Kerr, J. (2009). Establishing professional relationships in practicum settings. *Teaching and Teacher Education*, 25, 790-797.

Fleming, M. & Stevens, D. (2015). *English Teaching in the Secondary School: Linking theory and practice*. London: Routledge.

Franke, A. & Dahlgren, L. O. (1996). Conceptions of mentoring: An empirical study of conceptions of mentoring during the school-based teacher education. *Teaching and Teacher Education*, 12(6), 627-642.

Fry, S (2007) *The Ode Less Travelled*. London: Arrow Press.

Furlong, J. (2014). *Research and the teaching profession: Building the capacity for a self-improving education system*. Final Report of the BERA-RSA Inquiry into the role of research in teacher education. London: BERA.

Gibbons, S. (2015). The importance of oracy. In S. Brindley & B. Marshall (Eds.), *MasterClass in English Education: Transforming teaching and learning* (pp. 45-57). London: Bloomsbury Academic.

Gibbons, S. (2016). *English and Its Teachers: A history of policy and practice*. London: Routledge.

Gibbs, G. (1988). *Learning by Doing: A guide to teaching and learning methods*. Oxford: Oxford Further Education Unit.

Giovanelli, M. & Mason, J. (2015). 'Well I don't feel that': Schemas, worlds and authentic reading in the classroom. *English in Education*, 49(1), 41-55.

Goodwyn, A. (1997). *Developing English Teachers: The role of mentorship in a reflective profession*. Buckingham: Open University Press.

Goodwyn, A. (2004). *English Teaching and the Moving Image*. London: Routledge.

Goodwyn, A. (2010). *The Expert Teacher of English*. Abingdon: Routledge.

Goodwyn, A. (2016a). *Expert Teachers: An international perspective*. London: Routledge.

Goodwyn, A. (2016b). Still growing after all these years? The resilience of the 'Personal Growth model of English' in England and also internationally. *English Teaching, Practice and Critique*, 15(2), 7-21.

Goodwyn, A. (2018). The Highly affective teaching of English: A case study in a global context. The Annual Conference of the British Educational Research Association. The University of Northumbria.

Goodwyn, A. & Fuller, C. (Eds.) (2011). *The Great Literacy Debate*. London: Routledge.

Graves, D. H. (2003). *Writing: Teachers and children at work*. New Hampshire: Heinemann.

Green, A. (2006). University to school: Challenging assumptions in subject knowledge development. *Changing English*, 13(1), 111-123.

Green, A. (2011). Getting started. In A. Green (Ed.), *Becoming a Reflective English Teacher* (pp. 1-5). Maidenhead: Open University Press.

Green, A. & Mcintyre, J. (2011). What is English? In A. Green (Ed.), *Becoming a Reflective English Teacher* (pp. 6-25). Maidenhead: Open University Press.

Griffith, A. & Burns, M. (2014). *Teaching Backwards*. Carmarthen: Crown House Publishing Limited.

Grimmett, H., Forgasz, R., Williams, J. & White, S. (2018). Reimagining the role of mentor teachers in professional experience: Moving to I as fellow teacher educator. *Asia-Pacific Journal of Teacher Education, 46*(4), 340–353.

Gross, J. (2015). Emotion regulation: Current status and future prospects. *Psychological Inquiry, 26*(1), 1–26.

Haggard, D. L., Dougherty, T. W., Turban, D. B. & Wilbanks, J. E. (2011). Who is a mentor? A review of evolving definitions and implications for research. *Journal of Management, 37*, 280–304. doi:10.1177/0149206310386227

Hargreaves, A. (1998). The emotional politics of teaching and teacher development: With implications for educational leadership. *International Journal of Leadership in Education, 1*(4), 315–336.

Hargreaves, A. (2000). Four ages of professionalism and professional learning. *Teachers and Teaching: Theory and practice, 6*(2), 151–182.

Hattie, J. & Timperley, H. (2007). The power of feedback. *Review of Educational Research, 77*(1), 81–112.

Hattie, J. & Yates, G. (2014). *Visible Learning and the Science of How We Learn.* Abingdon: Routledge.

Hawkey, K. (2006). Emotional intelligence and mentoring in pre-service teacher education: A literature review. *Mentoring & Tutoring, 14*(2), 137–147.

Heilbronn, R. (2011). The reflective practitioner. In R. Heilbronn & J. Yandell (Eds.), *Critical Practice in Teacher Education. A study of professional learning.* London: IOE.

Higgins, M. C. & Thomas, D. A. (2001). Constellations and careers: Toward understanding the effects of multiple developmental relationships. *Journal of Organizational Behavior, 22*, 223–247.

Hobson, A., Ashby, P., Malderez, A. & Tomlinson, P. (2009). Mentoring beginning teachers: What we know and what we don't. *Teaching and Teacher Education, 25*, 207–216.

Hobson, A. & Malderez, A. (2013). Judgementoring and other threats to realizing the potential of school-based mentoring in teacher education. *International Journal of Mentoring and Coaching, 2*(2), 89–108.

Hochschild, A. (2012). *The Managed Heart: Commercialization of human feeling* (3rd ed.). Palo Alto, CA: University of California Press.

Hodgson, J. (2014). Surveying the wreckage: The professional response to changes to initial teacher training in the UK. *English in Education, 48*(1), 7–25.

Howell, W. S. (1982). *The Empathic Communicator.* Belmont, CA: Wadsworth Publishing Co.

Hoyle, E. & John, P. (1995). *Professional Knowledge and Professional Practice.* London: Cassell.

Hramiak, A. & Hudson, T. (2011). *Understanding Learning and Teaching in Secondary Schools.* Essex: Pearson.

Hudson, P. & Hudson, S. (2014). *Mentoring for Effective Teaching (MET).* Paper presented at the 21st European Mentoring and Coaching Conference, Venice, Italy.

Iser, W. (1978). *The Act of Reading: A theory of aesthetic response.* London (etc.): Routledge and Kegan Paul.

Israel, M., Kamman, M., McCray, E. & Sindelar, P. (2014). Mentoring in action: The interplay among professional assistance, emotional support, and evaluation. *Exceptional Children, 81*(1), 45–63.

Iyer-O'Sullivan, R. (2015). From bit to whole: Reframing feedback dialogue through critical incidents. In A. Howard & H. Donaghue (Eds.), *Teacher Evaluation in Second Language Education.* London: Bloomsbury.

Izadinia, M. (2017). Pre-service teachers' use of metaphors for mentoring relationships. *Journal of Education for Teaching, 43*(5), 506–519.

Jegede, O., Taplin, M. & Chan, S. (2000). Trainee teachers' perception of their knowledge about expert teaching. *Educational Research, 42*(3), 287–308.

References

Jerome, L. & Bhargava, M. (2015). *Effective Medium-term Planning for Teachers*. London: SAGE.

Jing-Schmidt, Z. (2007). Negativity bias in language: A cognitiveaffective model of emotive intensifiers. *Cognitive Linguistics*, 18(3), 417-443.

John, P. (2000). Awareness and intuition: How student teachers read their own lesson. In T. Atkinson & G. Claxton (Eds.), *The Intuitive Practitioner* (pp. 84-107). London: Oxford University Press.

John, P. (2006). Lesson planning and the student teacher: Thinking the dominant model. *Journal of Curriculum Studies*, 38(4), 483-498.

Katz, L. G. (1995). *Talks with Teachers: A Collection*. Norwood, NJ: Ablex.

Kelchtermans, G. (2009). Who I am in how I teach is the message: Self-understanding, vulnerability and reflection. *Teachers and Teaching: Theory and practice*, 15(2), 257-272.

Kerry, T. & Shelton-Mayes A. (Eds.) (1995). *Issues in Mentoring*. London: Routledge.

Kiely, R., Sandmann, L. & Truluck, J. (2004). Adult learning theory and the pursuit of adult degrees. *New Directions for Adult and Continuing Education*, 2004(103), 17-30.

Kolb, D. A. (1983). *Experiential Learning: Experience as the source of learning and development*. Upper Saddle River, NJ: Prentice Hall.

Kroll, J. (2016). What is meant by the term group mentoring? *Mentoring and Tutoring: Partnership in Learning*, 24, 44-58.

Lakoff, G. & Johnson, M. (1980). *Metaphors We Live By*. London: University of Chicago Press.

Lam, D. & Gale, J. (2000). Cognitive behaviour therapy: Teaching a client the ABC model - the first step towards the process of change. *Journal of Advanced Nursing*, 31(2), 444-451.

Leavis, F. & Thompson, D. (1933). *Culture and Environment*. London: Chatto and Windus.

Lieberman, A. & Wood, D. R. (2002). *Inside the National Writing Project: Connecting Network Learning and Classroom Teaching*. New York: Teachers College Press.

Lindsay, D. & Yandell, D. (2014). English as a curriculum subject. In J. Davison & C. Daly (Eds.), *Learning to Teach English in the Secondary School: A companion to school experience* (4th ed., pp. 35-47). New York: Routledge.

Locke, T. (2015). *Developing Writing Teachers*. New York: Routledge.

Lord, P., Atkinson, M. & Mitchell, H. (2008). *Mentoring and Coaching for Professionals: A Study of the Research Evidence*. Available at: www.nfer.ac.uk/mentoring-and-coaching-for-professionals-a-study-of-the-research-evidence

Lortie, D. (1975). *Schoolteacher*. Chicago, IL: University of Chicago.

Loughran, J. (2010). *What Expert Teachers Do*. Abingdon: Routledge.

Lunt, I. (2008). Ethical issues in professional life. In B. Cunningham (Ed.), *Exploring Professionalism* (pp. 73-120). London: Institute of Education, University of London.

Manguel, A. (1997). *A History of Reading*. London: Flamingo.

Marable, M. & Raimondi, S. (2007). Teachers' perceptions of what was most (and least) supportive during their first year of teaching. *Mentoring & Tutoring*, 15(1), 25-37.

Margolis, J., Hodge, A. & Alexandrou, A. (2014). The teacher educator's role in promoting institutional versus individual teacher well-being. *Journal of Education for Teaching*, 40(4), 391-408.

Marinez Aguado, J. (2016). What type of feedback do student teachers expect from their school mentors during practicum experience? The case of Spanish EFL student teachers. *Australian Journal of Teacher Education*, 41(5), 36-51.

Martin, J. R. & White, P. R. R. (2005). *The Language of Evaluation: Appraisal in English*. Basingstoke: Palgrave Macmillan.

Mason, J. (2002). *Researching Your Own Practice: The discipline of noticing*. London: RoutledgeFalmer.

Mathieson, M. (1975). *The Preachers of Culture*. London: Rowan and Littlefield.

Maynard, T. & Furlong, J. (1995a). Learning to teach and models of mentoring. In T. Kerry & A. Shelton-Mayes (Eds.), *Issues in Mentoring* (pp. 10-14). London: Routledge.

Maynard, T. & Furlong, J. (1995b). *Mentoring Student Teachers: The growth of professional knowledge*. London: Routledge.
McCallum, F. & Price, D. (2010). Well teachers, well students. *Journal of Student Wellbeing*, 4(1), 19-34.
McCallum, F. & Price, D. (2017). *Teacher Wellbeing: A review of the literature*. Sydney, Australia: The Association of Independent Schools of NSW.
McCann, T. (2013). Mentoring matters. *English Journal*, 102(6), 88-90.
Meek, M. (1988). *How Texts Teach What Readers Learn*. Stroud: Thimble Press.
Megginson, D. & Clutterbuck, D. (1995). *Mentoring in Action* (1st ed.). London: Kogan Page.
Mercado, L. & Mann, S. (2015). Mentoring for teacher evaluation and development. In A. Howard & H. Donaghue (Eds.), *Teacher Evaluation in Second Language Education*. London: Bloomsbury.
Mercer, N. (2000). *Words and Minds. How we use language to think together*. London: Routledge.
Ministry of Education and Research (Norway) (2010). *Differentiated Primary and Lower Secondary Teacher Education Programmes for Years 1-7 and Years 5-10*. Oslo: Ministry of Education and Research.
Montgomery, B. L. (2017). Mapping a mentoring roadmap and developing a supportive network for strategic career advancement. *SAGE Open*, April-June, 1-13.
Muijs, D. & Reynolds, D. (2010). *Effective Teaching: Evidence and practice* (3rd ed.). London: SAGE.
Nagin, C (2006). *Because Writing Matters*. San Francisco, CA: Jossey Bass.
NCTE (2004). *NCTE Beliefs about the Teaching of Writing*. Available at: https://wrd.as.uky.edu/sites/default/files/NCTE%20Beliefs%20about%20the%20Teaching%20of%20Writing.pdf
New Teacher Center (2011). *NTC Continuum of Mentoring Practice*. Santa Cruz, CA: New Teacher Center.
Nias, J. (1996). Thinking about feeling: The emotions in teaching. *Cambridge Journal of Education*, 26(3), 293-316.
Nicols, S., Schutz, P., Rodgers, K. & Bilica, K. (2017). Early career teachers' emotion and emerging teacher identities. *Teachers and Teaching*, 23(4), 406-421.
Ofsted (2015). *Ofsted Inspections: Myths*. Available at: www.gov.uk/government/publications/school-inspection-handbook-from-september-2015/ofsted-inspections-mythbusting
Ohio Department for Education (2015). *Ohio Standards for Professional Development*. Ohio: Department for Education. Available at: ohio.gov/Topics/Teaching/Professional-Development/Organizing-for-High-Quality-Professional-Development
O'Leary, M. (2014). *Classroom Observation*. Abingdon: Routledge.
Orland-Barak, L. & Klein, S. (2005). The expressed and the realised: Mentors' representations of a mentoring conversation and its realisation in practice. *Teaching and Teacher Education*, 21, 379-402.
Parsloe, E. & Wray, M. (2000). *Coaching and Mentoring*. London: Kogan Page.
Peters, T. & Austin, N. (1985). *A Passion for Excellence: The Leadership Difference*. London: Collins.
Philpott, C. (2013). Who has all the answers in education (and why should you believe them)? In H. Scott, C. Mercier & C. Philpott (Eds.), *Professional Issues in Secondary Teaching* (pp. 7-22). London: SAGE.
Polanyi, M. (1958). *Personal Knowledge: Towards a post-critical philosophy*. Chicago, IL: University of Chicago Press.
Pollard, A. (2014). *Reflective Teaching in Schools* (4th ed.). London: Bloomsbury.
Quigly, A. (2014). *Teach Now! English*. Oxon: Routledge.
Ragins, B. (2016). From the ordinary to the extraordinary: High quality mentoring relationships at work. *Organizational Dynamics*, 45, 228-244.

Ramaprasad, A. (1983). On the definition of feedback. *Behavioural Science, 28*(1), 4-13.

Rehman, A. & Al-Bargi, A. (2014). Teachers' perspectives on post observation conferences: A study at a Saudi Arabian university. *Theory and Practice in Language Studies, 4*(8), 1558-1568.

Rhodes, C., Stokes, M. & Hampton, G. (2004). *A Practical Guide to Mentoring, Coaching and Peer-networking*. Abingdon: Routledge.

Richards, I. A. (1929). *Practical Criticism: A study of literary judgement*. Cambridge: Cambridge University Press.

Riggenbach, J. (2013). *The CBT Toolbox: A workbook for clients and clinicians*. Eau Claire, WI: Premier Publishing and Media.

Roberts, R. (2014). An exploration of how three School Direct trainee teachers observe lessons taught by 'expert' teachers – how have they learnt to observe? EdD Assignment (unpublished). Reading: Institute of Education, University of Reading. Summary available at: www.innovatemyschool.com/ideas/trainee-teachers-learning-from-observing

Roberts, R. (2019). Critical Conversations: The role of evaluative language in mentor meetings in Initial Teacher Training (EdD). University of Reading.

Rosenblatt, L. M. (1978). *The Reader, the Text, the Poem: The transactional theory of the literary work*. London: Southern Illinois University Press.

Sachs, J. (2016). Teacher professionalism: Why are we still talking about it? *Teachers and Teaching, 22*(4), 413-425.

Sadler, D. (1989). Formative assessments and the design of instructional systems. *Instructional Science, 18*(4), 119-144.

Scholes, R. (1985). *Textual Power*. New Haven, CT: Yale University Press.

Schön, D. (1983). *The Reflective Practitioner. How professionals think in action*. New York: Basic Books.

Schutz, W. (1994). *The Human Element*. San Fancisco, CA: Jossey-Bass.

Shulman, L. (1986). Those who understand: Knowledge growth in teaching. *Educational Researcher, 15*(2), 4-14.

Smith, J. & Wrigley, S. (2017). *Introducing Teachers' Writing Groups*. Abingdon: Routledge.

Stevens, D. & Lowing, K. (2008). Observer, observed and observations: Initial teacher education English tutors' feedback on lessons taught by student teachers of English. *English in Education, 42*(2), 162-198.

Stone, D., Patton, B. & Heen, S. (2010). *Difficult Conversations: How to discuss what matters most* (2nd ed.). London: Penguin.

Sullivan, A. & Brown, M. (2015). Reading for pleasure and progress in vocabulary and mathematics. *British Educational Research Journal, 41*(6), 971-991.

Swales, J. (1988). Discourse communities, genres and English as an international language. *World Englishes, 7*(2), 211-220.

Teaching Schools Council (2016). *National Standards for School-based Initial Teacher Training (ITT) Mentors*. London: Crown.

Timperley, H. (2001). Mentoring conversations designed to promote student teacher learning. *Asia-Pacific Journal of Teacher Education, 29*(2), 111-123.

Tomlinson, P. (1995). *Understanding Mentoring*. Buckingham: Open University Press.

Tripp, R. T. (Ed.) (1970). *The International Thesaurus of Quotations*. Available at: www.bartleby.com/73/484.html

Turner, S. & Braine, M. (2016). Embedding wellbeing knowledge and practice into teacher education: Building emotional resilience. *Teacher Education Advancement Network Journal, 8*(1), 67-82.

Turvey, A. & Anderson, G. (2011). Tasks, audience and purposes: Writing and the development of teacher identities within pre-service teacher education. In R. Heilbronn & J. Yandell (Eds.), *Critical Practice in Teacher Education. A study of professional learning*. London: IOE.

Tyler, R. (1949). *Basic Principles of Curriculum and Instruction.* Chicago, IL: University of Chicago Press.
Walker, R. & Adelman, C. (1975). *A Guide to Classroom Observation.* London: Routledge.
Ward, S. C. & Connolly, R. (2008). Let them eat Shakespeare: Prescribed authors and the National Curriculum. *Curriculum Journal, 19*(4), pp. 293-307.
WHO (2014). Mental health: A state of well-being. Available at: www.who.int/features/factfiles/mental_health/en
Wilson, E. (2013). *School-based Research: A guide for education students* (2nd ed.). London: SAGE.
Wilson, E. (2017). *School-based Research: A guide for education students* (3rd ed.). Los Angeles, CA: SAGE.
Winch, C. (2013). Curriculum design and epistemic ascent. *Journal of Philosophy of Education, 47*(1), 128-146.
Wright, T. (2012). *How to be a Brilliant English Teacher.* Abingdon: Routledge.
Wright, T. (2018). *How to be a Brilliant Mentor* (2nd ed.). Abingdon: Routledge.
Yandell, J. (2017). Knowledge, English and the formation of teachers. *Pedagogy, Culture & Society, 25*(4), 583-599, DOI: 10.1080/14681366.2017.1312494
Yandell, J. & Brady, M. (2016). English and the politics of knowledge. *English in Education, 50*(1), 44-59.
Yuan, R. & Lee, I. (2016). 'I need to be strong and competent': A narrative inquiry of a student-teacher's emotions and identities in teaching practicum. *Teachers and Teaching, 22*(7), 819-841.

INDEX

A Level 26, 65, 131, **133**, 152, 159
Aderibigbe, S., Colucci-Gray, L. & Gray, D. 126
AITSL 9
Akcan, S. & Tatar, S. 121
Alexander, R. 83, 87, 127
Allen, M. & Toplis, R. 141
Anderson, E. & Shannon, A. 41
Aristotle 49
assessment: 128, 132, **151**, 157-159; assessment-for-learning 73-74, 109-110; assessment-of-learning **107**; criteria 70; framework 82; student teacher 7, 44, 118, **119**, 125, 152, 160, 161; pupil **40**, **46**, 54-56, 70-71, 88, 109-111
assignment 32, 60

Baldridge, J. 137
Ball, S. J. 141
Ballantyne, R., Packer, J. & Hansford, B. 41
barriers 24, 129-130, 139, 154
Barton, G. 88
behaviour: 11, 39, 63, 118, 137, 142, 149; behaviour codes and expectations 30, 49; behaviour for learning 131; behaviour management 34, 37, **40**, 42, 45, 64, 71, 74, 108, 131, 136, 146; behaviour policy 45, 131, 143, 144, 159
Bleiman, B. 88
books 40, 46, 109, 153, 158, 162
Brandt, C. 121
Brindley, S. & Marshall, B. 31
Brindley, S. 30, 31, 32, 81, 85
Brooks, V., Abbot, I. & Duddleson, P. 33
Bullock, A. 88

Capel, S., Leask, M. & Turner, T. 148, 149
Chapman, G. & White, P. 134

Child, A. & Merrill, S. 14
Cho, C., Ramanan, R. & Feldman, M. 14
CIPD 6
Clark, C. & Cunningham, A. 84
Clarke, S., Westbrook, J., & Dickinson, P. 31
Cliff Hodges, G. 31, 84, 85, 86, 87, 162
Clutterbuck, D. 11, 13, 98
Coe, R., Aloisi, C., Higgins, S. & Major, L. E. 80
cognition 66
Cognitive Behaviour Therapy 63-66
Cohen, L., Manion, L. & Morrison, K. 113
collaboration: 64, 67-89, 101, 106; collaborative practice 7, 57, 67-89, 90, 115, 129, **133**; collaborative planning 71-74
community **10**, 29, 32, 38, 59, 131, **134**, 141, 148, 162
Connelly, F. M. & Clandinin, D. J. 61
counselling 12, 13, 53, 58, 61-62, 130
Cox, B. 24, 80
creative writing 38, 46, 117
creativity 56, 86, 89, 98
Cremin, T. 84
critical thinking 27, 29, 114
criticism: 32, **65**, 120, 124, 130, 134, 139, 162; critical analysis 22; Practical Criticism 22-23
Cunningham, B. 141
CUREE 6
curriculum 19, 23, 31, 33, **40**, 69, 93, 97, **133**, 142, 145, 156; *see also* National Curriculum; cross-curricular 35, 132, **133**, 160; curriculum vitae 154

Daloz, L. A. 11, 13, 98
data **40**, 53, 54, 57, 73, 109-110, 144, 152-153, 155, 158

Davis, L., Little, M. & Thornton, W. 98-99
Davison, J., Daly C. & Moss, J. 31
Day, C. & Leitch, R. 42
Day, C. 115
Dean, G. 84
Department for Education 7, 8, **9-10**, 14, 30, 35, 37, 41, 44, 53, 54, 55, 56, 57, 58, 82, 95, 106, 116, 146, 147, 149, 151, 154, 156, 157, 160
Department of Education and Science and the Welsh Office 19
Dickens, C. 79, 84, 85
Didau, D. 109
discourse 38, 82, 83, 86, 114
Dixon, J. 17, 18
Dodds, P., Clark, E., Desu, S., Frank, M., Reagan, A., Williams, J. ... Danforth, C. 122
Doecke, B. 30, 32
Donaghue, H. 118
drama 34, 38, 69, 71, 75, 128, **133**, **134**, 144
Driscoll, L. G., Parkes, K. A., Tilley-Lubbs, G. A., Brill, J. M. & Pitts Bannister, V. R. 6

Eagelton, T. 22
Elbow, P. 88
Elliott, V., Baird, J., Hopfenbeck, T. & Ingram, J. 56
English and Media Centre 26, 91
English as an additional language 12, 131, **133**
Enow, L. & Goodwyn, A. 102, 156, 157, 162
Eraut, M. 96, 97
Ericsson, A. & Pool, R. 116, 117
evaluation: 42, 48, 63, 71, 74, 92, 95, 98, 99, 106, **107-108**, 109, 110, 118, **119**, **128**, 134, 139, 155; self-evaluation 42, 63
Evertson, C. M. & Smithey, M. W. 126
expectation **10**, 29, 36, 39, 44, **45-47**, 48-49, 55, 95, 98, 104, 133, 143, 150, 154, 157, 160

Fautley, M. & Savage, J. 108
feedback 39, 45-48, 55, 62, 67-69, 98, 116-125, 158, 159
Ferrier-Kerr, J. 44
Fleming, M. & Stevens, D. 31
Franke, A. & Dahlgren, L. O. 126
Fry. S. 34
Furlong, J. 8

GCSE 17, 20, 23, 25, 26, 30, 40, 55, 82, 94, 95, 131, **133**, 143, 159

Gibbons, S. 21, 82
Gibbs, G. 127-128, 134
Giovanelli, M. & Mason, J. 84
Goodwyn, A. 19, 20, 21, 23, 24, 25, 26, 33, 39, 113, 114, 115
Goodwyn, A. & Fuller, C. 21, 31
Graves, D. H. 88, 89
Green, A. 30, 43, 79
Green, A. & Mcintyre, J. 31, 81
Griffith, A. & Burns, M. 105
Grimmett, H., Forgasz, R., Williams, J. & White, S. 44
Gross, J. 134

Haggard, D. L., Dougherty, T. W., Turban, D. B. and Wilbanks, J. E. 6
Hargreaves, A. 42, 97, 141
Hattie, J. & Timperley, H. 118
Hattie, J. & Yates, G. 114
Hawkey, K. 43
Heilbronn, R. 93, 94
Higgins, M. C. & Thomas, D. A. 7
Hobson, A., Ashby, P., Malderez, A. & Tomlinson, P. 7
Hobson, A. & Malderez, A. 120
Hochschild, A. 43, 134
Hodgson, J. 33
Howell, W. S. 114
Hoyle, E. & John, P. 141, 142
Hramiak, A. & Hudson, T. 145, 146
Hudson, P. & Hudson, S. 120, 145

identity: 14, 31, 43, 61, 66, 136, 139, 144; professional identity 44-47, 49, 141, 149
induction 110, 112
intervention 58, 62, **99**, 130, 141, 146
Iser, W. 87
Israel, M., Kamman, M., McCray, E. & Sindelar, P. 41
Iyer-O'Sullivan, R. 120
Izadinia, M. 41

Jegede, O., Taplin, M. & Chan, S. 113
Jerome, L. & Bhargava M. 105
Jing-Schmidt, Z. 122
John, P. 102, 103, 104, 106, 109, 111

Kelchtermans, G. 120
Kerry, T. & Shelton-Mayes, A. 41

Index

key stage: 35, 132, 151, 152; Key Stage 2 20; Key Stage 3 20, **40**; Key Stage 4 20, **40**
Kiely, R., Sandmann, L. & Truluck, J. 39
knowledge; pedagogical subject knowledge 82; subject knowledge 27-29, 32, 33-34, 37-38, 68, 79-90, 114, 116, 131, **133**, 146, 162; tacit knowledge 113-114
Kolb, D. A. 93, 94
Kroll, J. 6

Lakoff, G. & Johnson, M. 38
Lam, D. & Gale, J. 64
language 19, 20-21, 24, 27, 33, 35, 38, 81, 82, 85, 88, 102, 104, 116, 120, 122-123, 125, 132-134, 154, 159; *see also* English as an additional language
Leavis. F. & Thompson, D. 22, 23, 24
Lieberman, A. & Wood, D. R. 88
Lindsay, D. & Yandell, D. 31
listening: 20, 124; listening to mentees 53, 58, 62; speaking and listening 25, 81-83, 84, 89, 132
literacy: 18, 21, 27, **133**, 144; critical literacy 19; National Literacy Strategy 21
literature 19, 20-21, 22-25, 33, **40**, 84, 105, 143, 159
Locke, T. 89
Lord, P., Atkinson, M. & Mitchell, H. 37
Lortie, D. 42
Loughran, J. 113
Lunt, I. 30, 142, 143

Manguel, A. 88
Marable, M. & Raimondi, S. 41
Margolis, J., Hodge, A. & Alexandrou, A. 63
Marinez Aguado, J.
marking 30, **46**, 53, 54-56, 70, 71, 106, 109, 110, 132, 157-158, 162
Martin, J. R. & White, P. R. R. 134
Mason, J. 114
Mathieson, M. 23
Maynard, T. & Furlong, J. 8, 11, 13, 67, 103, 110
McCallum, F. & Price, D. 59, 61, 62, 63, 64
McCann, T. 103, 106
media: 19, 20, 23, 114, 134, 162; social media 34, 131
Meek, M. 84
meeting: weekly (debrief) meeting 110, 126-139
Megginson, D. & Clutterbuck, D. 36, 37
Mercado, L. & Mann, S. 118, 120

Mercer, N. 82, 98
Ministry of Education and Research (Norway) 9
Montgomery, B. L. 6
motivation 21-22, 24, 38, 42, 86, 134, 139, 148, 161
Muijs, D. & Reynolds, D. 80, 143

Nagin, C. 89, 90
National Curriculum 17, 23, 27, 30, 31, 32, 82, 103, 129, 131, 143
NATE 91, 162
NCTE 89
New Teacher Center 10
Nias, J. 42
Nicols, S., Schutz, P., Rodgers, K. & Bilica, K. 122
non-fiction 35, 128
novel 19, 71, 105
NQT 20, 134, 150-162

O'Leary, M. 121
objectives 21, 43, 71-73, **108**, **122**, 129, 133, 155, 156
observation: 62-63, 75, 93, 112, 153; of the mentee 33, 67-68, 108, 112-125, 137, 157, 159-160; mentee observations of others 103-104
Ofsted 115, 134, 144, 162
Ohio Department for Education 10
oracy 82-83, 162
Orland-Barak, L. & Klein, S. 127

Parsloe, E. & Wray, M. 121
pedagogy 1, 21, 22, 29, 33, 34, 35, **46**, 68, 75, 82-83, 85-87, 89-91, 103, 139, 143
pedagogical subject knowledge 37, 80, 82, 89, 114
Peters, T. & Austin, N. 39
PGCE 38, 60, 79, 82, 123, 150, 151, 154, 155, 158, 160, 162
Philpott, C. 28
planning: 19, 26, 30, **45-46**, 53, 54, 56-57, 71-74, 80-81, 83, 86, 87, 90, 95, 101-111, 115, 128-129, 132, **133**, 142, 155-157, 159, 162; action planning 40; collaborative planning 71-74
plays 69, 74
poetry 34, **65**, 68, 71, 72, 115, **128**
Polanyi, M. 113
Pollard, A. 7
praise 39, 41, 121, 123, 132, 134, 139
preparation 56, 103, 158

problems: navigating problems 47-49, 53, 58, 61-66
profession: 1, 7, **10**, 21, 27, 30, 49, 79, 138, 140, 150, 161; professional 140-143
progress: pupil progress 12, 42, 56, 57, 88, 105, 106, **107**, 108, 110-111, 116, 129, 132, 146, 158; student teacher progress 11, 36, 37, 43, **47**, 49, 54, 61, 63-64, 68, 71-73, 98, 105, 108, 110, 112, 118, 123, 126, 129-131, 134, 138-139, 144, 150, 152, 153, 157, 161

Quigley, A. 105

Ragins, B. 14, 109
Ramaprasad, A. 118
reading 2, 18, 20, 21, 24, 25, 31, **47**, 64, 66, 74, 82, 84-88, 104, 113, 130, 131, 150, 156
reflection: **10**, 12, 17, 20, 33, 34, 43, 44, 55, 56, 60, 67, 69-70, 71, 73, 74, 75, 79, 84, 96, 97, 98, 101, 103, 106, **108**, 109, 111, 115, 116, 118, *119*, 120, 121, 126, 127-128, 130, 149, 155, 162; mentor reflection tasks 6, 7, 14, 23, 29, 32, 47, 54, 55, 56, 57, 58, 60, 61, 62, 64, 87, 89, 90, 95, 99, 100, 101, 102, 110, 141, 143, 147, 153, 157; reflective practice 43, 92-93, 99-100
reflexivity 90, 92, 93-95, 97, 143, 149
Rehman, A. & Al-Bargi, A. 37
relationships 25, 35, 36-49, 64, 71, 75, 84, 109, 116, 123, 136, 147, 148
Rhodes, C., Stokes, M. & Hampton, G. 121
Richards, I. A. 22, 23, 24
Riggenbach, J. 64
Roberts, R. 37, 42, 114, 118, 120, 123, 134, 135, 138
roles 5, 7, 55, 124, 141-142, 146, 147, 149, 150
Rosenblatt, L. M. 22, 24, 87

Sachs, J. 141
Sadler, D. 126
scheme of work 69, 93, 129, 139
Scholes, R. 32
Schön, D. 12, 33, 44, 93, 96
Schutz, W. 41, 120, 122, 134
Shulman, L. 37, 38

Smith, J. & Wrigley, S. 88, 89
standards: 7, 35, 39, 84, 137, 162; Teachers' Standards 8, **9-10**, 35, 40, 55, 68, 95, 97, 98, 103, 106, 115, 116, 122, 124, 125, 128, 129, 130, 132, **133**, 141, 147, 149, 150, 152, 154, 155, 157, 158, 159, 160, 161; Mentor Standards 1, 7, 14, 37, 40, **45-47**, 49
Stevens, D. & Lowing, K. 27
Stone, D., Patton, B. & Heen, S. 136, 137
Sullivan, A. & Brown, M. 84
Swales, J. 38

target: 7, 114, 116, 137; target-setting 155
Teaching Schools Council 1
textbooks 56
Timperley, H. 127
Tomlinson, P. 33, 41, 120
Turner, S. & Braine, M. 49, 63, 136
Turvey, A. & Anderson, G. 99
Tyler, R. 102

UKLA 91

values 7, 19, 24, 31, 38, 49, 61, 63, 86, 94, 138, 140, 143, 144, 146, 147, 149
verbal feedback 98, 119-124

Walker, R. & Adelman, C. 114
Ward, S. C. & Connolly, R. 31
well-being 42, 53, 58-66, 130, 136, 145, 161
WHO 59
Wilson, E. 95
Winch, C. 38
workload 1, 43, 48, 53, 54-58, 66, 110, 130, 157
Wright, T. 81, 128, 129, 137
writing 18, 20, 21, 22, 25, 32, 38, 41, 43, **46**, 54, 70, 71, 80, 81, 82, 83, 85, 88-90, 99, 117, 128, 129, 132, 143, 151, 158
written feedback **45**, 55, 116, 124, 125, 134, 139, 158

Yandell, J. & Brady, M. 84
Yandell, J. 27
Yuan, R. & Lee, I. 43, 134

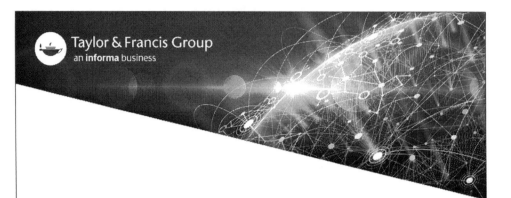